Demystifying Legal Reasoning

Demystifying Legal Reasoning defends the proposition that there are no special forms of reasoning peculiar to law. Legal decision makers engage in the same modes of reasoning that all actors use in deciding what to do: open-ended moral reasoning, empirical reasoning, and deduction from authoritative rules. This book addresses common-law reasoning, when prior judicial decisions determine the law, and interpretation of texts. In both areas, the popular view that legal decision makers practice special forms of reasoning is false.

Larry Alexander is a Warren Distinguished Professor of Law at the University of San Diego School of Law. He is the author of *Is There a Right of Freedom of Expression?* (Cambridge, 2005); (with Emily Sherwin) *The Rule of Rules: Morality, Rules, and the Dilemmas of Law* (2001); *Constitutionalism: Philosophical Foundations* (Cambridge, 1998); (with Paul Horton) *Whom Does the Constitution Command?* (1988); several anthologies; and more than 160 articles, book chapters, and review essays in jurisprudence, constitutional law, criminal law, and normative ethics. He has been a member of the faculty at the University of San Diego School of Law since 1970. He is coeditor of the journal *Legal Theory* (Cambridge), and he serves on the editorial boards of *Ethics, Law and Philosophy,* and *Criminal Law and Philosophy.* He is co–executive director of the Institute for Law and Philosophy at the University of San Diego, and he is past president of AMINTAPHIL.

Emily Sherwin is Professor of Law at Cornell Law School. She specializes in jurisprudence, property, and remedies. She is the author (with Larry Alexander) of *The Rule of Rules: Morality, Rules, and the Dilemmas of Law* (2001) and has published numerous book chapters, articles, and reviews in her subjects of specialty. She was a member of the faculty at the University of Kentucky College of Law from 1985 to 1990 and the University of San Diego School of Law from 1990 to 2003, when she moved to Cornell University. She is a member of the advisory committee for the American Law Institute's Restatement (Third) of Restitution and Unjust Enrichment and a regular participant in roundtable conferences of the University of San Diego's Institute for Law and Philosophy.

Cambridge Introductions to Philosophy and Law

William A. Edmundson, *Georgia State University*

This introductory series of books provides concise studies of the philosophical foundations of law, of perennial topics in the philosophy of law, and of important and opposing schools of thought. The series is aimed principally at students in philosophy, law, and political science.

Demystifying Legal Reasoning

LARRY ALEXANDER
University of San Diego School of Law

EMILY SHERWIN
Cornell Law School

CAMBRIDGE
UNIVERSITY PRESS

CAMBRIDGE UNIVERSITY PRESS
Cambridge, New York, Melbourne, Madrid, Cape Town, Singapore, São Paulo, Delhi

Cambridge University Press
32 Avenue of the Americas, New York, NY 10013-2473, USA

www.cambridge.org
Information on this title: www.cambridge.org/9780521703956

First published 2008

Printed in the United States of America

A catalog record for this publication is available from the British Library.

Library of Congress Cataloging in Publication Data

Alexander, Larry, 1943–
Demystifying legal reasoning / Larry Alexander, Emily Sherwin.
p.   cm. – (Cambridge introductions to philosophy and law)
Includes bibliographical references (p.) and index.
ISBN   978-0-521-87898-2 (hardback) – ISBN   978-0-521-70395-6 (pbk.)
1. Law – Methodology.   2. Logic.   3. Reasoning.   I. Sherwin, Emily, 1955–   II. Title
III. Series.

K213.A429 2008
340′.1–dc22   2007045107

ISBN   978-0-521-87898-2 hardback
ISBN   978-0-521-70395-6 paperback

Contents

Introduction

Legal reasoning, meaning reasoning about the requirements and application of law, has been studied for centuries.[1] This is not surprising: legal

---

[1] Early works include Sir Edward Coke, *The First Part of the Institutes of the Law of England*, §138 ¶97b (1628), reprinted in II *The Selected Writings of Sir Edward Coke* 577, 701 (1639) (Steve Sheppard, ed., Indianapolis: Liberty Fund 2003); Christopher St. German, *Doctor and Student* (1523) (T. F. T. Plucknett and J. L. Barton, eds., London: Seldon Society 1974); Thomas Hobbes, *A Dialogue between a Philosopher and a Student of the Common-Lawes* (1681) (Joseph Cropsey, ed., Chicago: University of Chicago Press 1971); Sir Matthew Hale, *The History of the Common Law of England* 39–46 (1713) (Charles M. Gary, ed., Chicago: University of Chicago Press 1971); 2 Henry Bracton, *On the Laws and Customs of England* 19–28 (ca. 1230–50) (Samuel E. Thorne and George E. Woodbine, eds. and trans., Cambridge, Mass.: Harvard University Press 1968); *The Treatise on the Laws and Customs of the Realm, Commonly Called Glanville* 1–3 (ca. 1187–89) (G. D. G. Hall, ed., London: Nelson 1965); 1 William Blackstone, *Commentaries on the Laws of England* 38–73 (Oxford: Clarendon Press 1765).

More recent works focusing on legal reasoning include Lloyd L. Weinreb, *Legal Reason: The Use of Analogy in Legal Argument* (Cambridge: Cambridge University Press 2005); Cass R. Sunstein, *Legal Reasoning and Political Conflict* (New York: Oxford University Press 1996); Steven J. Burton, *An Introduction to Law and Legal Reasoning* (Boston: Little, Brown 1995); Henry M. Hart Jr. and Albert M. Sacks, *The Legal Process: Basic Problems in the Making and*

decision making is tremendously important to peace, prosperity, human dignity, and daily life. Yet, at least since Sir Edward Coke described the common law as "an artificial perfection of reason," legal reasoning has been surrounded by an air of mystery.[2] More recent works on legal reasoning have produced neither clarity nor consensus on what legal deliberation entails; if anything, they have compounded the problem. Legal decision making is frequently described as a "craft" involving special forms of reasoning that are accessible only to those with long experience in applying law.[3] Seasoned judges and lawyers are said to reason

---

Application of Law (William N. Eskridge Jr. and Phillip P. Frickey, eds., New York: Foundation Press 1994); Steven J. Burton, *Judging in Good Faith* 35–68 (Cambridge: Cambridge University Press 1992); Oliver Wendell Holmes, *The Common Law* (New York: Dover Publications 1991); Melvin Aron Eisenberg, *The Nature of the Common Law* (Cambridge, Mass.: Harvard University Press 1988); Ronald Dworkin, *Law's Empire* (Cambridge, Mass.: Harvard University Press 1986); Ronald Dworkin, *Taking Rights Seriously* 14–130 (Cambridge, Mass.: Harvard University Press 1978); Karl N. Llewellyn, *The Common Law Tradition: Deciding Appeals* (Boston: Little, Brown 1960); Roscoe Pound, *Law Finding through Experience and Reason* (Athens: University of Georgia Press 1960); Benjamin N. Cardozo, *The Nature of the Judicial Process* (New Haven: Yale University Press 1949); Edward H. Levi, *An Introduction to Legal Reasoning* (Chicago: University of Chicago Press 1948).

[2] "[T]he common law itself is nothing else but reason; which is to be understood of an artificial perfection of reason, gotten by long study, observation, and experience, and not of every man's natural reason. . . ." Coke, *supra* note 1, at 577, 701. *See Prohibitions Del Roy*, 12 *Edward Coke, Reports* 63 (1607), reprinted in I *The Selected Writings of Sir Edward Coke* 478 (Steve Sheppard, ed., Indianapolis: Liberty Fund 2003) (maintaining that the king cannot render legal judgments because he lacks "the artificiall reason and judgment of Law").

  For helpful discussions of Coke and of early understandings of legal "reason," see J. W. Tubbs, *The Common Law Mind: Medieval and Early Modern Conceptions* 45–52, 148–68 (Baltimore: Johns Hopkins University Press 2000) (suggesting that Coke's term "artificial reason" referred to reasoning skills obtained through special training, reasoning developed through debate among learned persons, or a combination of the two); Gerald J. Postema, *Classical Common Law Tradition, Part II*, 3 *Oxford U. Commonwealth L.J.* 1, 1–11 (2003) (describing artificial reason as pragmatic, public-spirited, contextual, nonsystematic, discursive, and shared); Gerald J. Postema, *Classical Common Law Tradition, Part I*, 2 *Oxford U. Commonwealth L.J.* 155, 176–80 (2002).

[3] *See* Anthony Kronman, *The Lost Lawyer* 170–85, 209–25 (Cambridge, Mass.: Belknap Press of Harvard University Press 1995); Llewellyn, *supra* note 1, at 213–35; Brett G. Scharffs, *The Character of Legal Reasoning*, 61 *Wash. & Lee L. Rev.* 733 (2004); Charles Fried, *The Artificial Reasoning of the Law, or What Lawyers Know*, 60 *Tex. L. Rev.* 35 (1981). *See also* Weinreb, *supra* note 1, at 123–46 (suggesting that analogical reasoning depends on a combination of psychological hardwiring and legal training and experience); Brian Leiter, *Heidegger and the Theory of Adjudication*, 106 *Yale L.J.* 253 (1996) (finding support in Heidegger for learned methods of legal reasoning that cannot be articulated); Daniel A. Farber, *The Inevitability of Practical Reasoning: Statues, Formalism, and the Rule of Law*, 45 *Vand. L. Rev.* 533 (1992) (discussing the need for "practical reason," gained from experience, in interpretation).

analogically from one case to another and to discover or construct "legal principles" that differ from the moral principles that govern decision making in other areas of life.[4]

Our own contribution to the subject of legal reasoning is fairly simple: we believe that legal reasoning is ordinary reasoning applied to legal problems.[5] Legal decision makers engage in open-ended moral reasoning, empirical reasoning, and deduction from authoritative rules. These are the same modes of reasoning that all actors use in deciding what to do. Popular descriptions of additional forms of reasoning special to law are, in our view, simply false. Past results cannot determine the outcomes of new disputes. Analogical reasoning, as such, is not possible. Legal principles are both logically incoherent and normatively unattractive. Nor do legal decision makers engage in special modes of interpreting texts. To the extent that judges purport to discern meanings in legal texts that differ from the meanings intended by the authors of those texts, they are making rather than interpreting law.[6]

We recognize that, as a descriptive matter, legal actors purport to apply special decision-making techniques. They study prior outcomes, seek analogies, and search for principles. We offer a limited defense of

---

[4] Efforts to explain and defend analogical reasoning in law can be found in Weinreb, *supra* note 1; Sunstein, *supra* note 1, at 62–100; Burton, *supra* note 1, at 25–41; Levi, *supra* note 1, at 1–6; Scott Brewer, *Exemplary Reasoning: Semantics, Pragmatics, and the Rational Force of Legal Argument by Analogy*, 109 *Harv. L. Rev.* 925, 925–29, 962–63 (1996).

    Legal principles are analyzed in Dworkin, *Law's Empire*, *supra* note 1, at 240–50, 254–58; Dworkin, *Taking Rights Seriously*, *supra* note 1, at 22–31. *See also* Hart and Sacks, *supra* note 1, at lxxix–lxxx, 545–96 (discussing "reasoned elaboration" of law).

[5] *See* Kent Greenawalt, *Law and Objectivity* 197–202 (New York: Oxford University Press 1992). *See also* Joseph Raz, *Ethics in the Public Domain* 310 (Oxford: Clarendon Press 1994) (application of law does not involve special forms of logic); Frederick Schauer, *Playing by the Rules: A Philosophical Examination of Rule-Based Decision-Making in Life and Law* 187 (Oxford: Clarendon Press 1991) ("nothing about precedent-based constraint uniquely differentiates it from rule-based constraint"); Eisenberg, *supra* note 1, at 94 (suggesting that reasoning by analogy is "substantively equivalent" to reasoning from precedent rules).

[6] Our views on these matters are set out in part in a variety of earlier writings. *See, e.g.*, Larry Alexander and Emily Sherwin, *Judges as Rule Makers*, in *Common Law Theory* 27–50 (Douglas Edlin, ed., Cambridge: Cambridge University Press 2007); Larry Alexander and Emily Sherwin, *The Rule of Rules: Morality, Rules, and the Dilemmas of Law* 98–179 (Durham: Duke University Press 2001); Emily Sherwin, *Judges as Rulemakers*, 73 *U. Chi. L. Rev.* 919 (2006); Emily Sherwin, *A Defense of Analogical Reasoning in Law*, 66 *U. Chi. L. Rev.* 1179 (1999); Larry Alexander, *The Banality of Legal Reasoning*, 73 *Notre Dame L. Rev.* 517 (1998); Larry Alexander, *Bad Beginnings*, 145 *U. Pa. L. Rev.* 57 (1996); Larry Alexander, *Constrained by Precedent*, 63 *S. Cal. L. Rev.* 1 (1989).

traditional legal methods of this kind. Our defense, however, is indirect, based on the capacity of traditional methods to counteract the situational disadvantages that affect judges as appliers of rules and as rule makers for future cases. We explain these techniques as ingrained practices that may have instrumental value for imperfect reasoners, not as specialized forms of reasoning.

Part 1 describes the circumstances that give rise to law and sets out our understanding of the most important problems of jurisprudence. This is familiar ground but nevertheless important as background for our analysis of legal reasoning. As will be clear, we owe significant debts to others who have studied the subjects we address here, in particular H. L. A. Hart and Frederick Schauer.[7]

Part 2 addresses legal reasoning in the application and development of common law. We have several aims in this part of the book. We hope to clarify the reasoning methods judges use, to demonstrate that a variety of other supposed methods of legal decision making are illusory, and to explain the different roles judges occupy within the legal system, as adjudicators and as lawmakers. In presenting our view of what common-law reasoning entails, we face a descriptive problem: courts often insist that they are reasoning in ways that we say they are not. To defend our limited view of legal reasoning and at the same time explain the apparent behavior of courts, we propose that a number of time-honored judicial techniques function not as actual decision-making tools but as indirect strategies to avoid the disadvantages that judges face in their dual capacities as adjudicators and lawmakers.

Part 3 takes up the methodology of interpreting canonical legal texts – a vast array that includes constitutions, statutes, administrative rules and orders, and judicially crafted rules, as well as the legally authoritative texts constitutive of private ordering (contracts, wills, trusts, deeds, leases, and so on). Our basic position is that interpretation, properly so-called, consists in recovering the intended meaning of the texts' authors. In defending that position, we explore its many competitors, such as textualism, dynamic interpretation, and the employment of highest-level purposes or concepts; and we also analyze the legal rules that compel departure

---

[7] *See* Schauer, *supra* note 5; H. L. A. Hart, *The Concept of Law* (Oxford: Clarendon Press 1961).

from interpretation as we define it and require that algorithms substitute for intended meanings. In addition, we examine the interpreter's predicament when there is no authors' intended meaning, or when that intended meaning is absurd or perverse. Finally, we ask whether interpreting a constitution is fundamentally different from interpreting other canonical legal texts and conclude that in most respects it is not.

Accordingly, as to both the common law and interpretation of legal texts, we find no ground for the claim that judges and other actors employ special methods of reasoning different from the methods employed by all reasoners in all contexts that call for decision making.

Law and Its Function

I

Settling Moral Controversy

I. Settlement

The need for legal reasoning comes about when members of a community confer authority on certain individuals to settle moral controversies.[1] The controversies that concern us arise in a community whose members agree on moral values at a fairly high level of generality and accept these values as guides for their own action.[2] Individuals who are fundamentally like-minded and well intentioned may nevertheless differ about the specific implications of moral values, or they may be uncertain about

---

[1] *See* Larry Alexander and Emily Sherwin, *The Rule of Rules: Morality, Rules, and the Dilemmas of Law* 11–15 (Durham: Duke University Press 2001). *See also* Joseph Raz, *Ethics in the Public Domain* 187–92 (Oxford: Clarendon Press 1994) (defending an "institutional" approach to law); Melvin Aron Eisenberg, *The Nature of the Common Law* 4–7 (Cambridge, Mass.: Harvard University Press 1988) (defending an "enrichment model" of the common law).

[2] *See* Gregory S. Kavka, *Why Even Morally Perfect People Would Need Government*, 12 Soc. Phil. & Pol'y 1 (1995).

the best ways to realize shared values. Recognizing that controversies of this kind are inevitable, the community can reduce the moral costs of disagreement and uncertainty by delegating a power of settlement to a chosen authority.

Settlement, as we use the term, is not simply choice of a solution. It entails reasoning, by which we mean conscious, language-based deliberation about reasons for the choice ultimately made.[3] The members of our imagined community have not agreed to flip a coin; they have selected a human authority to translate the values that serve as reasons for action within the community into solutions to practical problems.[4] Given the flaws of human reasoning, the solutions the authority endorses may not

---

[3] The nature of "reasoning" and the degree to which reasoning guides human decision making are much-debated subjects in the field of psychology. *See, e.g.*, Steven A. Sloman, *Two Systems of Reasoning*, in *Heuristics and Biases: The Psychology of Intuitive Judgment* 379–96 (Thomas Gilovich, Dale Griffin, and Daniel Kahneman, eds., Cambridge: Cambridge University Press 2002) (surveying evidence of parallel systems of "reasoning": associative and rule-based).

We do not intend to enter into or comment on this debate. Our definition of reasoning as conscious deliberation is a working definition sufficient to describe what we believe is required by the notion of authoritative settlement. Reasoning, for us, is distinct from intuition or affective response. The point we wish to make is that when a community confers power on an authority to settle moral controversy, it calls on the authority to deliberate – to engage in a process that is at least susceptible to explanation and justification. Whatever the psychology of personal moral judgment may be, a political authority must bring its power of reason, in this sense, to bear in decision making.

For a definition of reasoning that is similar to ours, though offered from a different point of view, *see* Jonathan Haidt, *The Emotional Dog and Its Rational Tail: A Social Intuitionist Approach to Moral Judgment*, 4 *Psychological Review* 814, 818 (2001) (moral reasoning is "conscious mental activity that consists of transforming given information about people"; [to say that] "moral reasoning is a conscious process means that the process is intentional, effortful, and controllable and that the reasoner is aware that it is going on"). For a philosophical analysis of forms of reasoning, *see* Simon Blackburn, *Think* 193–232 (Oxford: Oxford University Press 1999).

[4] We assume general agreement among members of the community on moral principles (we assume this because the function of rules in resolving moral uncertainty is easiest to see when there is no need to coerce compliance with moral principles). However, we take no substantive position either on the content of moral principles or on the possibility of moral options, moral ties, gaps in moral principles, or incommensurable moral choices. Our analysis is political in the sense that we are concerned not with law as the embodiment of moral truth but with law as a means by which communities seek to implement shared moral values.

We do make at least one substantive assumption, which is that members of the community believe that, at least in some situations, certainty, conflict avoidance, and coordination are of greater moral importance than vindication of their own views about what actions governing moral principles require. This is why they have conferred rule-making authority on certain officials. This assumption leaves room, however, for options and choices that are not governed by legal rules or determined by legal decisions – options that are outside the province of law.

be justified in the sense that they are morally correct. But, because the authority's task is to settle what the community's values require in practice, its conclusions must be susceptible to justificatory argument. They cannot refer to intuition alone.

If the authority chosen to settle controversies could be on the scene whenever a dispute or uncertainty arose, there would be no need for anything more than a series of decisions about what outcome is best in each instance, all things considered. Normally, however, it is neither practical nor desirable for authorities to be constantly on hand; therefore, the community will need a form of settlement that can guide future decision making. The way to accomplish this broader form of settlement is through authoritative rules.[5]

A rule, for this purpose, is a general prescription that sets out the course of action individual actors should follow in cases that fall within the predicate terms of the rule. To settle potential controversies effectively, the rule must prescribe, in understandable and relatively uncontroversial terms, a certain response to a certain range of factual circumstances.[6] It must claim to prescribe, and be taken as prescribing, what all actors subject to the rule should do in all cases it covers. It must also require its subjects to respond as prescribed without reconsidering what action would best promote the reasons or values that lie behind the rule. We call rules of this kind "serious rules," as distinguished from advisory rules or "rules of thumb" that purport to guide but not to dictate action.[7]

For example, suppose that a rule-making authority enacts the rule "No one shall keep a bear within one thousand feet of a private

---

[5] We have made the case for rule-bound decision making at length elsewhere. *See, e.g.*, Alexander and Sherwin, *supra* note 1, at 17–21, 53–122; and *see* Frederick Schauer, *Playing by the Rules: A Philosophical Examination of Rule-Based Decision-Making in Life and Law* 53–54 (Oxford: Clarendon Press 1991). We offer an abbreviated form of our argument in favor of deductive reasoning in Chapter 2; for the most part, however, our strategy in this book is to debunk the alternatives to deduction from rules that are commonly attributed to judges. We conclude that legal reasoning is ordinary reasoning applied to legal subject matter. Ordinary reasoning, for us, includes empirical analysis, moral reasoning, and deduction from serious rules. *See* Chapter 2, *infra*.

[6] On the need for determinacy to accomplish settlement, see Alexander and Sherwin, *supra* note 1, at 30–31; Schauer, *supra* note 5, at 53–54.

[7] For further discussion of the nature, function, and problems of "serious" authoritative rules, *see* Alexander and Sherwin, *supra* note 1, at 53–95; Schauer, *supra* note 5, at 42–52, 77–134; Joseph Raz, *The Morality of Freedom* 57–62 (Oxford: Clarendon Press 1986); Joseph Raz, *The Authority of Law* 16–19, 22–23, 30–33 (Oxford: Clarendon Press 1979).

residence."[8] The motivating reason for this rule may be to protect the safety and peace of mind of the inhabitants of residential neighborhoods. At a deeper level, the rule may reflect the assumptions that human interests rank higher than the interests of bears and that the liberty of property owners to use their property as they wish is subject to a duty not to inflict harm on others. In some situations, the rationale for the rule may not apply with its ordinary force: the bear may be a gentle, declawed former circus animal, kept in a sturdy double cage. But the rule makes no exceptions: its upshot is that bear owners must keep their bears elsewhere, irrespective of the underlying purpose of the rule.[9] Rule subjects therefore need not consult the rule's purposes in order to determine what the rule requires of them.

We use the term "rule" in a fairly inclusive way.[10] The rules we are interested in are posited by human beings; in this respect, they differ from nonposited moral principles. The rules' prescriptions are serious in the manner we have just described. Aside from these characteristics, the rules we are concerned with may be quite general or fairly specific, so long as they are general enough to settle some range of future cases. They may be posited in canonical form or implicit in material such as judicial opinions, as long as they are traceable to human decision making and determinate enough to guide action without the need for further assessment of the reasons that motivate them.[11]

Communities designate authorities to make rules because and to the extent that they deem authoritative settlement to be superior to

---

[8] This rule could take the form of a public regulation, such as a zoning ordinance; a private land use regulation, such as a covenant; or a judicial ruling that a bear in a residential setting is a nuisance per se. *Cf.* Lakeshore Hills, Inc. v. Adcox, 413 N.E.2d 548 (Ill. App. 1980) (preliminary injunction for removal of a 575-pound pet bear based on subdivision covenants).

[9] *See* Alexander and Sherwin, *The Deceptive Nature of Rules*, 142 U. Pa. L. Rev. 1191, 1192–93 (1994) (suggesting that rules deceive their audience by implying that the conduct they prescribe is the right course of action in all cases to which they apply).

[10] For a careful analysis of the variety of forms rules can take, *see* Schauer, *supra* note 5, at 1–16.

[11] We discuss canonicity and the possibility of implicit rules in Chapter 2, *infra* text at notes 45–46. On canonicity as a criterion for authoritative rules, *see* Frederick Schauer, *Prescriptions in Three Dimensions*, 82 Iowa L. Rev. 911, 916–18 (1997). We agree with Schauer that authoritative rules need not be posited in explicit terms. Because we believe the meaning of rules is a function of the rule maker's intent, we do not agree that rules can come into being without being created by a rule maker. *See id.* at 916–17. For us, rules must have authors; they may, however, have multiple authors, and interpreters of rules may become authors of rules. We take these matters up in detail in Chapters 5 and 6, *infra*.

individual decision making. The preference for settlement derives from
the moral costs of controversy and uncertainty and from the ability of the
chosen authorities to design rules that further the community's values
and ends. In particular, settlement avoids strife; it solves coordination
problems that arise when one person's reasons for action depend on the
actions of others; and it limits the need for costly deliberation.[12] If rule-
making authorities are wiser than most members of the community,
or have more deliberative resources at their command, authoritative
settlement is also more likely than unconstrained reasoning to resolve
controversy in morally desirable ways.[13]

We emphasize that authoritative rules address the problems of controversy and uncertainty, not the problem of misbehavior. In a nonideal
community, disputes may occur because particular individuals defect
from prevailing values or refuse to accept moral constraint. We set aside
disputes of this kind because we wish to show that settlement is necessary
even in the most auspicious social circumstances. In any event, when the
problem is defection from well-defined values rather than moral uncertainty, rules are not necessary: the community can refer directly to the
values it accepts and, guided by those values alone, punish or exact
reparations from errant individuals.

Conversely, doubt and disagreement make rules essential even when
all members of the community agree on the values they wish to pursue. Everyone may agree that private property is morally justified and
socially valuable, that owners should have the greatest possible freedom
to use and enjoy their property that is compatible with the interests of
others, and that human safety is of great importance, and yet differ about
whether keeping a pet bear interferes unreasonably with the enjoyment

---

[12] *See* Alexander and Sherwin, *supra* note 1, at 13–15; Schauer, *supra* note 5, at 137–55. On the
value of coordination, *see, e.g.*, Heidi M. Hurd, *Moral Combat* 214–21 (Cambridge: Cambridge
University Press 1999); Tom D. Campbell, *The Legal Theory of Ethical Positivism* 6, 50, 53,
58 (Aldershot: Dartmouth Publishing 1996); Jules L. Coleman, *Authority and Reason*, in *The
Autonomy of Law: Essays on Legal Positivism* 304–5 (Robert P. George, ed., Oxford: Clarendon
Press 1996); Raz, *The Morality of Freedom*, *supra* note 7, at 49–50; Neil MacCormick, *The
Concept of Law and* The Concept of Law, in *The Autonomy of Law*, *supra* at 162, 182, 190;
Donald H. Regan, *Authority and Value: Reflections on Raz's Morality of Freedom*, 62 S. *Calif.
L. R.* 995, 1006–10 (1989); Gerald J. Postema, *Coordination and Convention at the Foundation
of Law*, 11 J. *Legal Stud.* 165, 172–86 (1982).

[13] On the importance of rule-maker expertise, see Campbell, *supra* note 12, at 51, 58; Coleman,
supra note 12, at 287, 305; Schauer, *supra* note 5, at 150–52.

of surrounding land. This type of disagreement provides the motive and justification for authoritative rules.[14]

In a well-developed legal system, rule-making power will not be confined to a single official. The community may designate different rule makers or rule-making bodies for different domains, and rule makers themselves may establish secondary rules that vest power in other sources.[15] Delegation of rule-making power from one authority to another may also be implicit in institutional arrangements. For example, when a primary rule maker designates others to adjudicate disputes that arise under rules, the interpreter has power, at least presumptively, to supplement the rules when they prove to be incomplete or indeterminate.[16] The interpreter then becomes a rule maker in its own right. An implicit delegation of rule-making authority also occurs when the primary rule maker chooses to promulgate a standard – that is, a vague prescription that is likely to be indeterminate in many of its applications – rather than a determinate rule of conduct.[17] The vagueness of standards typically stems from their use of evaluative terms about which there is disagreement or uncertainty and therefore a need for settlement. Yet the standard itself, because it uses these terms, fails to provide settlement. Therefore, the standard functions as a delegation by the rule maker to actors in the first instance, and then to adjudicators called on to apply the standard, to act as rule makers.

Alternatively, official rule makers may decline to issue a prescription in any form, leaving individual actors free to choose their own courses of action within a certain domain. Or, if pluralism in interpretation of values and ends appears more important than settlement, the community may decline to confer rule-making authority within a domain. Even within

---

[14] *See* Alexander and Sherwin, *supra* note 1, at 11–15.

[15] On primary and secondary rules, see H. L. A. Hart, *The Concept of Law* 78–79, 89–96 (Oxford: Clarendon Press 1961).

[16] *See* id. at 94–95.

[17] On prescriptions in the form of standards, *see, e.g.,* Cass R. Sunstein, *Legal Reasoning and Political Conflict* 27–28 (New York: Oxford University Press 1996); Louis Kaplow, *Rules versus Standards: An Economic Analysis*, 42 *Duke L.J.* 557, 560–62 (1992); William Powers Jr., *Structural Aspects of the Impact of Law on Moral Duty within Utilitarianism and Social Contract Theory*, 26 *U.C.L.A. L. Rev.* 1263, 1270–93 (1979); Isaac Ehrlich and Richard A Posner, *An Economic Analysis of Legal Rulemaking*, 3 *J. Legal Stud.* 257, 261–71 (1974).

On deliberately indeterminate standards as delegations of authority, see Raz, *The Authority of Law*, *supra* note 7, at 193–245.

an unregulated domain, however, rules may guide action as individuals formulate general propositions to govern their own deliberations. In situations of this kind, individual actors act as their own rule makers.[18]

II. The Dilemma of Rules

Serious rules are necessary for effective settlement of moral and practical controversy. At the same time, serious rules generate a dilemma that renders authoritative settlement a psychological mystery, if not an impossibility. We have discussed this dilemma at length elsewhere; our present purposes require only a brief summary.[19]

If a rule is to settle doubt and controversy, it cannot simply track the values it is designed to promote. Instead, it must simplify moral and practical problems and translate disputed concepts into concrete terms. As a consequence, the rule will sometimes dictate a result that differs from what its motivating reasons require.[20] The rule "No bears within one thousand feet of a private residence" will prevent some bear lovers from rescuing circus animals, or result in their punishment, when the bear in question is unlikely to cause harm.

Nevertheless, from the point of view of the rule-making authority, as well as the community it governs, the best form of settlement may be a per se rule: no bears. The reason is that unconstrained decision makers make mistakes. Bear owners may make more errors, or errors of greater magnitude, in assessing potential harm case by case than they would make by following the rule consistently. If so, then it is rational and morally correct for the authority to issue a serious rule and insist on full compliance.

The dilemma of serious rules arises when one shifts to the perspective of individuals who are governed by the rules, the rule subjects. Setting aside for the moment the possibility of sanctions for disobeying the rule, if a bear owner believes that his bear is unlikely to cause harm and needs

---

[18] See Richard A. Fumerton, *Reason and Morality: A Defense of the Perspective* 208–23, 234–39 (Ithaca: Cornell University Press 1990) (discussing an act consequentialist's need for rules).

[19] For a full analysis of the dilemma of rules, see Alexander and Sherwin, *supra* note 1, at 53–95. Frederick Schauer makes a similar observation in his discussion of the "asymmetry of authority." *See* Schauer, *supra* note 5, at 128–34.

[20] *See* Schauer, *supra* note 5, at 31–34, 48–54.

a home, he may believe that following the rule is not the morally correct course of action, and it will not be rational for him to follow it.[21]

Yet, if we return to the perspective of the authority, the matter looks different because the bear owner may be wrong. By hypothesis, the moral and practical costs of potential mistakes are higher than the costs of full compliance with the rule; this is why the authority issued the rule. Therefore, it continues to be rational and morally correct for the authority to insist on compliance by all owners of bears. There is, in other words, a gap between the rational and morally correct course of action for the rule-making authority (issue and enforce the rule) and the rational and morally correct response on the part of the rule subject (disobey).[22]

We do not believe this gap can be closed, at least as long as rule subjects act rationally. Rule subjects might adopt the attitude Frederick Schauer calls "rule-sensitive particularism," taking into account the impact that failure to comply would have on the settlement value of the rule (the value of peace, coordination, expertise, and decision-making efficiency).[23] Rule-sensitive particularism is rational, and is

---

[21] *See* Hurd, *supra* note 12 at 62–94; Heidi M. Hurd, *Challenging Authority*, 100 *Yale L.J.* 1011 (1991). *See also* Gregory Kavka, *The Toxin Puzzle*, 43 *Analysis* 33 (1983); Gregory Kavka, *Some Paradoxes of Deterrence*, 75 *J. Phil.* 285 (1978) (explaining why it is impossible to form certain intentions). The rationality of following rules is a debated question; however, we are not persuaded that commitment, consent, or any other mental sleight of hand can make it rational, at the time of application of a rule, to act in a way that one believes to be wrong, all things considered. *See* Alexander and Sherwin, *supra* note 1, at 75–77. For contrary suggestions, *see, e.g.,* Scott J. Shapiro, *The Difference That Rules Make*, in *Analyzing Law* 33, 45–54 (Brian Bix, ed., Oxford: Clarendon Press 1998); Raz, *The Morality of Freedom, supra* note 7, at 88–99; David Gauthier, *Commitment and Choice: An Essay on the Rationality of Plans*, in *Ethics, Rationality, and Economic Behavior* 217 (Francesco Farina, Frank Hahn, and Stefano Vanncucci, eds., Oxford: Clarendon Press 1996); Edward F. McClennon, *Pragmatic Rationality and Rules*, 26 *Phil. and Pub. Aff.* 210 (1997); Mark C. Murphy, *Surrender of Judgment and the Consent Theory of Political Authority*, 16 *Law and Phil.* 115 (1997).

[22] *See* Larry Alexander, *The Gap*, 14 *Harv. J. L. & Pub. Pol.* 695 (1991). Because we believe this gap is unavoidable, we cannot accept Joseph Raz's suggestion that authoritative rules simply are, as an analytical matter, exclusionary in the sense that they preempt consideration of the reasons on which they depend. *See* Alexander and Sherwin, *supra* note 1, at 75–77; Raz, *The Morality of Freedom, supra* note 7, at 57–62; Raz, *The Authority of Law, supra* note 7, at 16–19, 22–23, 30–33.

[23] *See* Schauer, *supra* note 5, at 94–100; Frederick Schauer, *Rules and the Rule of Law*, 14 *Harv. J. L. & Pub. Pol.* 645, 676 n. 66 (1991) ("Given that result *a* is indicated by rule *R*, you [the rule subject] shall reach result *a* unless there are reasons for not following rule *R* in this case that outweigh the sum of the reasons underlying rule *R* and the reasons for setting forth those underlying reasons in the form of a rule").

probably required as a matter of correct reason. But it will not close the gap between the authority and rule subjects as long as some rule subjects may conclude that the reasons for violating rules outweigh all the reasons that motivate the rule, including the value of settlement. Indeed, rule-sensitive particularism is always threatened with unraveling and becoming nothing more than case-by-case, all-things-considered particularism. For in a community of rule-sensitive particularists, everyone would realize that no one was treating rules as serious rules. Therefore, the settlement value of rules would be reduced, which in turn would mean less expected compliance with rules and therefore less settlement value, and so on until the rules collapsed completely as serious rules.

Alternatively, rule subjects might resolve to follow rules unless the action prescribed by a rule is obviously wrong in a particular case – an attitude Schauer describes as "presumptive positivism."[24] This attitude, however, is not fully rational: the rule subject must resist acting on his or her best judgment unless the moral mistake in the application of the rule is not just likely but overwhelmingly likely.[25] In any event, even if we assume that a limited inquiry into reasons for action is psychologically feasible, there remains a possibility that rule subjects will err in applying the presumption called for by this approach. If so, the gap persists, particularly when the primary value of the rule lies in coordination.[26]

The rule-making authority can attempt to close the gap by providing for sanctions against those who violate rules. In terms of rationality, if not morality, enforcement may close the gap between rule makers and actors deciding whether to obey the rules, if violators are uniformly punished, and if avoiding punishment counts as a reason for action.[27] However,

---

[24] See Schauer, *supra* note 5, at 196–206.

[25] See Gerald J. Postema, *Positivism, I Presume? . . . Comments on Schauer's Rules and the Rule of Law*, 14 Harv. J. L. & Pub. Pol. 797, 815–16 (1991).

[26] For a fuller explanation of our reasons for rejecting presumptive positivism, *see* Alexander and Sherwin, *supra* note 1, at 68–73. Briefly: on the most plausible interpretation of presumptive positivism, the presumptive positivist takes a "peek" at both reasons for following the rule (including rule value) and reasons for violating the rule, then violates the rule if the reasons for doing so greatly exceed the reasons for compliance. If the presumptive positivist understands that other actors will treat the rule in the same way, and that in doing so they will sometimes err in favor of violating the rule, the coordination value of the rule quickly erodes and the presumption loses force.

[27] Possible concern about harm to oneself from justifiable sanctions should not count as a moral reason for action; even so, grave harm to oneself or incidental harm to others may at

a secondary gap arises when judges are asked to impose sanctions on subjects who have done what the judge perceives (or what the subjects perceive) to be right in a particular situation. In such a case, it is morally and rationally problematic for the judge to enforce the rules.[28] Moreover, to the extent that this secondary gap between rule maker and judges prevents uniform punishment, the primary gap between rule maker and subjects recurs.[29]

In fact, people do follow rules. They comply with rules they have designed for themselves and with rules imposed by authorities they recognize as legitimate, without reassessing underlying reasons for action. We suspect that the explanation for compliance lies in habit, socialization, and an element of self-deception. In our present inquiry into legal reasoning, we assume that some such combination of psychological mechanisms allows subjects and judges to follow and enforce rules in most cases. Nevertheless, the dilemma of serious rules remains in the background as we discuss deduction of legal conclusions from rules.

III. The Possibility of Determinate Rules

Another important background feature of our analysis of legal reasoning is the assumption that rules can provide determinate answers to legal questions in a significant number of cases. The purpose of rules is to settle controversy about what shared moral values and societal ends require in particular cases. To perform this function effectively, the rules must be understood by most of their subjects in a similar way. Because the premise that rules have determinate meaning is vital to our understanding of legal reasoning, we must briefly address rule skepticism.[30]

some point take on a moral dimension. *See* Postema, *supra* note 25, at 819, 822 (sanctions work by "*corruption* of the decisionmaking process").

[28] *See* Hurd, *supra* note 12, at 253–94; Rolf E. Sartorius, *Individual Conduct and Social Norms* 56–57 (1975); Heidi M. Hurd, *Justifiably Punishing the Justified,* 90 Mich. L. Rev. 2203, 2279–334 (1992).

[29] *See* Alexander and Sherwin, *supra* note 1, at 77–86.

[30] For arguments in support of the determinacy of rules, see Kent Greenawalt, *Law and Objectivity* 34–89 (New York: Oxford University Press 1992); Schauer, *supra* note 5, at 53–68; Hart, *supra* note 15, at 132–44; Jules L. Coleman and Brian Leiter, *Determinacy, Objectivity, and*

Critics of rule-oriented legal theory have, in various ways, challenged the assumption that rules can communicate determinate instructions to their subjects. Some are broadly skeptical about the capacity of law to constrain decision making.[31] Others believe in the possibility of legal constraint but argue that constraint comes not from rules but from professional norms or specialized modes of reasoning, such as reasoning by analogy.[32]

Particularly among proponents of analogical reasoning, the claim of indeterminacy often takes the form of an assertion that legal rules, being general, cannot determine their own application to particular cases.[33] This argument obviously runs contrary to our own conception of rule-oriented decision making, in which the critical feature of serious rules is precisely their capacity to dictate their application to particular cases. It might also seem puzzling to an ordinary rule subject, for whom many rules appear to provide comprehensible instructions about what to do.

What, then, does it mean to say that rules cannot determine their own application? One way to understand this claim of indeterminacy is

---

Authority, 142 *U. Pa. L. Rev.* 549 (1992); Lawrence B. Solum, *On the Indeterminacy Crisis: Critiquing Critical Dogma*, 54 *U. Chi. L. Rev.* 462 (1987).

[31] *See, e.g.,* Andrew Altman, *Legal Realism, Critical Legal Studies and Dworkin*, 15 *Phil. & Pub. Aff.* 205 (1986); Anthony D'Amato, *Pragmatic Indeterminacy*, 85 *Northwestern U. L. Rev.* 171–74 (1990); David Kairys, *Law and Politics*, 52 *G.W. L. Rev.* 243 (1984); Joseph Singer, *The Player and the Cards: Nihilism and Legal Theory*, 94 *Yale L.J.* 1 (1984). *See also* Hanoch Dagan, *The Realist Conception of Law* 8–12 (unpublished manuscript on file with the authors) (surveying indeterminacy arguments by American Legal Realists).

[32] *See, e.g.,* Lloyd L. Weinreb, *Legal Reason: The Use of Analogy in Legal Argument* 88–91, 103–5 (Cambridge: Cambridge University Press 2005); Steven J. Burton, *An Introduction to Law and Legal Reasoning* 18–20, 44, 52–57 (Boston: Little, Brown 1995); Karl Llewellyn, *The Bramble Bush: On Our Law and Its Study* 72–75 (Dobbs Ferry, N.Y.: Oceana Publishing 1960); Karl N. Llewellyn, *The Common Law Tradition: Deciding Appeals* 11–12, 178–235 (Boston: Little, Brown 1960).

[33] Lochner v. New York, 198 U.S. 45, 76 (1905) (Holmes, J., dissenting) ("General propositions do not decide concrete cases"); Burton, *supra* note 32, at 44 ("It may seem that rules can dictate the result in a case when this is not so."), 50 ("rules do not determine the scope of their own applications"), 57 ("the language of an enacted rule, announced before any case governed by the rule has materialized, describes an abstract class. The statement of conditions . . . points at the class of cases, not at the particular facts of any problem case"); Weinreb, *supra* note 32, at 89–90 ("because words, as symbols with meaning, are general, and phenomena, as such, are particular, and because words, however precise, do not fully distinguish phenomena in all their variety . . . there remains a gap between a rule and its application that no further statement of the rule or specification of the facts will close completely"), 91 ("no rule dictates a decision, in the manner of a deductive argument").

that the full extension of a rule – all cases to which it applies – is never clear from the rule's terms. This is true as far as it goes. If a rule prohibits bear owners from keeping their bears in "residential neighborhoods," cases are sure to arise involving mobile homes or hotels that may or may not be residential and may or may not count as neighborhoods. Ambiguity at the margins of usage, however, is not fatal to rule-governed legal reasoning if the meaning of the rule is clear in a significant number of cases. Rules will sometimes leave important controversies unsettled. How often this will occur is a difficult empirical question, but common experience suggests that indeterminacy is not pervasive.[34]

Another interpretation is that the claim that rules are indeterminate is a general claim about language. It may be that, in a certain technical sense, the words of a rule have no "meaning" apart from their use in particular cases because there are no facts in the world that correspond to the meaning of abstract language.[35] This argument is linguistically interesting but unimportant for purposes of legal reasoning. Whatever the true nature of linguistic meaning, basic social understandings allow courts and rule subjects to make sense of the language of rules.

Assume, for example, that the governing rule prohibits the keeping of bears "within one thousand feet of a private residence without the owner's consent." This rule contains some tricky words: ownership is a complicated legal construct, and a full definition of consent involves contestable moral conclusions.[36] Yet, the more typical forms of ownership are widely known, and most people understand that in a case of disputed land use, consent normally means express permission. Thus, in at least some instances, and probably in many, the words of the no-bear rule, coupled with minimal linguistic and social expertise on the part of rule subjects, dictate the rule's application. As Frederick Schauer puts it,

---

[34] *See* Greenawalt, *supra* note 30, at 36–41; Hart, *supra* note 15, at 132–36.

[35] *See* Saul A. Kripke, *Wittgenstein on Rules and Private Language: An Elementary Exposition* (Cambridge, Mass.: Harvard University Press 1982). Kripke is discussing Ludvig Wittgenstein, *Philosophical Investigations* §203 (Oxford: Blackwell 1997). *See also* Margaret Jane Radin, *Reconsidering the Rule of Law*, 69 B.U. L. Rev. 781, 797–811 (1989) (relying on Wittgenstein to refute traditional understandings of the rule of law). For discussion of Kripke's argument, see Schauer, *supra* note 5, at 64–68; Coleman and Leiter, *supra* note 30, at 568–72.

[36] *See, e.g.*, Peter Westen, *The Logic of Consent: The Diversity and Deceptiveness of Consent as a Defense to Criminal Conduct* (Aldershot: Ashgate 2004); Alan Wertheimer, *Consent to Sexual Relations* (Cambridge: Cambridge University Press 2003).

among members of a community who share a language and a sense of its "universal context," words and their intended meanings have "semantic autonomy."[37] (For us, if not for Schauer, semantic autonomy does not imply the autonomy of words from the author's intended meanings – an autonomy we reject.[38] Semantic autonomy means only the autonomy of those intended meanings from the purposes the words and their meanings are intended to achieve. Autonomy in this sense is enough to make rules determinate in core cases.)

A more significant version of the claim that legal rules cannot determine their own application is the claim that the meaning of any rule depends on its purpose. On this view, rules are promulgated as means for realizing certain underlying values and ends, and the only way to ascertain their application to particular cases is to ask what those values and ends require in the circumstances.[39] Assuming the no-bear rule is designed to protect the safety of surrounding residents, a bear owner, or a court, might conclude that it should not apply to a very docile, well-caged bear 999 feet from a single residence occupied by a retired lion tamer. Thus, even in a linguistically simple case, the words of the rule do not determine whether an entry is legally permissible.

In our view, this argument overlooks the settlement function of serious rules. Given the possibility that those who apply rules will err in assessing the implications of a rule's purposes for individual cases, the best way to promote those purposes may be to identify a course of action that, if universally followed, will result in fewer errors overall. In other words, the benefits of the rule as a means of advancing purposes and realizing certain values come precisely from its semantic autonomy – the independence of what it prescribes from the purposes it serves. At best, the argument that rules are indeterminate because their meaning in particular cases depends on their purposes expresses a contestable view about the best way to pursue social ends rather than a logical implication of rules.[40]

---

[37] See Schauer, *supra* note 5, at 55, 57.

[38] Schauer suggests that rules may take on social meanings separate from their authors' intent. Id. at 218–21. We disagree, although we recognize that the question of authorship is sometimes complex. See Chapter 6, *infra*.

[39] See, e.g., Lon L. Fuller, *Positivism & Fidelity to Law: A Reply to Professor Hart,* 71 Harv. L. Rev. 630, 663–69 (1958).

[40] See Schauer, *supra* note 5, at 59–61. Schauer points out that the same criticism applies to a claim of legal indeterminacy made by some semantic realists. The claim is, roughly, that the

Another variant of the indeterminacy argument takes a different form but is ultimately similar in effect. Rule skeptics sometimes assert that rules cannot determine the outcomes of particular cases because the application of any rule depends on a prior classification of facts.[41] For example, Steven Burton states that, at the point of application of a rule, "[t]he connection between the abstract class and the case remains to be drawn. . . . Drawing this all-important connection – placing a case in a legal class – requires a judgment of importance to mark the particular facts that justify the classification."[42]

Burton has something more in mind than the obvious truth that the outcome of any decision depends on the decision maker's skill and integrity in finding facts.[43] Rather, his claim appears to be that the decision maker must judge which facts count as important features of the case in order to determine whether the case fits within the words of the rule. But why should this be so? If we are correct that the words of a rule, read in light of common social understandings about usage and context, have semantic autonomy, it should follow that rules themselves pick out the important features of individual cases. Burton may be using the term "classification" to refer to an assessment of the relationship between specific facts and the underlying purposes of the rule: if, and only if, certain facts are important to the purposes of the rule, or to the overall question of what outcome is best, should they be classified as falling within the terms of the rule.[44] If this is the argument, however, it suffers from the same weakness as the argument from the purposive interpretation of rules: it depends on an inadequate view of the operation of rules.

The last indeterminacy argument we address is an argument about the body of legal rules as a whole. Centuries of legislative and judicial rule

---

meaning of words corresponds to the best current understanding of the things described, and the best understanding of law is a function of the values it serves. This argument relies implicitly on the contestable view that adjudication is best understood as entailing direct, rather than indirect, pursuit of values.

Our own understanding of rules includes the view that interpretation of rules should refer to the intent of rule makers. *See* Chapter 5, *infra*. This might be thought to introduce a source of indeterminacy. A crucial feature of rule makers' intent, however, is the decision to employ a rule. In other words, the rule maker intends the rule to possess a degree of semantic autonomy from the purposes the rule maker intends it to implement.

[41] *See* Burton, *supra* note 32, at 18–20, 44, 52–57; Weinreb, *supra* note 32, at 88–91, 103–5.
[42] Burton, *supra* note 32, at 57.
[43] On the effects of fact finding, see Greenawalt, *supra* note 30, at 45–48.
[44] *See* Burton, *supra* note 32, at 97–102.

making have produced a tangled accumulation of rules. Even if we assume that individual rules have a degree of semantic autonomy, the number and complexity of existing rules, combined with a certain amount of interpretive play, make it likely that, in a case of any difficulty, two or more different rules will point to different outcomes. As a consequence, legal rules do not determine the outcome of particular cases: decision makers face a choice among rules, a choice for which the rules themselves provide no guidance.[45]

The claim of indeterminacy is significant, but we do not think it seriously threatens the possibility of governance by rules. As Frederick Schauer has pointed out, the extent of overlap among rules is an empirical question.[46] Moreover, rather than simply choosing among rules that appear to conflict, judges can and do avoid conflict by ranking and refining the rules. The very fact that legal actors try to reconcile conflicting rules belies the suggestion that the multiplicity of rules undermines legal constraint.[47]

A related argument against rule-oriented views of law holds that even if rules are capable of conveying determinate meaning, simple rules that permit deductive reasoning are rare in our legal system. Instead, legal norms typically are phrased as broad standards calling for "reasonable" conduct or "fair" dealing between parties. This is an empirical question, but we believe that deduction plays a larger role in law than may at first appear. A legal standard phrased in evaluative terms that are just as likely as underlying moral principles to generate uncertainty is not a rule and, indeed, will not support deductive reasoning. In our view, the reasoning involved in applying a standard of this kind is simply unconstrained moral and empirical reasoning. Purely evaluative standards, however, are just as rare in law as fully determinate rules. Legal standards typically not only are bounded by rules that constrain their scope but also frequently have a core of determinate meaning, or have rulelike terms that limit the applicable criteria for moral and empirical reasoning and operate as rules to that extent. ("Drive

---

[45] See Llewellyn, *The Bramble Bush, supra* note 32, at 72–75; Dagan, *supra* note 31, at 10–13.

[46] See Schauer, *supra* note 5, at 194–95; Coleman and Leiter, *supra* note 30, at 572–578.

[47] See Schauer, *supra* note 5, at 195–96. Schauer puts this in terms of judicial psychology: according to Schauer, it is an empirical question whether judges faced with conflicting rules choose the rule that best supports their all-things-considered (or political) conclusion or attempt instead to resolve the conflict.

reasonably in light of the weather" is a standard that is limited to driving and is evaluative only with respect to weather conditions.) A working legal system is likely to contain a sufficient number of determinate rules and hybrids of the sort just described to provide significant, if not pervasive, deductive constraint.

IV. The Nature of Law

Legal reasoning is, of course, about law. So it might seem that to address properly the subject of legal reasoning, we must first specify what we mean by law. We do not think this is the case: nothing in our analysis of legal reasoning requires an answer to the jurisprudential question of what counts as law. Nevertheless, it may be useful to summarize briefly how we might respond to that question.

In classic debates about the identity of law, the principal divide has been between natural law and positivism.[48] Those who support the natural-law position hold that because law purports to guide action and impose obligations, the validity of any proposition as law depends on its conformity to moral standards. Positivists, on the other hand, hold that the status of a norm as law depends on social facts and, in particular, on the fact that the norm was posited by a source generally recognized as a lawmaking authority. Moral evaluation is not necessary – and, on some versions of positivism, not permissible – in determining the identity and content of law. Another difference between natural law and positivism is methodological: natural-law theorists look at law from the committed stance of insiders, who look to law for their own practical guidance, whereas positivists look at law from the external

---

[48] *See generally*, Brian H. Bix, *Natural Law: The Modern Tradition*, in *Oxford Handbook of Jurisprudence and Philosophy of Law* 61 (Jules Coleman and Scott Shapiro, eds., New York: Oxford University Press 2002); John Finnis, *Natural Law: The Classical Tradition*, in *Oxford Handbook of Jurisprudence and Philosophy of Law, supra*, at 1; Kenneth Einar Himma, *Inclusive Legal Positivism*, in *Oxford Handbook of Jurisprudence and Philosophy of Law, supra*, at 125; Andrei Marmor, *Exclusive Legal Positivism*, in *Oxford Handbook of Jurisprudence and Philosophy of Law, supra*, at 104; *Postscript to H.L.A. Hart's* The Concept of Law, Parts I and II, 4 *Legal Theory* 249–547 (1998). Our own position can be found in Alexander and Sherwin, *supra* note 1, at 183–211.

position of observers analyzing the practices of those who are committed to law.[49]

In some ways, our understanding of the function and operation of law fits more comfortably within a positivist theory of law than a natural-law theory. Communities recognize lawmaking authorities because they want the benefits of settlement; effective settlement requires serious rules; and serious rules, even the best serious rules possible, produce morally defective outcomes in some cases.

At the same time, however, our view of law is linked to morality in several ways. We recognize that the positivist's route to settlement relies on insiders' recognition of lawmaking authority and insiders' compliance with particular laws, both of which are moral matters. The settlement function that justifies legal authorities and their posited norms – the very phenomena that are the focus of positivism – is itself a moral function. Its aim is to reduce the moral costs of anarchy, costs that will occur even among those who are morally motivated. Moreover, as we stated at the outset, the act of settlement entails moral reasoning: the authority's rules, if not actually justified, must be the product of a conscious process that is susceptible to justificatory argument. Only then can members of the community view them as an exercise of the authority they have conferred, authority to settle what the community's values require.

Thus, for us, positivism and natural law are complementary rather than conflicting positions that describe two different facets of "law." Indeed, a central feature of our analysis of law is the dilemma of rules described earlier, a dilemma that arises from this dual character of law and raises doubts about the possibility of law in the positivist sense.

In this book, we approach the problem of legal reasoning within a mainly positivist framework. We focus on how judges respond to posited law and how they distinguish between reasoning from posited law and reasoning in the absence of posited law. Moreover, our analysis proceeds from a detached perspective of the kind associated with positivism.

Ultimately, we argue that courts function in two ways: they reason deductively from rules posited by others; or they posit law, relying on

---

[49] *See* Hart, *supra* note 15, at 38–41, 79–88; Finnis, *supra* note 48, at 15–18; Jules Coleman, *Methodology*, in *Oxford Handbook of Jurisprudence and Philosophy of Law*, *supra* note 48, at 311, 314–42; Stephen R. Perry, *Interpretation and Methodology*, in *Law and Interpretation: Essays in Legal Philosophy* 97 (Andrei Marmor, ed., Oxford: Clarendon Press 1995).

moral and empirical judgment, as any lawmaker must. For us, there is no middle ground in which courts discover nonposited law in past decisions or texts, or combine morality and posited law to construct legal principles. At the same time, however, we are sensitive to both the moral ends of law (settlement and its benefits) and the dilemma that judges and rule subjects face when posited law appears to dictate morally erroneous results.

PART TWO

Common-Law Reasoning: Deciding Cases When Prior Judicial Decisions Determine the Law

We have assumed that even in an ideal community whose members share basic values and are disposed to act on them, settling controversies over specific applications of those values will be a high priority. Accordingly, the community will vest a power of settlement in chosen authorities. The community's primary lawmaking authorities, being unable to preside over every dispute that arises, will design and enforce general, serious rules.

In many cases, the primary authority's rules will prove sufficiently determinate to settle controversy without further official involvement. But this will not always be the case. Rules will require interpretation, a problem we take up in later chapters. Rules also will require enforcement: even if all actors within the community are disposed to act on the same values that animate the authorities' rules, some may be mistaken about what the rules require and others may believe that, in a given case, what the rule prescribes is wrong. Finally, the set of rules promulgated by lawmaking authorities will not provide answers to all questions that might arise in disputes. For all these reasons, the community, or the primary rule-making authority, will need to create adjudicative authorities – judges with power to apply rules and settle particular disputes.

It is possible to conceive of a legal system in which judges perform a purely adjudicative function. Judicial decisions would not be publicized and, consequently, would have no prospective effect.[1] Actual legal systems, however, have not evolved this way, perhaps as a result of community demand for settlement.[2]

In the early period of English common law, for example, the role of courts was confined almost entirely to retrospective adjudication.[3] Judges announced their views orally, and the only written records of decisions were uninformative formal entries and scanty collections of observers' notes.[4] Precedents were invoked from memory and were cited, if at all, as evidence of law rather than embodiments of law.[5] The common law itself was conceived of as an amalgam of custom and reason taken up by judges.[6] Over time, however, judicial decisions became increasingly

---

[1] Bentham favored an arrangement along these lines. *See* Gerald J. Postema, *Bentham and the Common Law Tradition* 403–8, 453–64 (Oxford: Clarendon Press 1989).

[2] *See* Melvin Aron Eisenberg, *The Nature of the Common Law* 4–5 (Cambridge, Mass.: Harvard University Press 1988) ("Our society has an enormous demand for legal rules that private actors can live, plan, and settle by").

[3] *See* Gerald J. Postema, *Classical Common Law Jurisprudence, Part II*, 3 *Oxford U. Commonwealth L.J.* 1, 11–17 (2003). For an account of the unwritten character of early common law and the increasing "textualization" of common law over time, *see* Peter M. Tiersma, *The Textualization of Precedent*, available from *Social Science Research Network*, http://ssrn.com/abstract=680901 (2005).

[4] *See* J. H. Baker, *An Introduction to English Legal History* 177–80, 196–98 (4th ed., London: Butterworth's Lexis-Nexis 2002); J. W. Tubbs, *The Common Law Mind: Medieval and Early Modern Conceptions* 42–46 (Baltimore: Johns Hopkins University Press 2000).

[5] *See* 1 William Blackstone, *Commentaries on the Laws of England* 71 (Oxford: Clarendon Press 1765); Tubbs, *supra* note 4, at 182; Tiersma, *supra* note 3, at 17; Gerald J. Postema, *Classical Common Law Jurisprudence, Part I*, 2 *Oxford U. Commonwealth L.J.* 155, 160–62 (2002); Postema, *supra* note 3, at 11–17. One manifestation of this idea was a judicial practice of declining to rule when the judges disagreed among themselves: if judges disagreed, the opinion of the majority was only weak evidence of the law. *See* Baker, *supra* note 4, at 198.

[6] *See* Postema, *supra* note 5, at 176–80; Postema, *supra* note 3, at 1–11. J. W. Tubbs suggests at least five possible understandings of the term "reason," as used in the Yearbooks and other English sources from the thirteenth to the seventeenth century: equity in the Aristotelian sense of corrections of the errors of general rules; natural law; reason in distinction to the will of judges; internal coherence; "tried reason" tested by experience; and Coke's notion of "artificial" reason gained through training and refined by learned argument. Tubbs, *supra* note 4, at 46–52, 68–73, 148–51, 161–68.

public, textualized, and authoritative, particularly in the United States.[7] Reports were regularized, secondary materials sorted precedents by legal type, and judges began to write opinions.[8] Lawyers focused increasingly on the texts representing judicial opinions, and judges as well as legal observers came to recognize a stronger connection between past and future decisions.[9]

The evolution of English common law suggests that adjudication is unlikely to remain purely that – adjudication – in a working legal system. At the least, decisions adjudicating controversies, as well as the reasoning on which they are based, will be known to the public. Once publicized, adjudicative decisions and their bases will serve not only as examples of legal reasoning but also as subjects of legal reasoning by courts and private actors.[10] The following chapters address the nature of this reasoning.

[7] See Tiersma, supra note 3, at 25–51; Baker, supra note 4, at 181–86.
[8] In the United States, statutes and state constitutions often require courts to issue written opinions. See Tiersma, supra note 3, at 38. Opinions issued by "the court" have replaced seriatim statements by individual judges, and reports are official. Id. 39–42.
[9] See David Lieberman, The Province of Legislation Determined 122–43 (Cambridge: Cambridge University Press 1989) (tracing the evolution of judicial attitudes toward lawmaking in the eighteenth century); Tiersma, supra note 3, at 52–69 (reporting findings on the frequency of explicit judicial statements and quotations of holdings).
[10] See Eisenberg, supra note 2, at 5.

II

Ordinary Reason Applied to Law

Natural Reasoning and Deduction from Rules

In our view, there are two plausible models of common-law reasoning, and only two.[1] The first is the "natural" model, in which courts resolve disputes by deciding what outcome is best, all things considered. In the courts' balance of reasons for decision, prior judicial decisions are entitled to exactly the weight they naturally command.[2] The second

---

[1] For earlier statements of our views on judicial treatment of precedent, see Larry Alexander and Emily Sherwin, *The Rule of Rules: Morality, Rules, and the Dilemmas of Law* 136–56 (Durham: Duke University Press 2001); Larry Alexander and Emily Sherwin, *Precedent*, in *Common Law Theory* (Douglas Edlin, ed., Cambridge: Cambridge University Press 2005); Larry Alexander, *Constrained by Precedent*, 63 S. Cal. L. Rev. 1 (1989).

[2] Michael Moore can be read as endorsing this model of the common law. Michael S. Moore, *Precedent, Induction, and Ethical Generalization*, in *Precedent in Law* 183, 210 (Laurence Goldstein, ed., Oxford: Clarendon Press 1987) ("one sees the common law as being nothing else but what is morally correct, all things considered – with the hooker that among those things considered are some very important bits of institutional history which may divert the common law considerably from what would be morally ideal"). However, Moore also expresses sympathy, at least procedurally, with the notion of reasoning from legal principles – a notion we criticize in Chapter 3. *See* id. at 201.

model of common-law reasoning is the "rule" model, in which courts treat rules announced by prior courts as serious rules of decision, but then revert to natural decision making when rules provide no answers.[3]

The difference between these two models of common-law reasoning is that the natural model treats judicial decisions as facts about the world, whereas the rule model treats them as sources of law. In the next chapter, we explain why, contrary to many popular views of common-law decision making, we believe that there are no other intelligible ways to reason from precedent.

I. The Natural Model of Common-Law Reasoning

The most obvious tools for courts to use in addressing controversies are moral and empirical reasoning. We assume that moral reasoning follows the Rawlsian method of wide reflective equilibrium: the reasoner makes an initial judgment about how a particular case should be resolved, formulates a tentative moral principle to support his or her initial judgment, and then tests the principle by picturing other actual and hypothetical examples of its application. If the principle yields results the reasoner judges to be wrong in test cases, the reasoner must refine the analysis. The reasoner can either reject the supporting principle and reconsider the initial judgment; hold to the initial judgment and attempt to reformulate the principle; or, if the reasoner is convinced that the principle as formulated is sound, reconsider his or her judgments about its other applications. By moving between principles and particulars in this way, the reasoner can reach a better understanding of both moral values and their implications for the case at hand.[4]

---

[3] See Alexander and Sherwin, The Rule of Rules, supra note 1, at 145–48 (endorsing a rule model); Frederick Schauer, Playing by the Rules: A Philosophical Examination of Rule-Based Decision-Making in Life and Law 185–87 (Oxford: Clarendon Press 1991) (endorsing a rule model); Alexander, supra note 1 (finding the rule model superior to alternatives). See also Melvin Aron Eisenberg, The Nature of the Common Law 52–55, 62–76 (Cambridge, Mass.: Harvard University Press 1988) (suggesting that courts generally accept a rule model of precedent, but coupling the rule model with a generous view of overruling powers).

[4] See John Rawls, A Theory of Justice 14–21, 43–53, 578–82 (Cambridge, Mass.: Belknap Press of Harvard University Press 1971); Howard Klepper, Justification and Methodology in Practical Ethics, 26 Metaphilosophy 201, 205–6 (1995); Norman Daniels, Wide Reflective Equilibrium and

Let us say, for example, that Heidi is a judge. In the case before her, Stephen has made plans to open a halfway house for released prisoners in a residential neighborhood.[5] Brian, who owns a home next to the proposed site for the halfway house, has sued to enjoin the project as a nuisance – that is, an unreasonable interference with Brian's use and enjoyment of his land. Brian argues that a halfway house will increase traffic and bring to the neighborhood unsavory characters who might have a bad influence on local children. Stephen's evidence shows that the halfway house will house only nonviolent criminals such as minor drug offenders and that prisoners are more likely to make a successful transition back into society if they spend time in a halfway house. Stephen has not yet invested significant resources in the project. We assume, as we shall assume throughout this chapter, that there are no pertinent public regulations or private land use agreements in the legal background of the case.

Heidi's initial sense of the case is that the halfway house should be allowed to open. The burden on landowners like Brian is not too great, and Stephen will have difficulty finding a suitable location if residential landowners are given a veto. To support this judgment, she formulates a principle: uses of land that do not pose a significant threat to the health or safety of surrounding owners should be permitted.

To test her principle, Heidi considers examples of some other activities that might be challenged as nuisances if carried on in a residential neighborhood, examples drawn from actual cases or from her imagination. In her view, a pet bear, a rifle range, a paintball arena, and a mortuary should not be allowed, whereas a day care center and a sewage treatment plant would be reasonable. Heidi's principle, allowing land uses that pose no significant threat to health or safety, confirms her judgment about the bear (risky), the rifle range (risky), the day care center (low risk), and probably the sewage treatment plant (not much risk). However, it does not exclude a paintball arena and a mortuary. At this point, Heidi might reformulate the principle: uses of land that pose no significant threat to

---

Theory Acceptance, 76 J. Phil. 256 (1979); John Rawls, *Outline of a Decision Procedure for Ethics*, 60 Phil. Rev. 177 (1951).

[5] *Cf.* Nicholson v. Connecticut Half-way House, Inc., 218 A.2d 383 (Conn. 1966) (injunction against halfway house on ground of nuisance).

health or safety and provide a needed service to the community should be permitted. The added requirement of public interest leaves open the possibility that homeowners could resist a paintball arena and is therefore more consistent with Heidi's judgments about particular cases. The mortuary remains a problem. Disposing of bodies might be deemed a needed service; if so, Heidi may need to reconsider her initial response to that case.

In any event, the issues posed by the halfway house dispute seem clearer now than when Heidi began. The method of reasoning she has used, however, is not uniquely legal. It is what any careful reasoner does in working through a moral problem.

Some controversies requiring settlement by courts will turn on the probable consequences of actions or the best means for implementing agreed ends, rather than on specification of moral principles. In such a case, courts must engage in empirical reasoning, gathering data and testing hypotheses. Empirical reasoning is probably more prominent when courts consciously formulate general rules for future cases than when they focus on the resolution of a single dispute, but it can enter into particularized decision making as well – for example, when the outcome of a dispute depends on an assessment of risk. The case of the halfway house illustrates the point: to decide the question of nuisance, Heidi must determine whether nonviolent ex-prisoners pose a substantial threat to the safety of neighbors.[6] Again, this type of assessment is not unique to law. There are legal procedures that may assist Heidi in assessing the risk of violence as well as procedures that may limit her ability to do so, but there is nothing especially "legal" about the method of reasoning involved.

Within a natural model of common-law decision making, moral and empirical reasoning are the only tools courts use to resolve disputes. This does not mean, however, that courts disregard past judicial decisions; past decisions enter into moral and empirical reasoning as facts about the world that can affect the outcome of a current case. Yet past decisions are not authoritative in the sense that they might dictate an outcome

---

[6] *See* id. at 385–86. Another common problem requiring empirical judgment is assessment of damages for harm extending into the future. *See generally* Douglas Laycock, *Modern American Remedies* 19–37, 201–31 (3d ed., New York: Aspen 2002).

that is contrary to the court's best judgment of what should be done, all things considered.

The principal way in which prior decisions affect current decision making within a natural model of precedent is as a source of expectations.[7] Expectations can form around judicial decisions in several ways. First, parties to a dispute may rely on the finality of the court's disposition. For example, suppose Claire plans to open a day care facility in Jules's neighborhood. Jules seeks an injunction on the ground that careless parents are likely to damage surrounding lawns as they drop off their children. Heidi concludes that the proposed facility is not a nuisance and denies the injunction. Claire and Jules will expect Heidi to reach the same result if Jules sues again, unless the facts have changed in some important way. Relying on this expectation, Claire may go forward with her day care investment and Jules may pave over a section of grass.

Apart from the immediate parties, others may observe the outcome of a litigated dispute and form an expectation that courts will reach similar conclusions in the future. Leo, who is thinking of opening a day care facility in a neighborhood similar to Jules's, may calculate that future courts will not view day care as a nuisance. Accordingly, he is now more likely to go forward with his plans.

Without more, a third-party expectation such as Leo's is not necessarily a justified expectation and therefore not a reason for decision within a natural model of the common law. Apart from the merits of the decision, which Leo is in no better position to assess now than he was before Heidi decided the case of *Jules v. Claire*, the reasonableness of Leo's prediction of consistent treatment depends on the likelihood that courts will in fact take his expectations into account as a reason for decision. In other words, his expectations are not justified unless there is some independent reason, other than his having formed them, for courts to protect them.

---

[7] *See* Henry M. Hart Jr. and Albert M. Sacks, *The Legal Process: Basic Problems in the Making and Application of Law* 55–58, 568–72 (William N. Eskridge Jr. and Phillip P. Frickey, eds., New York: Foundation Press 1994); Schauer, *supra* note 3, at 137–45, 155–58; Eisenberg, *supra* note 3, at 10–12 (discussing "replicability" as a criterion for sound law); Stephen R. Perry, *Judicial Obligation, Precedent, and the Common Law*, 7 Oxford J. Legal Stud. 215, 248–49 (1987).

There is, however, a general social interest in facilitating private expectations.[8] Another way to put this is that there is a social interest in coordination. Lack of coordination among individual actors is a common source of moral and practical error: the best course of action for one person often depends on the actions others take. Yet the actions of others are difficult to predict, especially when their choices too depend on others' unforeseeable acts.[9]

In a legal system in which judicial decisions are publicly accessible, courts can provide coordination by acting consistently over time. Individual actors can then predict with some degree of confidence that others will conform their conduct to the express or implied requirements of past decisions. Suppose that Sai is about to make a career decision that turns in part on the availability of local day care in Leo's suburb. If Heidi refuses to enjoin Claire's facility in the case of *Jules v. Claire*, and if Sai believes that later courts are likely to give weight to expectations of judicial consistency because of their social importance, Sai has an additional reason to anticipate that he will have easy access to day care and can make a better-informed decision about his career. Moreover, because the value of coordination provides courts with an independent reason for consistency with past decisions, apart from avoiding harm to the specific individuals who formed expectations based on those decisions, Leo's and Sai's expectations about the course of future adjudication are now justified expectations. As such, they become moral reasons for judicial consistency in their own right.

Another reason sometimes given for consistency with past decisions under a natural model of common-law decision making is equal treatment: as a moral matter, similarly situated parties should be treated alike; therefore, when two like cases arise over time, the later court should conform its decision to the decision of the earlier court. Suppose, for example,

---

[8] *See* Hart and Sacks, *supra* note 7; Andrei Marmor, *Should Like Cases Be Treated Alike?*, 11 *Legal Theory* 33, 155 (2005); L. L. Fuller and William R. Perdue Jr., *The Reliance Interest in Contract Damages*, 46 *Yale L.J.* 52, 62–63 (1946).

[9] For discussion of the value of coordination, *see, e.g.*, Schauer, *supra* note 3, at 162–66; Joseph Raz, *The Morality of Freedom* 49–50 (Oxford: Clarendon Press 1986); Gerald J. Postema, *Coordination and Convention at the Foundation of Law*, 11 *J. Legal Stud.* 165, 172–86 (1982); Donald H. Regan, *Authority and Value: Reflections on Raz's Morality of Freedom*, 62 *S. Cal. L. Rev.* 995, 1006–10 (1989).

that *Jules v. Claire*, the day care case, is now pending before Heidi. Jules cites a prior case in which another judge, Rick, granted an injunction prohibiting Ben from opening a day care facility in a residential neighborhood. Many would say that Rick's prior decision gives Heidi a reason, if not a conclusive reason, to enjoin Claire: Ben and Claire should be treated alike.[10]

Equal treatment, on this view, is a moral value in its own right, independent from other moral principles. If protection of residents from traffic and noise were definitive moral reasons to enjoin Ben, and if Claire's facility will cause traffic and noise to the same or a greater extent, then Claire should be enjoined as well. The reason for doing so, however, is not equality but traffic and noise. Equal treatment enters in when other moral principles do not require Heidi to reach the same result in Claire's case that Rick reached in Ben's case. Equal treatment is also distinct from the parties' expectations: the argument from equal treatment applies even when there is no suggestion that Jules has changed his position in reliance on the outcome in Ben's case.

A related point is that equal treatment matters only when the prior decision appears to have been wrong. If Heidi believes that Rick was correct in his judgment that the noise and traffic generated by Ben's day care facility amounted to a nuisance, and if she also believes that Claire's case and Ben's case are alike, equal treatment need not enter into her reasoning because protection of residents against noise and traffic provides the ground for a like result. Only if Heidi believes that Rick was correct about Ben, and that Claire should win against Jules, does equal treatment become a consideration.

Although the principle "Treat like cases alike" is widely accepted as a cornerstone of fairness, we believe it has no place in common-law reasoning about the implications of past decisions.[11] One reason is that

---

[10] *See, e.g.*, Moore, supra note 2, at 183; Kent Greenawalt, *How Empty Is the Idea of Equality?*, 83 *Columbia Law Review* 1167, 1170–71 (1983).

[11] *See* John E. Coons, *Consistency*, 75 *Cal. L. Rev.* 59, 102–7 (1987). For more general critiques of equality as a moral ideal, *see* Peter Westen, *Speaking of Equality: An Analysis of the Rhetorical Force of "Equality" in Moral and Legal Discourse* 119–23 (Princeton: Princeton University Press 1990); Christopher J. Peters, *Equality Revisited*, 110 *Harv. L. Rev.* 1210 (1997). *See also* Marmor, *supra* note 8 (acknowledging that equal treatment has no role to play when there are reasons for decision, but offering a limited defense of the principle of equal treatment in the absence of determinative reasons for decision).

real cases are never truly alike: Claire's day care facility is sure to differ in some ways from Ben's. Moreover, the only access Heidi has to the facts of Ben's case is the recital of facts in Rick's opinion. Rick's opinion, written with other purposes in mind, may filter out facts that differentiate the cases in important ways.

More important, even if we assume that the past and present parties are similarly situated in all relevant ways, we fail to see how equal treatment of this type can count as a moral good. For purposes of Heidi's reasoning, the current case must be viewed only from Heidi's perspective, and Heidi believes that Rick's prior decision enjoining a day care center was a moral error. *One moral error is not a reason for another.* Ben may have suffered an unjust loss in his case, but his loss is a consequence of the prior error, not of Heidi's decision for Claire, and a contrary decision – to enjoin Claire – will not make good the loss.

Let us elaborate on this point, for the argument that equal treatment is a moral imperative can be seductive. Equal treatment of a certain type *is* a moral imperative in particular situations. For example, when what justice requires is solely comparative, as some claim it to be in matters of retribution, and still more claim it to be in matters of distribution of resources or opportunities, then if *A* receives a certain punishment or a certain distribution of benefits, and *B* is identical to *A* in terms of retributive or distributive desert, then it follows that *B* should receive what *A* received in equal measure. The general point is banal: under any moral principle that dictates that *A* and *B* should be treated the same, if *A* is given treatment *T*, morality demands that *B* be given treatment *T*.

In the cases we are considering, however, the present judge believes that in the prior case, the losing party was treated in a way that was morally wrong. The question before us is whether any moral notion of equality demands that if one party is treated wrongly, it is right to treat another party in the same way – a way that would be wrong in the absence of the prior case. Does killing half of an ethnic group as an act of genocide create any reason based on equality, however weak, to complete the task? We think the answer is obviously no: equality furnishes absolutely no reason to extend past immoralities.

The same is true of judicial decisions: reliance aside, the fact that judges have strayed from the standard of morally correct treatment in the past does not alter the obligation of present judges to apply the correct moral principle to any and all litigants. If, to the contrary, equal treatment were a moral imperative requiring consistency with past decisions (including mistaken ones), morally incorrect decisions would corrupt morality itself. Moreover, if the set of past cases included both morally correct and morally incorrect decisions, the very notion of equality would lose coherence, with correct and incorrect decisions pulling in different directions.

There are cases in which equal treatment may be a legitimate consideration for judges. If the current decision is likely to place a prior litigant at a competitive disadvantage, avoiding further harm may be a reason for like treatment. If, for example, Ben's business will suffer if Claire is allowed to locate in a residential neighborhood, the potential new harm to Ben may be a (nonconclusive) reason to enjoin Claire. But it is Ben's further harm, not the value of equality, that is doing the work here. Equal treatment may also be warranted, on grounds of distributive justice, when the moral merits of a case are in balance.[12] If Ben's case was essentially a coin flip on the merits, and the same is true of Claire's case, perhaps Ben and Claire, who run comparable businesses, should be treated alike. Courts, however, do not flip coins: they generally feel obliged to reach a conclusion as to which party has the superior right.[13] Once a court has determined that one party has a stronger claim, that party should prevail without regard to past mistakes.

In sum: within a natural model of common-law decision making, courts engage in moral and empirical reasoning to determine what outcome is best, all things considered. Past decisions are relevant to the extent that they have generated justified expectations of consistency in the future. For those who reject our views about equal treatment, past decisions are also relevant to the extent of the weight properly accorded to equality (a mystery we leave to believers). Past decisions are not, however, authoritative: the overall balance of reasons for a decision, including expectations and (if you will) equal treatment, determines the outcome of judicial reasoning.

[12] *See* Marmor, *supra* note 8.
[13] One manifestation of this attitude is the reluctance of courts to adopt sharing remedies in close cases. *Cf.* R. H. Helmholtz, *Equitable Division and the Law of Finders*, 52 *Fordham L. Rev.* 313 (1983) (supporting equitable division but conceding that courts rarely grant remedies of this kind as a matter of common law).

II. The Rule Model of Common-Law Reasoning

An alternative model of common-law decision making builds on the natural model but adds one important feature: courts treat rules announced
by prior courts as authoritative in later cases that fall within the rules'
terms. When no rule applies, courts continue to engage in moral and
empirical reasoning to resolve disputes. If, however, the case is governed by a precedent rule, courts turn instead to interpretation and
deductive reasoning.[14]

To make clear the full implications of the rule model of the common
law, we must first return briefly to the natural model. Rules have a role
in the process of natural reasoning. As we explained in Chapter 1, rules
capture the rule maker's expertise, provide coordination for individual
actors who need to predict what others will do, and simplify the process
of decision making. For a natural reasoner, preservation of these rule-
based benefits may be a reason to conform to the rule: if disregarding the
rule would result in a loss of rule-based benefits, and that loss is likely to
outweigh the moral costs of following the rule, then it is right, all things
considered, to follow the rule.

For example, suppose Heidi is presiding over a suit to enjoin Mike's
Mortuary from opening for business in a residential neighborhood. Heidi
discovers a prior opinion by her fellow judge, Rick, stating that mortuaries in residential neighborhoods are nuisances.[15] If Heidi endorses the
natural model of decision making, she will not accept the no-mortuary
rule as authoritative: the result she reaches will be based on the balance of moral reasons for decision. Nevertheless, the rule may affect her
judgment insofar as it serves as a source of coordination or may have
engendered reliance.

Within a natural model of reasoning, however, a rule announced
in a past case has only the weight it commands in all-things-considered

---

[14] We take up the problem of interpretation in Part 3. In our view, all rules should be interpreted
according to the intent of their authors (taking into account the authors' decision to employ
a rule). Interpretation of common-law rules follows the same fundamental principles as
interpretation of statutes and other texts; it differs only in that both the rule and its "author"
may be more difficult to identify.

[15] *See* 8 A.L.R.4th 324 (2004) (collecting cases); Dr. Martin M. Moore, *Improving the Image and
Legal Status of the Burial Services Industry*, 24 *Akron L. Rev.* 565 (1991).

moral reasoning. In other words, judges approach previously announced judicial rules as rule-sensitive particularists,[16] taking into account the value of maintaining the rule as one of many reasons for decision. As we said in the preceding chapter, however, rule-sensitive particularism is always threatened with collapse into pure case-by-case particularism: if all judges are rule-sensitive particularists and all judges know this, then the value they accord to rules as rules in their reasoning will approach zero, and they will end up reasoning like pure particularists. Thus, if Heidi concludes through the process of reflective equilibrium that no plausible moral principle supports the exclusion of mortuaries from residential neighborhoods, and if she is not convinced that a no-mortuary rule has significant coordination benefits, she will ignore the rule and hold for Mike's.

The rule model of precedent entails a different attitude toward rules. In this model, prior judicial rules operate as serious rules, preempting the question whether the reasons for the rule justify the outcome it prescribes in a particular case.[17] If Heidi, presiding over the suit against Mike's Mortuary, discovers a no-mortuary rule in a prior opinion, her inquiry into the risks, aesthetics, and social benefits of mortuaries is finished. Subject to certain qualifications (discussed later), she must grant an injunction.[18]

The rule model of common-law decision making also entails a different role for judges. Under a rule model, rules announced in judicial opinions acquire authoritative status. Accordingly, judges now function as lawmakers as well as adjudicators. Traditionally, common-law judges were reluctant to assume lawmaking authority: their task, as they saw it, was not to make law but to find it embedded in social and legal practice and the dictates of reason.[19] Modern judges, however, are more forthright

---

[16] See Schauer, *supra* note 3, at 94–100; Frederick Schauer, *Rules and the Rule of Law*, 14 Harv. J. L. & Pub. Pol. 645, 676 n. 66 (1991). Rule-sensitive particularism is discussed in Chapter 1, *supra* note 23 and accompanying text.

[17] See Raz, *supra* note 9, at 17–62; Joseph Raz, *The Authority of Law* 16–19, 22–23, 30–33 (Oxford: Clarendon Press 1979).

[18] We discuss refinements of the rule model later in the chapter. *See* text at notes 33–58, *infra*.

[19] See J. W. Tubbs, *The Common Law Mind: Medieval and Early Modern Conceptions* 182 (Baltimore: Johns Hopkins University Press 2000); Sir Matthew Hale, *The History of the Common Law of England* 45 (1713) (Charles M. Gary, ed., Chicago: University of Chicago Press 1971); 1 William Blackstone, *Commentaries on the Laws of England* 69–70 (Oxford: Clarendon Press

in their exercise of lawmaking power.[20] The rule model assumes that judges have such a power.

III. Comparing the Models

In a world in which all judges were perfect reasoners, the natural model of the common law would undoubtedly be superior to the rule model. The natural model seeks the best outcome in every case. The rule model, in contrast, guarantees that some outcomes will be wrong.

The errors of the rule model of common law have several sources. First, the rule model incorporates the basic problem of rules: rules must be stated in terms that are general and determinate enough to guide future conduct and decisions; therefore, they do not perfectly capture the less determinate values they are designed to promote. It follows that in some of the cases they cover, they will prescribe the wrong result.[21]

A second source of error is bad rules. Rules prevent error by translating the expertise of the rule maker into prescriptions for action, by facilitating coordination, and by reducing the costs of decision making;

1765); Gerald J. Postema, *Classical Common Law Jurisprudence, Part I*, 2 *Oxford U. Commonwealth L.J.* 155, 166–67 (2002). *But cf.* J. H. Baker, *An Introduction to English Legal History* 200 (4th ed., London: Butterworth's Lexis-Nexis 2002) (suggesting that the ranks of judges have always included both "timid souls" and "bold spirits").

For modern descriptions of legal decision making that come close to the classic understanding, *see* Lloyd L. Weinreb, *Legal Reason: The Use of Analogy in Legal Argument* 147–52 (Cambridge: Cambridge University Press 2005) (associating the rule of law with the idea that courts "are not to decide for themselves what the law is but are to seek it out, to discover and apply it as it is," but also maintaining that the process of declaring law entails judgment as well as reason). *See also* Ronald Dworkin, *Taking Rights Seriously* 82 (Cambridge, Mass.: Harvard University Press 1977) ("Judges should apply the law that other institutions have made; they should not make new law"); A. W. B. Simpson, *The Common Law and Legal Theory*, in *Oxford Essays in Jurisprudence* 77, 84–86 (2d ser., A. W. B. Simpson, ed., Oxford: Clarendon Press 1973) ("common law rules enjoy whatever status they possess not because of the circumstances of their origin, but because of their continued reception").

[20] *See* Eisenberg, *supra* note 3, at 4–7 (1988) (maintaining that courts inevitably make law, not only as a by-product of adjudication but also to enrich the body of legal rules); Benjamin N. Cardozo, *The Nature of the Judicial Process* 125 (New Haven: Yale University Press 1949) ("Since the days of Bentham and Austin, no one, it is believed, has accepted [the theory that judges do not legislate] without deduction or reserve").

[21] *See* Schauer, *supra* note 3, at 31–34, 48–54; Chapter 1, *supra* text at note 17.

but they also cause error by prescribing wrong outcomes, through bluntness or otherwise.[22] They are justified only when, judged by the values on which they are based, they will prevent more error than they cause.[23] Some rules fail to meet this standard, either because they were poorly conceived from the outset or because circumstances have changed since they were issued.

For several reasons, judicial rules are particularly likely to lack justification or to lose their justification over time. Judges are not necessarily expert rule makers, and, as we explain more fully in later sections, the task of resolving a particular dispute may further hinder their ability to craft sound rules.[24] Another problem is that once judicial rules are recognized as authoritative, they are hard to eliminate. Judges traditionally have been reluctant to overrule established rules of law, and in any event it is difficult to formulate a standard for overruling that does not jeopardize the benefits of authoritative rules.[25]

Despite the inescapable flaws of serious judicial rules, the rule model of common-law decision making has advantages that we believe justify courts in adopting it. In the world as it exists, judges are not perfect reasoners: judges operating under the natural model of decision making will seek to reach the best decision, all things considered, but they will not always succeed. The important comparison, in other words, is not between full implementation of values and flawed implementation of values, but between the flaws of unconstrained reasoning and the flaws of rules. The rule model is preferable if there is reason to think that a greater sum of moral errors will occur if judges always decide what is best, all things considered, than if they treat previously announced judicial rules as serious rules of decision.

---

[22] On the benefits of rules, *see* Chapter 1, *supra* text at notes 11–13.

[23] *See* Raz, *supra* note 9, at 70–80 (discussing the "normal justification" of authority).

[24] *See* Frederick Schauer, *Do Cases Make Bad Law?*, 73 *U. Chi. L. Rev.* 883, 893–912 (2006); Alexander and Sherwin, *The Rule of Rules, supra* note 1, at 132–33 (noting the possibility of cognitive bias); Emily Sherwin, *A Defense of Analogical Reasoning in Law*, 66 *U. Chi. L. Rev.* 1179, 1191–92 (1999) (same). *But cf.* Jeffrey J. Rachlinski, *Bottom-Up and Top-Down Decisionmaking*, 73 *U. Chi. L. Rev.* 993, 940–64 (2006) (suggesting that courts and legislatures have different cognitive advantages and disadvantages for different purposes). We discuss this problem in greater length in Chapter 4, *infra* text at notes 16–32.

[25] We discuss the problem of overruling in, *infra* text at notes 56–61, and in Chapter 4, *infra* text at notes 36–44.

As we have said, the capacity of rules to prevent error depends primarily on the expertise of rule makers and the coordination value of the rules. In the context of the common law, the makers of rules are judges in past cases. Comparing past judges to present judges, rule-maker expertise does not go far to make the case for a rule model of the common law. In the case of Mike's Mortuary, for example, we can assume that Rick, who announced the rule that mortuaries in residential neighborhoods are nuisances, has no greater capacity for moral and empirical reasoning about property rights than Heidi, the current judge. Moreover, the salient image in Rick's mind at the time of his decision probably was the mortuary at issue in his case, which may not have been representative of mortuaries generally.[26] Therefore, rather than representing special expertise, the no-mortuary rule may be myopic.

Some judicial rules stand on better epistemic ground than others. If the mortuary rule has been followed over time by a multitude of judges, it may be entitled to greater respect as a reflection of collective judgment.[27] A further consideration is that judicial rules have a wider audience than future judges. In comparison to private judgment, a judicial rule may sometimes have the advantage. In the mortuary case, Rick has studied evidence and heard opposing arguments by advocates about the risks, burdens, and benefits associated with mortuaries in residential neighborhoods. Private decision makers, in contrast, may have less information at their command, and their judgment may be distorted by self-interest. On the other hand, in some settings private actors will have the best information about their own activities, so the argument from expertise remains weak.[28]

---

[26] *See infra* text at notes 31–32, and Chapter 4, *infra* text at notes 26–32 (discussing cognitive biases likely to affect rule making in the context of adjudication).

[27] *See* Sir Edward Coke, *The First Part of the Institutes of the Law of England*, §138, ¶97B (1628), reprinted in II *The Selected Writings of Sir Edward Coke* 577, 701 (Steve Sheppard, ed., Indianapolis: Liberty Fund 2003) (quoted in Introduction, n. 2); Edmund Burke, *Reflections on the Revolution in France, and on the Proceedings in Certain Societies in London Relative to That Event* (1790), in Edmund Burke, *Selected Writings and Speeches* 424, 469–70 (Peter J. Stanlis, ed., Washington, D.C.: Regnery Gateway 1963); Simpson, *supra* note 19, at 94. *But cf.* Tubbs, *supra* note 19, at 161–63 (suggesting that Coke's views evolved over time, as he came to place more emphasis on "reason" and less on antiquity).

[28] *See generally* Robert C. Ellickson, *Order without Law: How Neighbors Settle Disputes* (Cambridge, Mass.: Harvard University Press 1991).

A much stronger argument is that judicial rules, when treated as serious rules, provide a new source of coordination. The coordination effect may be easier to see if we alter the mortuary example in the following way: in the precedent case, Rick announces a rule that mortuaries are permissible in residential neighborhoods as long as they pass municipal safety inspections. If this rule is authoritative for future judges, mortuary entrepreneurs can make plans to locate in suburbs without the worry that surrounding landowners will sue to prevent them from opening. If Heidi is free to decide in the next case what outcome is best, all things considered, these entrepreneurs are less able to predict how landowners will respond. Because lack of coordination results in decisional error, the community has reason to favor judicial creation of authoritative legal rules. Serious judicial rules also can simplify decision making, both by future judges and by potential disputants, who must guess the course of judicial decision making and settle or litigate accordingly.[29]

Thus, the rule model of common law offers at least some of the benefits of rules generally. It creates a new set of rule-making authorities (judges) who, while they may lack special expertise, can increase the level of coordination within the community. Mortuary owners will know where they can and cannot build. Homeowners will know whether mortuaries can build near their homes. Judges need not revisit the morality of mortuary nuisance.

We have noted that the natural model of common-law decision making also takes account of judicial rules. Within the natural model, judges can – and, as a matter of sound moral reasoning, must – take account of the value of consistently applied rules as a reason to follow rules announced in prior cases. But because natural reasoners approach rules as rule-sensitive particularists, most if not all of the benefits of rules will be lost under the natural model of decision making.

To see why, suppose first that the no-mortuary rule appears to reflect collective wisdom (a form of expertise). Many judges have held over time that mortuaries in residential neighborhoods are nuisances. Heidi

---

[29] This may not affect the volume of litigation. *See* George L. Priest, *Private Litigants and the Court Congestion Problem*, 69 *B.U. L. Rev.* 527, 534 (1989) (discussing the effects of docket congestion on the expected value of judgments). However, it should make decision making easier for at least some parties.

endorses the natural model of decision making and acts as a rule-sensitive particularist. She recognizes that the rule bears indicia of expertise, but she also understands general rules are by nature overinclusive, and she believes that Mike's Mortuary is a particularly well-run and tasteful establishment. She may reason that even if past judges were well informed about mortuaries generally, the balance of reasons underlying the rule does not apply to Mike's. Accordingly, she may refuse to issue an injunction. This is all very well if Heidi is correct, but she may be wrong. And if judges in Heidi's situation (or private parties predicting what judges will do in Heidi's situation) are wrong more often than they are correct in second-guessing the rule, the community would be better off if all judges treated the rule as a serious rule.

More important for our purposes, rule-sensitive particularism runs into serious difficulties in accounting for the coordination benefits of rules. Suppose again that Heidi follows the natural model of decision making. She understands that Rick's no-mortuary rule has the capacity to coordinate the conduct of landowners and prospective morticians. She also believes that the rule should not apply to Mike's Mortuary because Mike's is tasteful and well run. The question she must ask in the course of all-things-considered reasoning is whether a decision for Mike's, contrary to the rule, will cause a reduction in the overall coordination benefits of the rule such that the loss of coordination outweighs the moral gain from (what she believes is) a correct understanding of liberty and property rights as applied to Mike's.

One difficulty is that the loss of coordination from any single departure from the rule may seem negligible. But the problem is more serious. The coordination benefits of a judicial rule depend on its consistent application in the courts: only then can actors assume that future judges (and other actors) will follow the rule. In a legal system dominated by the natural model of judicial reasoning, Heidi will expect most other judges to approach judicial rules as rule-sensitive particularists. Rather than simply following the no-mortuary rule, they will ask whether all relevant considerations, including maintenance of the coordination benefits of the rule, recommend enjoining a particular mortuary from opening in a particular neighborhood. Some will conclude that they should not grant an injunction; and, given the inevitability of reasoning errors, some who reach this conclusion will be wrong. The prospect that other rule-sensitive particularists will not follow the rule reduces the rule's capacity to coordinate conduct, and therefore reduces the weight that Heidi, as well as other rule-sensitive particularist judges, will allocate to the coordination value of the rule in their calculations of what decision is best. In other words, if judges cannot predict confidently that the rule will be widely followed, no judge will calculate that his or her departure from the rule will damage an otherwise effective source of coordination. In this way, rule-sensitive particularism as a universal practice unravels into pure particularism stripped of serious rules and their benefits.[30]

The situation changes if some judges treat precedent rules as serious rules. If some judges give preemptive effect to rules, but would cease to do so if they observed rule-sensitive particularist judges disregarding the rule, then the potential coordination value of the rule gives rule-sensitive particularists a reason to follow the rule. But even when judicial response is divided – some following the rule model and some acting as natural reasoners – the coordination value of rules is unstable at best. Only a widely accepted rule model of common-law decision making preserves the full potential of precedent rules to provide coordination.

A further problem is that, to the extent that precedent rules retain some capacity to coordinate conduct, judges acting as natural reasoners may fail to give coordination its due weight in the balance of reasons for decision. The difficulty is cognitive: psychological research suggests that decision makers tend to focus on facts that are especially salient and, in doing so, tend to disregard or undervalue background probabilities. This bias, which Kahneman and Tversky have called the "availability heuristic," is one of a number of cognitive biases that facilitate decision making but also distort human reasoning in systematic ways.[31] Tangible

---

[30] For more examples, *see* Alexander and Sherwin, *The Rule of Rules, supra* note 1, at 61–68.

[31] *See, e.g.,* Amos Tversky and Daniel Kahneman, *Availability: A Heuristic for Judging Frequency and Probability,* in *Judgment under Uncertainty: Heuristics and Biases* 163 (Daniel Kahneman, Paul Slovic, and Amos Tversky, eds., Cambridge: Cambridge University Press 1982); Scott Plous, *The Psychology of Judgment and Decision Making* 121–30 (Philadelphia: Temple University Press 1993); Norbert Schwarz and Leigh Ann Vaughn, *The Availability Heuristic Revisited: Ease of Recall and Content of Recall as Distinct Source of Information,* in *Heuristics and Biases: The Psychology of Intuitive Judgment* 103 (Thomas Gilovich, Dale Griffin, and Daniel Kahneman, eds., Cambridge: Cambridge University Press 2002). Fred Schauer has made the connection between availability and judicial decision making. *See* Schauer, *supra* note 24, at 894–95. *See also* Timur Kuran and Cass R. Sunstein, *Availability Cascades and Risk Regulation,* 51 *Stan. L. Rev.* 683 (1999) (discussing the effect of availability on legislation);

facts move quickly to the front of one's mind, while statistical regularities remain obscure; as a result, the more readily available features of a problem claim disproportionate attention.

In legal disputes, the most salient facts are likely to be the circumstances of the litigants before the court. In the mortuary case, Heidi's attention will naturally be drawn to the character of the plaintiffs' neighborhood, the emotional impact a mortuary is likely to have on the plaintiffs,[32] and the specifics of Mike's proposed mortuary. Meanwhile, the availability heuristic predicts that Heidi's interest will not be similarly engaged by the possibility that departing from the rule might undermine potential coordination benefits for mortuaries and homeowners making plans in other neighborhoods.

Thus, even if the actual coordination value of a rule is not entirely eroded by the prospect that some judges will not follow the rule, judges may systematically underemphasize coordination value in their calculation of what is best, all things considered. The rule model of judicial decision making prevents this form of error by preempting all-things-considered analysis. In this way, it both preserves the actual coordination value of the rule and builds in protection against judicial miscalculation of that value.

A further point of comparison between the rule model of judicial decision making and the natural model is the complexity of the decision-making process. The rule model requires interpretation of rules, but once the court has determined that a precedent rule covers the case before it, all that remains is to follow the prescription of the rule. Under the natural model, in contrast, the existence of a precedent rule complicates rather than simplifies decision making. A rule-sensitive particularist judge must make at least a quick assessment of the rule's meaning to determine whether it is likely to apply, and then must determine what weight the possible benefits of maintaining the rule should have in the balance of reasons for decision.

A definitive comparison of the two models of judicial decision making we have discussed – the rule model and the natural model – would require

Cass R. Sunstein, *What's Available?: Social Influences and Behavioral Economics*, 97 Nw. U. L. Rev. 1295 (2003) (same).
[32] *See* Moore, *supra* note 15, at 570–71.

empirical knowledge that we do not have. The critical question is whether the rule model ultimately results in less decisional error than the natural model. The answer depends on, among other things, the number and magnitude of likely reasoning errors by judges, the social value of various benefits of rules that might be lost under a natural model of reasoning, and the number and magnitude of errors that result from compliance with a contingent set of overinclusive rules – matters that are extremely difficult to quantify or compare. We are inclined to think that, given the frequency of human error and the demand for settlement we observe in society, the rule model is the better choice. In any event, it is at least possible, as a matter of logic, that deduction from imperfect serious rules will produce better results overall than all-things-considered evaluation of what decision is best.

Although there are reasons to think that judges can do better by following precedent rules than by natural reasoning, there are difficulties with the rule model of decision making. Most prominently, the rule model confers a broad rule-making authority on judges. We have already noted that, because judges' first task is to resolve particular disputes, they are not ideally positioned to design sound rules. Later in this chapter, we discuss possible qualifications to the rule model that impose some restraint on judicial lawmaking and also provide judges with a means of escape from precedent rules that are seriously flawed.

Another set of difficulties is descriptive: judges purport to act, and are widely believed to act, in ways that are not consistent with the rule model of decision making. As rule makers, they decline to exercise the full range of legislative power the rule model makes available to them. As rule appliers they "distinguish" seemingly applicable rules based on factual differences among cases. In Chapter 4, we return to the rule model and consider whether these features of judicial practice can be explained as strategies to counteract the disadvantages of rule making in the context of adjudication.

This brings us back to the point with which we began the present chapter: despite appearances to the contrary, we believe that the two models of decision making we have described, the natural model and the rule model, are the only plausible models of judicial reasoning. Moreover, neither of these models entails special "legal" forms of reasoning. Both rely on methods of reasoning used by all decision makers: moral reasoning, empirical reasoning, and, in the case of the rule model, deduction from authoritative rules. In our view, these are all the tools that judges need, and all the tools they use in fact.

IV. A Closer Look at the Rule Model: Implications and Puzzles

We have suggested that, at least under some conditions, judges can best implement the shared values of a community by treating rules announced by past judges as serious rules that determine the results of present cases. A central premise of the rule model of judicial decision making is that judges act as rule makers: judges have authority not only to resolve disputes but also to issue binding general rules to govern future disputes. The assumption that judges have power to establish legal rules leads to a number of further questions about the scope of judicial rule-making authority and the nature of judicial rules. We do not claim to have a complete set of answers; our objective in the following sections is simply to identify some of the puzzles judges might face in implementing a rule model of the common law.

A. PROMULGATION OF RULES

The first question that arises under a rule model of the common law is, When should judges announce rules? Legislatures issue rules in response to social problems that come to their attention in a variety of ways. Their rules typically are prospective and designed to deal as comprehensively as possible with the problems they have taken up.[33] Judges traditionally have taken a different approach, issuing rules in response to particular disputes brought before them by litigants. Judicial rules typically provide an answer to the dispute before the court and do not stray far beyond what is necessary to resolve that dispute.[34]

---

[33] *See, e.g.*, Rachlinski, *supra* note 24, at 937 (summarizing differences between legislative and adjudicative perspectives). Rachlinski states that "Courts *must* resolve the disputes before them and need not declare principles. Legislatures *must* declare general principles and cannot resolve single disputes." Id.

[34] *See, e.g.*, Cass R. Sunstein, *One Case at a Time* 4 (Cambridge, Mass.: Harvard University Press 1999) (citing the principle that "courts should not decide issues unnecessary to the

Nothing in the rule model of judicial decision making dictates that courts must adhere to this pattern of narrowly conceived, retrospective rules. The rule model treats precedent rules as serious rules. Yet, because rules are general in nature, precedent rules will always extend beyond the exigencies of the cases in which they are announced.[35] It follows that the rule model confers plenary legislative power on judges.[36] There may be constitutional limits on judicial lawmaking, as well as pragmatic reasons for judges to abstain from exercising plenary power,[37] but there are no inherent constraints on judicial authority to make rules.

Suppose, for example, that Heidi is deciding the case of Edward, who is keeping a pet bear in his home. Neighboring homeowners claim the bear is a nuisance and have requested an injunction requiring Edward to remove it from the neighborhood. After moral reflection, Heidi reaches three conclusions. First, bears typically should not be permitted in residential neighborhoods. Second, the possibility of reasoning errors and the need for clarity, coordination, and decision-making simplicity justify a serious rule: "Bears in residential neighborhoods are nuisances." Third, Edward's bear, which is small, friendly, and declawed and has spent its life

resolution of a case"); A. W. B. Simpson, *The Ratio Decidendi of Case and the Doctrine of Binding Precedent,* in *Oxford Essays in Jurisprudence* 148, 160–61, 167 (A. G. Guest, ed., London: Oxford University Press 1961). The idea that judicial rule making should not exceed the requirements of particular controversies is reflected in various justiciability doctrines adhered to by American courts. *See, e.g.,* Schauer, *supra* note 24, at 913–15.

[35] *See* Schauer, *supra* note 24, at 4–7 (discussing judicial lawmaking); Frederick Schauer, *Giving Reasons,* 47 *Stan. L. Rev.* 633, 638–42 (1995) (pointing out that reasons judges give for their decisions are necessarily broader than the decisions themselves and thus operate in the manner of rules).

[36] *Cf.* Raz, *supra* note 17, at 194–201. Raz acknowledges that judges make law, and that, in doing so, they should act "as one expects Parliament to act, i.e. by adopting the best rules they can find." Id. at 197. Yet he suggests that the lawmaking function of courts differs from that of legislatures, because judge-made law is revisable by later courts and therefore "less 'binding' than enacted law." Id. at 195. He also insists that judges act as "gap-fillers" and that "only the ratio" of judicial decisions is binding on future judges ; as a consequence, "[t]here are no pure law-creating cases." Id. at 194–95. These limitations may be descriptive of actual practice, but Raz does not explain why they should be taken as logically necessary features of judicial rule-making power.

[37] For discussion of considerations bearing on the exercise of judicial power, *see, e.g.,* Helen Hershkoff, *State Courts and the "Passive Virtues": Rethinking the Judicial Function,* 114 *Harv. L. Rev.* 1833 (2001); Alexander M. Bickel, *The Supreme Court, 1960 Term – Forward: The Passive Virtues,* 75 *Harv. L. Rev.* 40 (1961).

in captivity, poses no significant threat to neighbors; therefore Edward should be allowed to keep his pet.

In the circumstances, Heidi has at least three options. She can decide for Edward and decline to announce a rule. She can announce the optimal rule ("Bears are nuisances") and apply it retrospectively to Edward. Or she can decide for Edward and announce the rule "Bears are nuisances" as a rule to govern future cases.

The rational choice – and, if Heidi's reasoning is morally sound, the morally optimal choice – is the third of these: decide for Edward and announce a prospective rule. In this way, Heidi can secure both a correct outcome for Edward and maximum settlement value for the future. If we assume, as the rule model assumes, that judges have authority to settle moral controversy by announcing serious rules, their authority appears to encompass this alternative. Those familiar with judicial practice in the United States, however, are likely to find this resolution of the case surprising and possibly unsettling.[38]

Now, suppose we carry the example further. In the course of her deliberation in Edward's case, Heidi reflects on the problem of noise in residential neighborhoods. This reflection leads her to a fourth conclusion, that the community would be better off if all residential homeowners mowed their lawns between two and four o'clock on Saturday afternoons. The coordination benefits of such a rule, she concludes, outweigh possible inconveniences to owners who prefer a different time. We expect that most people would find it unseemly, as well as contrary to the ideals of due process and democratic representation, for Heidi to issue a rule, "Homeowners must mow between two and four o'clock on Saturday afternoons."[39] Yet once we recognize that judges

---

[38] For an arguable instance of prospective ruling, see Wilson v. Layne, 526 U.S. 603 (1999) (developing standards for qualified immunity). See also Hershkoff, supra note 37, at 1844–52, 1859–61 (discussing advisory opinions and moot decisions).

   Prospective *overruling*, as a way to rid the legal system of undesirable rules while minimizing the harm to parties who have relied on precedent rules, has had some supporters. See Beryl Harold Levy, *Realist Jurisprudence and Prospective Overruling*, 109 *U. Pa. L. Rev.* 1 (1960); cf. Eisenberg, *supra* note 3, at 127–32 (favoring a very limited use of the technique). The United States Supreme Court, however, has disapproved the practice. See Harper v. Virginia Dept. of Taxation, 509 U.S. 86 (1993); James B. Beam Distilling Co. v. Georgia, 501 U.S. 529 (1991); Griffith v. Kennedy, 479 U.S. 314 (1987).

[39] In traditional terms, this is a clear example of "dicta," which later courts are free to reject as outside the scope of binding precedent. See Steven J. Burton, *An Introduction to Law and Legal Reasoning* 37–38, 60 (Boston: Little, Brown 1995); Simpson, *supra* note 34, at 160–61.

have rule-making authority, the logic of authority places no limit on her power to issue the rule. To the extent that judges refrain from issuing rules of this kind, the disability is self-imposed.[40]

B. IDENTIFICATION OF PRECEDENT RULES

Another question about the rule model of the common law arises from the perspective of later judges: what acts and statements by past courts count as binding precedent rules? Legislative rules may require interpretation, but identifying the rule is not a problem. Because courts traditionally have been reluctant to legislate overtly, their rules can be harder to recognize. Judicial opinions typically focus on the immediate task before the court – resolution of a particular case. They are likely to contain a narrative description of the facts of the dispute, references to precedent cases, and a more or less complete explanation of the court's reasoning, but they may not explicitly announce a rule for future cases.[41]

---

[40] The statement in the text is intended to make an analytical point only. The primary rule-making authority designated by the community (typically, a legislature) will find it necessary to delegate the task of adjudicating particular disputes to judges. If we are correct about the moral function of precedent rules, the primary authority will also find it desirable, from a moral point of view, to confer rule-making authority on judges. It may be that, for reasons pertaining to the political legitimacy of adjudicative decision making and the freedom of citizens from arbitrary coercion, the primary authority will also find it desirable to place some constraints on judicial rule making. (For example, the authority might require judges to comply with the clear dictates of legal rules duly enacted by representative legislatures.) But there is nothing in the nature of adjudication that limits the scope of the adjudicator's rule-making power. In fact, as we note, any recognition of rule-making power in adjudicators entails that adjudicators can legislate beyond the necessities of the case before them.

For purposes of our present analysis, we set aside a range of important political questions about the legitimacy of judicial rule making. For example, judicial rule making may conflict with the ideal of representative democracy. In a working legal system, direct election of judges can ease this conflict, although even elected judges are expected to approach disputes as impartial arbiters rather than as representatives of particular political constituencies. In keeping with our general approach to problems of political legitimacy, however, we make no assumptions about the selection and qualifications of judges within our imaginary community, or about the degree to which the primary rule-making authority may choose to limit judicial rule making.

[41] Tiersma finds an increasing tendency on the part of judges to state their holdings explicitly, yet he also notes that many courts continue to avoid "textualized" holdings. *See* Peter Tiersma, *The Textualization of Precedent*, available from *Social Science Research Network*, http://ssrn.com/abstract=680901 (2005), at 51–69. *See also* Frederick Schauer, *Opinions as Rules*, 62 *U. Chi. L. Rev.* 1455 (1995) (pointing out the advantages of increasingly explicit rule making in judicial opinions).

Several necessary conditions for the existence of a serious precedent rule follow from our understanding of the function of authoritative rules. As we explained in Chapter 1, communities recognize rule-making authorities for the purpose of settling controversy and uncertainty about the application of shared moral values.[42] To perform the function of settlement, rules must be general enough to prescribe results in classes of future cases, determinate enough to provide answers without direct consideration of the values the rules are designed to serve, and "serious" in the sense that they preempt further reasoning and determine results.[43]

The settlement function of rules also dictates that precedent rules must be posited by a rule-making authority – in this case, a prior judge.[44] Authoritative rule making is an intentional act. The task of the rule maker is to determine the best prescription for future cases that can be captured in the form of a rule. Rule-making authorities, including judges, are expected to bring their powers of reason and expertise to bear on the choice of rules. It follows, for us, that authoritative rules take their meaning from their author's intent. We will have more to say about intent-based interpretation of rules in Chapter 5. For now, the important point is that precedent rules come into existence when they are posited by a past judge and mean what that judge intends them to mean.[45]

The requirement that precedent rules must be posited does not necessarily mean that they must appear in canonical form in a prior opinion. Often a rule is detectable in explanatory remarks and citations even if the precedent court did not state the rule explicitly and flag it as a prescription for future cases. As long as the judge had a rule in mind and the rule is capable of restatement in determinate, canonical form, positing can occur in an informal way.[46] Recognition of informal rules expands the

---

[42] See Chapter 1, *supra* text at notes 1–2.
[43] See Alexander and Sherwin, *The Rule of Rules, supra* note 1, at 28–34; Schauer, *supra* note 3, at 17–111.
[44] See Alexander and Sherwin, *The Rule of Rules, supra* note 1, at 26–28 (distinguishing between rules and moral principles on the ground that rules are posited whereas moral principles are not).
[45] If the rule is posited by a court composed of multiple judges, there is a problem of collective intent. We address this problem in Chapter 6, *infra*.
[46] On canonicity of rules, *see* Frederick Schauer, *Prescriptions in Three Dimensions*, 82 *Iowa L. Rev.* 911, 916–18 (1997); Schauer, *supra* note 3, at 68–72. If canonicity entails that a rule be posited by a particular source as an intentional act at a particular time, we view canonicity as an essential feature of authoritative rules; we do not agree with Schauer's suggestion that

capacity of the common law to settle future controversy: given prevailing patterns of judicial opinion writing, insistence on explicit rules would result in too few rules and too little settlement.

Thus, it is possible, and probably desirable, to include implicit precedent rules within the rule model of the common law. At the same time, it is important to maintain a distinction between rules implicitly posited by prior courts and norms drawn (or "abduced") by later courts from the data of past decisions.[47] A precedent rule exists only when the precedent judge intended to adopt or endorse a rule and the rule can be stated in a form that is capable of governing future disputes. If these conditions are met, the precedent court can fairly be viewed as the author of the rule. If, however, the conditions we have described are not present, the current judge is not following a precedent rule. The current judge is either constructing a norm from the facts and outcomes of prior cases or simply positing a new rule. As we explain in our discussion of legal principles in Chapter 3, a norm constructed from past facts and outcomes is not posited (either by the past judge or by the current judge); nor does it constrain the current judge's decision in any meaningful way.[48]

For example, suppose Heidi is presiding over the case of John, who is planning to open a music store in a residential neighborhood. Neighboring homeowners have asked Heidi to enjoin John from opening his store, arguing that the noise it will generate makes it a nuisance.[49] Heidi discovers a prior decision in which a court held an aerobics studio to be a nuisance in a residential neighborhood. The opinion in that case referred

---

a pattern of decisions can produce a rule. *See* Schauer, *Prescriptions in Three Dimensions, supra,* at 917–18. If canonicity entails that the rule must be posited *in the form of a rule,* we do not view it as essential; we require only that a rule-making authority has done something from which a rule capable of statement in determinate form can be inferred.

[47] Abduction is a term coined by Charles Peirce to describe the process by which a reasoner links observed phenomena to possible explanatory hypotheses. *See* Scott Brewer, *Exemplary Reasoning: Semantics, Pragmatics, and the Rational Force of Legal Argument by Analogy,* 109 *Harv. L. Rev.* 925, 945–48 (1996).

[48] *See* Chapter 3, *infra* text at notes 61–63, 71–77.

[49] Schauer uses a similar example to illustrate his argument that prescriptions can be inferred from a pattern of prior particularistic decisions. *See* Schauer, *supra* note 46, at 916–17. In our example, however, the prescription is inferable, not from the pattern of prior decisions, but from the pattern of citations offered by a precedent judge. The pattern of citations, unlike the pattern of decisions itself, is evidence of rule-maker intent.

to the likelihood of noise and explained that an aerobics studio would place too great a burden on surrounding owners. It also cited cases from other jurisdictions holding that a trumpet academy, an amusement park, and an ice cream truck were nuisances in residential neighborhoods but a chess tournament was not. Heidi can infer from this opinion that the precedent judge applied a rule, "Noisy activities are not permitted in residential neighborhoods."

Suppose, however, that instead of the opinion just described, Heidi finds an array of past cases holding that an aerobics studio, a trumpet academy, an amusement park, and an ice cream truck were nuisances in residential neighborhoods but a chess tournament was not. In each case, the court stated only that the activity in question placed an unreasonable burden on surrounding owners. In this version of the example, Heidi has no basis for inferring a rule against noisy activities in residential neighborhoods. She can posit a serious rule to this effect, or construct a principle that appears to fit the pattern of prior decisions, but there is no precedent rule in place to prescribe the decision she should reach in John's case.

Precedent rules must be posited, general, determinate, and preemptive: this much is implied by the concept of authoritative rules. The rule model of common law, in itself, places no further limits on what should count as a precedent rule. As we have noted, however, judges, as adjudicators, are not ideally situated to make rules. To counteract the risk of flawed precedent rules, they might adopt additional preconditions for recognition of binding precedent rules.[50]

One possible way to protect against misconceived rules would be to deny precedential effect to rules that appear to have been posited without serious deliberation. The procedural history of a decision might reveal that the court announced a rule and intended it to operate as a rule in future cases, but that the parties never engaged in full debate about the future consequences of the rule.[51] If so, later courts could disregard the rule.

---

[50] We return to the problem of judicial rule making in Chapter 4, *infra*, where we raise the possibility that various judicial practices may serve as indirect strategies for improving the quality of precedent rules.

[51] *See, e.g.*, Conley v. Gibson, 355 U.S. 41 (1957) (announcing a pleading rule not debated by the parties); State v. Shack, 277 A.2d 369 (1971) (announcing a trespass rule, although no active party defended the position of the owner).

A requirement of adequate deliberation might not be practical, however, at least in the context of current legal practice. Evidence of deliberation, such as judicial notes and records of oral argument, tends to be
scant and difficult to obtain. Further, regular inquiry into the deliberations leading up to adoption of rules might undermine the prescriptive
effect of precedent rules. Following a rule against one's best judgment is
not rational; therefore, a legal system that relies on serious precedent rules
to settle controversy necessarily depends on a general disposition among
judges to follow precedent rules without much reflection.[52] Intensive
scrutiny of the deliberations of past judicial rule makers could undermine the practice of unreflective rule following.

A second possible check on undesirable judicial rules is a precondition
of acceptance over time. According to this condition, precedent rules
would become binding when, but only when, they had been "taken
up" by a sufficient number of judges.[53] A condition of acceptance over
time limits the precedential effect of judicial rules to rules that have been
studied and approved by multiple judges working in a variety of contexts:
rules come to represent a kind of collective wisdom.[54]

One difficulty with a precondition of acceptance over time is indeterminacy. There is no nonarbitrary point at which a rule has been sufficiently "taken up" by subsequent courts, and quantifying the extent of
acceptance required would be impractical. The indeterminacy of acceptance, however, is like the indeterminacy of baldness and heaps: there
comes a point at which one knows it has occurred.[55]

---

[52] On the rationality of rule following, *see* Heidi M. Hurd, *Moral Combat* 62–94 (Cambridge:
Cambridge University Press 1999); Heidi M. Hurd, *Challenging Authority*, 100 *Yale L.J.* 1011
(1991). *See also* Alexander and Sherwin, *The Rule of Rules, supra* note 1, at 53–96 (explaining
why it may be rational to endorse rules but not to follow them); Schauer, *supra* note 3,
at 128–34 (explaining the "asymmetry of authority"). On the importance of a practice of
unreflective rule following and the difficulties of maintaining such a practice, *see* Alexander
and Sherwin, *supra*, at 87–88; Larry Alexander and Emily Sherwin, *The Deceptive Nature of
Rules*, 142 *U. Pa. L. Rev.* 1191, 1201 (1994).

[53] This position has support in judicial practice, particularly in earlier periods of the common
law. *See* Postema, *supra* note 19, at 167 (explaining the classical view that common law was
not posited by judges but found in "*reasonable usage* – usage observed and confirmed in a
public process of reasoning"). *See also* Simpson, *supra* note 19, at 85–86 (taking the view that
common law exists by virtue of its "reception" over time); Tubbs, *supra* note 19, at 149–51
(discussing the notion of "tried reason").

[54] *See* sources cited *supra*, at note 27.

[55] *See* Dominic Hyde, "Sorites Paradox," in *Stanford Encyclopedia of Philosophy*
(Edward N. Zalta, ed., Fall 2005), http://plato.stanford.edu/archives/fall2005/entries/sorites-
paradox/: "The name 'sorites' derives from the Greek word *soros* (meaning 'heap') and

A more difficult question analytically is what exactly must be accepted. The intended meaning of a rule may change as judges apply the rule over time. For example, a prior opinion contains the rule "Domestic household animals are permissible in residential neighborhoods." The judge who announced the rule intended the term "household animals" to include horses and chickens. Subsequent courts have continued to apply the rule. Recently, however, courts applying the rule have used the term "household animals" in a more restrictive way, to mean pets such as dogs and cats. As we have explained, one implication of the settlement function of rules is that the meaning of rules is a function of their authors' intent. This raises the question, if precedent rules are not binding until taken up by later judges, who is the author whose intent governs the meaning of the rule?

The authority of the original judge is incomplete because that judge alone cannot establish a binding precedent rule: the endorsement of subsequent judges is necessary to place the rule in force. This suggests that the subsequent judges who accept a precedent rule are its authors. The meaning intended by subsequent judges cannot be the meaning of the rule because that meaning has not yet been accepted over time. Nor, for that matter, can the original judge's intended meaning be the meaning of the rule, because that meaning has not met the test of acceptance. It appears, therefore, that no effective precedent rule exists until a further round of acceptance occurs, with all endorsers concurring in the meaning of the rule as posited by some prior judge. This further requirement, of course, adds greatly to the indeterminacy of the rule, and so is at odds with the objective of settlement that motivates the rule model of the common law.

C. THE PERSISTENCE OF PRECEDENT RULES

A third question that arises under the rule model is whether and how later courts can overrule precedent rules. An initial point is that altering

---

originally referred, not to a paradox, but rather to a puzzle known as *The Heap*: Would you describe a single grain of wheat as a heap? No. Would you describe two grains of wheat as a heap? No. . . . You must admit the presence of a heap sooner or later, so where do you draw the line?"

a precedent in any way overrules the rule. Serious precedent rules are effective as a means of coordinating conduct and otherwise reducing error because, and to the extent that, later judges follow them automatically without looking behind the rules to see if their underlying reasons require a different result. It follows that when a current judge "narrows" a rule by carving out an exception for a particular case in which the rule's prescription appears to be a mistake, the judge is not applying a modified version of the rule but disregarding the rule and establishing a new rule in its place. As we explain more fully in the next chapter, the original rule places no constraint at all on the current judge; in effect, the rule is overruled.[56]

Some power to overrule precedent rules is essential to the success of the rule model of judicial decision making. The most persuasive criticism of the rule model is that serious rules entrench error.[57] Rules may be poorly designed or may become obsolete, and, as we have noted, judicial rules are especially susceptible to flaws. Without some qualification, the rule model appears to require that judges follow all rules according to their terms, and so to lock in past errors.

Perpetual entrenchment of flawed rules, however, is not a necessary implication of serious precedent rules. Under the rule model, precedent rules are preemptive in the sense that judges, in their role as adjudicators, must follow previously announced rules even if the reasons behind the rules appear to require a different outcome in the case before the court. Yet the rule model also gives judges rule-making authority, and in their role as rule makers, judges can override rules they believe are flawed.[58]

Overruling of precedent rules is appropriate in two circumstances, and only two. First, a precedent rule may not be justified as a rule, either because it was misconceived or because it has become obsolete. Rules lack justification if they cause more error by prescribing erroneous

---

[56] *See* Chapter 3, *infra* text at notes 44–51.

[57] *See* Edward H. Levi, *An Introduction to Legal Reasoning* (Chicago: University of Chicago Press 1948) ("change in the rules is the indispensable dynamic quality of law"); Frederick Schauer, *Formalism*, 97 *Yale L.J.* 509, 542 (1988) (acknowledging the inherent conservatism of rules, but defending rule-based decision making).

[58] Melvin Eisenberg appears to share this view. *See* Eisenberg, *supra* note 3, at 104–5 (maintaining that overruling is governed by the same principles as development of law; thus, "[a]s an event in the history of a doctrine, overruling often involves no sharp changes of course).

outcomes than they prevent by coordinating conduct and averting the errors of natural reasoning. Second, a precedent rule may be justified, in that it improves on unconstrained decision making, but not optimal: the rule may prevent more error than it causes, but prevent less error, or cause more error, than an alternative rule. In that case, overruling is appropriate if but only if the benefits of the alternative rule are greater than the costs of disrupting the patterns of coordination that have formed around the existing rule. At least in theory, judges have the same power as legislatures to repeal rules when either of these conditions obtains. In contrast, overruling is not appropriate simply because the precedent rule prescribes erroneous outcomes in some cases. Errors of this kind are an inevitable feature of determinate general rules. If the rule is justified in the sense that brings about a net reduction in error, and is preferable to any alternative rule, the rule model requires judges to follow the rule even when it prescribes the wrong result.

Suppose, for example, that Heidi is presiding over the case of Martha, who keeps a pet pit bull in her home. Heidi discovers a precedent case in which the judge announced a rule, "Pit bulls in residential neighborhoods are nuisances." If this rule is sound as applied to most pit bulls and superior to any alternatives, Heidi must apply it to Martha's pit bull even if she is convinced that Martha's pet is gentle, well behaved, and unlikely to do harm. If, however, Heidi believes that the rule "Pit bulls are nuisances" is based on faulty empirical reasoning by a prior judge whose attention was focused on a rare case of mauling, she can overrule the rule by announcing a modified rule or simply declaring that no rule shall apply.

Logically, under a rule model of the common law, the powers of judges and legislators to make and then unmake rules are coextensive. Traditionally, however, judges have been reluctant to overrule precedent rules, at least overtly.[59] For several reasons, this may be a wise course. The first is that judges have more opportunities to overrule rules than

---

[59] *See, e.g.*, Raz, *supra* note 17, at 189 (noting that courts overrule "more sparingly" than they distinguish); Robert S. Summers, *Precedent in the United States (New York)*, in *Interpreting Precedents: A Comparative Study* 355, 394–97 (D. Neil MacCormick and Robert S. Summers, eds., Aldershot: Dartmouth Publishing 1997) (describing limited categories of "justified overruling"; Grant Lamond, *Do Precedents Create Rules?*, 11 *Legal Theory* 1, 12 (2005) (stating that courts distinguish much more freely than they overrule).

legislatures: they are likely to revisit rules frequently as parties bring disputes one by one before multiple courts. Their assessment of rules will sometimes be incorrect, and even when their assessment is correct, frequent overruling will undermine the settlement benefits of common-law rules generally.

A second reason for caution in overruling precedent rules is that judges, unlike legislators, combine their oversight of rules with the task of adjudication. The separate standards we have outlined for applying sound rules and overruling unsound rules place judges in a difficult position psychologically. When a precedent rule is justified overall – when it will prevent more error than it produces if it is regularly applied – the rule model of decision making calls for judges to follow the rule without consulting the reasons behind the rule. Yet judges must consider the same set of reasons to determine whether to overrule. If, judged by those reasons, the rule will cause more error than it prevents, the rule is unjustified and should be overruled. If, judged by its underlying reasons, the precedent rule will cause more error or prevent less error than an alternative rule, and if the benefits of a change outweigh the costs of disruption, the rule is suboptimal and again should be overruled. The problem is that, if the reasons underlying the rule are available to judges for the purpose of overruling, they will be hard to suppress for the purpose of application.

Assume, for example, that the rule that pit bulls are nuisances is based on a balance between the welfare that owners derive from their dogs and the risk of injury to others. Heidi cannot decide for Martha on the ground that these reasons do not support an injunction in the case of Martha's dog; however, she is free to decide that they do not support a rule against pit bulls. Locally, these two conclusions are distinct: one concerns the outcome of the case, and the other concerns the overall performance of the rule. In practice, however, it will be difficult for Heidi to compartmentalize in this way, particularly when she is convinced that an injunction is the wrong outcome for Martha.

Perhaps this dilemma could be avoided or at least minimized by a serious rule governing the occasions for overruling. For example, a court or legislature might posit a rule such as "Overrule precedent rules that have not been followed for thirty years," or "Overrule precedent rules that have been questioned by later judges in ten or more cases." A rule of this kind, however, suffers from several difficulties. It is uncomfortably blunt because the subject matter of legal rules and the frequency of litigation in different areas of law vary greatly. Moreover, the underlying assumption that judges have power to overrule rules creates a problem of regress. The overruling rule (and any higher-order overruling rule for overruling rules) can be overruled. Ultimately, therefore, the question when to overrule can be resolved only through moral judgment.

Given the limitations and dilemmas we have described, the best approach to overruling is difficult to discern. Never overruling will lead to too much bad law. On the other hand, overruling whenever a precedent rule fails to meet the test of moral justification (net reduction of error over the long run) will undermine the settlement value of rules. The middle ground is a practice of overruling precedent rules when and only when they are *obviously* and *significantly* flawed in terms of their predicted long-term effects.[60]

This middle-ground standard is surely not ideal. It operates as a presumption of unspecifiable weight against overruling precedent rules. It does not eliminate the conflict between overruling rules that the court believes are unjustified and the demand of rules that they be applied preemptively without regard to their merits in particular cases; and, in any event, applying this presumption – just like following a rule when it departs from its background justification – is not rational when a judge believes the rule is only moderately, not egregiously, flawed. Overruling according to this formula, however, appears to be the only practical alternative for judges operating within the rule model of precedent, as *never* overruling flawed rules or *always* overruling them both seem too extreme. (As a theoretical matter, the dilemma of overruling infelicitous rules replicates the general dilemma of rule following, a dilemma for which we can offer no satisfactory theoretical solution.)[61]

---

[60] This approach to precedent would ask judges to "peek" at the justification of the rule, in the manner Frederick Schauer recommends in his discussion of "presumptive positivism." *See* Schauer, *supra* note 16, at 677. Although we reject presumptive positivism as a solution to the general dilemma of rules, it appears to provide the best available answer to the question when a rule should be jettisoned altogether. See Alexander and Sherwin, *The Rule of Rules*, *supra* note 1, at 68–73.

[61] See Alexander and Sherwin, *The Rule of Rules*, *supra* note 1, at 53–95. *But see* Alan H. Goldman, *The Rationality of Complying with Rules: Paradox Resolved*, 116 *Ethics* 453 (2006).

Finally, we should point out that the problem of when to overrule mischievous or suboptimal precedent rules arises not only in common-law adjudication but also in adjudication under canonical texts, such as constitutions and statutes. Courts establish precedent rules under canonical texts in two ways. First, if the canonical text in question is itself a standard – a delegation from the text's enactors to future decision makers to apply evaluative criteria within the boundaries set by rules – courts, in applying that standard, may "rulify" it. That is, they may apply the governing standard indirectly through rules that they craft for that purpose. And a later court may believe that such a judicially crafted rule fails to realize the standard optimally or at all. It will then face a decision whether to overrule the precedent rule that is no different from the decision courts face about when to overrule common-law rules.

On the other hand, the canonical text may be a rule, but one the meaning of which is unclear. The precedent rule will then be a court's substitution of a clearer formulation for the enactors' formulation, although the substitution is supposed to be equivalent to the original formulation in its meaning. If the later court believes the precedent court misinterpreted the canonical text, it will have to weigh the authority of the canonical text, correctly interpreted, against the authority of the precedent rule. Some theorists believe the precedent rule should always be overruled if it is not faithful to the governing canonical text. Others believe the precedent rule should be overruled only if it is both mistaken as an interpretation and also causes more mischief than its overruling would cause. Either approach is coherent, though the latter requires difficult moral calculations by courts and tempts them to be less than faithful interpreters of canonical texts with which they disagree. We take no position on this controversy here.

III

The Mystification of Common-Law Reasoning

We argued in the preceding chapter that there are two and only two plausible models of judicial reasoning: the natural model and the rule model. The natural model incorporates two forms of reasoning: moral reasoning through the method of reflective equilibrium and empirical reasoning. The rule model adds a third form of reasoning, deduction from authoritative rules. These forms of reasoning are not unique to law but are common to all subjects of human deliberation. In our view, they are the only tools judges need to decide cases and the only tools they use in fact.

This is not the prevailing view. Texts on judicial reasoning, as well as judges themselves, often maintain that the primary decision-making method of the common law is reasoning by *analogy*.[1] Analogical

---

[1] *See, e.g.,* Lloyd L. Weinreb, *Legal Reason: The Use of Analogy in Legal Argument* (Cambridge: Cambridge University Press 2005); Edward H. Levi, *An Introduction to Legal Reasoning* 1–6 (Chicago: University of Chicago Press 1948). For explanations and defenses of analogical

reasoning is the special art of lawyers and judges and the means by which the common law has successfully adapted to changing social conditions.[2] Commentators also maintain that courts reason from *legal principles*, a method closely linked to the method of analogy.[3]

In this chapter, we intend to demonstrate that judges cannot be doing what they claim. One cannot "reason" by analogy, and legal principles are chimerical. We argue as well that if analogies and legal principles could in fact operate as elements in judicial reasoning, they would tend to lead judges into error, without the compensating benefits of settlement.

Our position raises several questions. One is descriptive: what are judges doing when they claim to reason by analogy or to apply legal principles? We suggest in the next chapter that, even if analogy-based decision making is unsound, *searching* for analogies and common principles that link past and present cases is a professional habit that might play a useful role in the development of common law. This habit of searching for analogies and legal principles is not equivalent to

reasoning in various forms, *see* Cass R. Sunstein, *Legal Reasoning and Political Conflict* 62–100 (New York: Oxford University Press 1996); Steven J. Burton, *An Introduction to Law and Legal Reasoning* 25–41 (Boston: Little, Brown 1995); Joseph Raz, *The Authority of Law* 183–89, 201–6 (Oxford: Clarendon Press 1979); Grant Lamond, *Do Precedents Create Rules?*, 11 *Legal Theory* 1 (2005); John F. Horty, *The Result Model of Precedent*, 10 *Legal Theory* 19 (2004); Scott Brewer, *Exemplary Reasoning: Semantics, Pragmatics, and the Rational Force of Legal Argument by Analogy*, 109 *Harv. L. Rev.* 925, 925–29, 962–63 (1996). *See also* Karl N. Llewellyn, *The Common Law Tradition: Deciding Appeals* 77–87 (Boston: Little, Brown 1960) (discussing "the leeways of precedent"); Karl Llewellyn, *The Bramble Bush: On Our Law and Its Study* 66–69 (Dobbs Ferry, N.Y.: Oceana Publishing 1960) (same).

[2] *See, e.g.*, Anthony Kronman, *The Lost Lawyer* 109–62, 170–85, 209–25 (Cambridge, Mass.: Belknap Press of Harvard University Press 1995); Levi, *supra* note 1, at 4; Charles Fried, *The Artificial Reason of the Law, or What Lawyers Know*, 60 *Tex. L. Rev.* 35, 57 (1981).

[3] Ronald Dworkin, *Law's Empire* 228–32, 240–50, 254–58 (Cambridge, Mass.: Harvard University Press 1986); Ronald Dworkin, *Taking Rights Seriously* 22–31 (Cambridge, Mass.: Harvard University Press 1978). *See also* Sunstein, *supra* note 1, at 30–31; Burton, *supra* note 1, at 105–11 (discussing "purposes" embedded in the common law); Henry M. Hart Jr. and Albert M. Sacks, *The Legal Process: Basic Problems in the Making and Application of Law* lxxix–lxxx, 545–96 (William N. Eskridge Jr. and Phillip P. Frickey, eds., New York: Foundation Press 1994) (discussing "reasoned elaboration" of law); Steven Burton, *Judging in Good Faith* 35–68 (Cambridge: Cambridge University Press 1992); Roscoe Pound, *An Introduction to Legal Philosophy* 56 (New Haven: Yale University Press 1922); Kenneth Henley, *Abstract, Principles, Mid-Level Principles, and the Rule of Law*, 12 *L. & Phil.* 121 (1993); Roscoe Pound, *Survey of the Conference Problems*, in *Conference: The Status of the Rule of Judicial Precedent*, 14 *U. of Cin. L. Rev.* 324, 328–31 (1940).

reasoning with them: analogies and legal principles do not themselves rationally decide cases.

A second question is why judges, teachers, and text writers find the idea of judicial reliance on analogies and legal principles so appealing. One explanation for the popularity of this account of judicial decision making is that it appears to provide a way out of the stark choice presented by the natural and rule models of decision making. If all judicial reasoning is natural reasoning, there is no meaningful "common law" that can curb the errors and biases of individual judges. The rule of law is imperiled, at least in the absence of legislation. If, on the other hand, precedent rules are serious rules, then judges must set aside their best moral judgment and decide as the rules require. Analogies and legal principles seem to offer a middle course: they constrain judicial judgment without displacing it. Our analysis, however, suggests that the compromise is illusory. Natural decision making and rule-governed decision making are the only courses open to judges.

I. Analogical Reasoning from Case to Case

In the purest sense, analogical reasoning in law means reasoning directly from one case to another.[4] The judge observes the facts and outcome of a past case, compares the facts of the past case to those of a pending case, then reaches a decision in the pending case based on similarities and differences between the cases. This form of reasoning has popular appeal for several reasons. As we have just noted, it promises a happy medium between constraint and flexibility. Judges must conform their decisions to the course of prior adjudication, but they are not precluded from assessing the merits of cases before them and they have considerable leeway to expand on or distinguish the past conclusions of their colleagues.[5] Analogical reasoning also conforms to a supposed principle

---

[4] *See* Weinreb, *supra* note 1, at 8, 78–90; Burton, *supra* note 1, at 27–41; Levi, *supra* note 1, at 1–2. Weinreb states, for example, that "the arguments of lawyers and judges resemble a Tinker-toy construction, one case being linked to another by factual similarities." Weinreb, *supra*, at 8.

[5] *See* Weinreb, *supra* note 1, at 160–62 (arguing that analogical reasoning is central to the "rule of law," properly understood as a combination of justice and certainty); Burton, *supra* note 1, at 31–41 (asserting that in drawing analogies, judges must make an unconstrained "judgment of importance"); Levi, *supra* note 1, at 2–3 ("It is not what the prior judge intended that is

of justice: treat like alike.[6] Another possible reason for the broad appeal of analogical reasoning is that findings of similarity and difference among cases may be acceptable to parties who disagree at the more abstract level of moral principle.[7]

Judges use, or claim to use, case-to-case analogies in three ways. First, the outcome of a precedent case may dictate a like outcome in the new case if the cases are factually similar.[8] Second, the outcome of a precedent case may dictate the outcome of a new case a fortiori, because the new case presents at least as strong a case for the same result.[9] These two versions of the analogical method are thought to be sources of constraint: the analogy between precedent case and new case is a reason, and possibly a conclusive reason, for the court in the new case to reach a result that parallels the result of the precedent case, even if the court believes, all things considered, that the result is wrong. In effect, the precedent court exercises authority by describing a set of facts and determining an outcome that can control the outcome of later cases.

The third way in which courts purport to reason by analogy is to "distinguish" precedent rules based on factual dissimilarities between the cases in which the rules were announced and new cases that appear to fall within the rules' terms.[10] Distinguishing is the flip side of a fortiori decision making, in that disanalogy provides an escape from authority. The precedent court exercises lawmaking authority by announcing a general rule, but the court in a new case can avoid the rule and return to natural reasoning.

---

of any importance; rather it is what the present judge, attempting to see the law as a fairly consistent whole, thinks should be the determining classification").

[6] See, e.g., Burton, supra note 1, at 26.

[7] See Sunstein, supra note 1, at 65–69.

[8] See, e.g., Goddard v. Winchell, 52 N.W. 1124 (1892) (determining ownership of a fallen meteor: meteors are like rocks). This use of analogy is discussed in Raz, supra note 1, at 201–6; Levi, supra note 1, at 1–2.

[9] See, e.g., Edwards v. Sims, 24 S.W.2d 619 (1929) (finding caves to be indistinguishable from underground minerals for purposes of trespass). This type of analogy is discussed in Lamond, supra note 1. Horty, supra note 1.

[10] See Hannah v. Peel, [1945] K.B. 509 (1945) (drawing distinctions among finders of lost property). This practice is discussed in Raz, supra note 1, at 183–89; Lamond, supra note 1, at 9–15.

A. CONSTRAINT BY SIMILARITY

The simplest and most common way in which courts use analogies is by finding that the case before them is similar to a precedent case and then proceeding to reach a parallel result. For example, suppose Heidi is called on to decide a nuisance action against Karl, who is keeping an ocelot in his house. Surrounding homeowners point to a past case in which the court enjoined Edward to remove his pet bear from a residential neighborhood. An ocelot, they say, is like a bear, so Heidi should likewise order Karl to remove it.

The homeowners in this case presumably are invoking the maxim that like cases should be treated alike. We have already explained why, in our view, like treatment has no moral value in sequential decision making.[11] But suppose we assume, for the purpose of argument, that the principle of like treatment is sound. The difficulty with the analogy between Karl's ocelot and Edward's bear – and with any analogy of this kind – is that, without more, it is impossible to say that the two cases are either alike or different.

As a factual matter, there are an infinite number of similarities and differences between the ocelot and the bear.[12] Both are predators that might harm a small child, both are difficult to domesticate, and both are furry mammals. On the other hand, Karl's ocelot is (we can assume) smaller than Edward's bear, it is a type of feline indigenous to Belize, and it has spots. Nothing in the outcome of Edward's case – Edward was made to give up his bear – picks out which of these similarities and differences are important for purposes of comparison. Karl can just as easily point to another past case in which Herman was allowed to keep a Dalmatian in a residential neighborhood. Herman's Dalmatian, he might say, was about the same size as his ocelot and, like his ocelot, it had spots. Where are we now?

Our point is that Heidi cannot *reason* that Karl's case and Edward's case should be decided alike because they are similar. To reason that they should be decided alike, she must determine that they are *importantly*

---

[11] *See* Chapter 2, *supra* text at notes 20–21.
[12] *See* Melvin Aron Eisenberg, *The Nature of the Common Law* 84 (Cambridge, Mass.: Harvard University Press 1988); Weinreb concedes this point but insists that courts can determine relevant similarity without the aid of rules. *See* Weinreb, *supra* note 1, at 109–15.

similar, and to reason that they are importantly similar, she must refer to some general proposition that links ocelots to bears. Without this additional link, the facts and outcome of Edward's case have nothing to say about Karl's case.[13]

In a recent book defending analogical reasoning in law, Lloyd Weinreb rejects the conclusion that analogies depend on supporting generalizations.[14] Weinreb cites as an example an opinion in which the New York Court of Appeals held the owner of a steamboat strictly liable for losses suffered by a passenger whose money was stolen from a stateroom.[15] The court cited two possible lines of precedent: a series of cases holding that innkeepers were strictly liable for thefts from guest rooms, and another series of cases holding that railroads were not strictly liable for thefts from sleeping cars. Ultimately, the court of appeals found steamboats to be more like inns than like railroads and held for the passenger.[16] In Weinreb's view, this demonstrates that courts can and do decide cases on the basis of factual similarity, without reference to general propositions that make certain similarities relevant to the outcome.[17]

We observe, first, that the court's failure to refer explicitly to a general rule linking steamboats to inns does not establish that it decided the case without the aid of a generalization. Judicial opinions, particularly opinions from the days of steamboats when courts were reticent about rule making, may not spell out every step of the courts' reasoning. In any event, our point is not that courts must engage in formal rule making in order to draw analogies but only that the reasoning they engage in

---

[13] See Eisenberg, *supra* note 12, at 87; Peter Westen, *On "Confusing Ideas": Reply*, 91 *Yale L.J.* 1153, 1163 (1982). Schauer suggests that it is possible to induce a rule from the facts stated in a prior opinion, based on natural kinds and cultural and linguistic conventions; however, the rule, rather than the facts, governs the later decision. See Frederick Schauer, *Playing by the Rules: A Philosophical Examination of Rule-Based Decision-Making in Life and Law* 183–87 (Oxford: Clarendon Press 1991). Similarly, Scott Brewer argues that judges can "abduce" an analogy-warranting rule from the facts of prior cases. From that point on, however, the analogy-warranting rule (confirmed by more abstract analogy-warranting rationales) determines the outcome of the present case. See Brewer, *supra* note 1, at 962–65. See also Weinreb *supra* note 1, at 19–39 (arguing that Brewer's account underestimates the force of pure analogy in decision making).

[14] See Weinreb, *supra* note 1, at 12–13, 77–103, 107–16.

[15] Adams v. New Jersey Steamboat Co., 151 N.Y. 163 (1896).

[16] Id. at 166–70.

[17] See Weinreb, *supra* note 1, at 44–45.

to reach decisions must refer to some general proposition that supports the analogy. The court of appeals may well have had in mind that businesses providing lodging are strictly liable for thefts from rooms if the accommodation is of such a type that guests are likely to expect protection, or that providers of lodging are in a better position than guests to furnish protection.[18]

If, on the other hand, Weinreb is correct that the court detected a similarity between steamboats and inns without relying on a supporting generalization, the analogy has no power of constraint. Suppose the court of appeals had reached the opposite conclusion, that steamboats are like railroads, and therefore that they are not strictly liable for thefts. As a matter of similarity, this is fair enough: steamboats and railroads are both mobile. Thus, if nothing more than brute similarity were involved, the steamboat-railroad analogy would be equally as valid as the steamboat-inn analogy and, consequently, equally incapable of determining the outcome of the case.

We can press our point further by examining more closely what might be involved in drawing an analogy. There are several ways in which Heidi might *reason* to the conclusion that ocelots and bears are importantly alike for the purpose of an action of nuisance. She might formulate a moral principle and test her initial judgment through the method of reflective equilibrium: the liberty of property owners to use their property as they wish is subject to a duty not to inflict an unreasonable risk of harm on others, and both ocelots and bears pose unreasonable risks of harm.[19] More likely, Heidi will refer to a rule that captures applicable moral principles in more concrete terms: dangerous wild animals should not be kept in residential neighborhoods, and both ocelots and bears are dangerous wild animals.[20] Once Heidi has arrived at a morally sound

---

[18] The court referred to "considerations of public policy" common to steamboats and inns, and also to passenger expectations in locked rooms and the opportunity for theft. Adams v. New Jersey, at 166–69. Brewer provides an "interpretive reconstruction" of the case as relying on an analogy-warranting rule turning on the passenger's confidence in the proprietor and the proprietor's opportunity for theft. See Brewer, *supra* note 1, at 1003–6.

[19] On reflective equilibrium, *see* John Rawls, *A Theory of Justice* 14–21, 43–53, 578–82 (Cambridge, Mass.: Belknap Press of Harvard University Press 1971); Chapter 2, *supra*, at note 4 and accompanying text.

[20] It may be that the "craft" often attributed to judges and lawyers is simply familiarity with many such low-level rules. *See* Kronman, *supra* note 2, at 109–62, 295; Llewellyn, *The Common Law Tradition*, *supra* note 1, at 213–32; Fried, *supra* note 2, at 57.

principle or rule, she can deduce from it that ocelots and bears are importantly similar and enjoin Karl.

Notice that when Heidi reasons in either of these ways – by reference to a moral principle or by reference to a less abstract rule – the outcome of the prior case against Edward plays no effective role in her decision. The reason for granting an injunction against Karl is not that his ocelot is similar to Edward's bear but that his ocelot falls within a general principle or rule that Heidi has now determined is sound and should apply. The principle or rule is both necessary and sufficient to decide Karl's case, and the fact that the same principle or rule applies to Edward's case as well has no effect on the outcome. Another way to put this is that the lawmaker who settles Karl's case is not the judge in Edward's case but the new judge, Heidi, who exercises authority by formulating a principle or rule. The reasoning Heidi uses to arrive at her decision is not a special "analogical" form of reasoning but ordinary moral reasoning and deductive reasoning.

A third way in which Heidi might be said to reason to the conclusion that Karl's ocelot should be treated in like manner as Edward's bear is by referring to a *legal principle* that establishes similarity between the cases. A legal principle is a general proposition that is consistent with existing legal materials, including the outcomes of past cases.[21] For example, suppose past cases include the decision enjoining Edward to remove his bear and another decision permitting Jerome to keep his pet crocodile. The combination of precedents might support the legal principle that dangerous furry wild animals are not permissible in residential neighborhoods. Heidi can then deduce from this principle that Karl's ocelot must be removed. This method of decision making, unlike the methods just described, accords a role to past outcomes. The legal principle (no dangerous furry wild animals) decides the case against Karl, but the prior decision in favor of Jerome limits the principle's content.

If, in fact, legal principles are viable entities, then analogical decision making on the basis of legal principles is a form of reasoning that is, arguably, unique to law. We take up the subject of reasoning from legal principles in the second half of this chapter.[22] For now, it is enough to

---

[21] See Dworkin, *Law's Empire, supra* note 3, at 230–32, 254–58; Dworkin, *Taking Rights Seriously, supra* note 3, at 115–18.

[22] See *infra* text at notes 54–55.

say that we reject the notion of legal principles as both incoherent and undesirable. It follows that for us, decisions that appear to treat past outcomes as grounds for decision in current cases are in fact instances of either ordinary moral reasoning or deduction from rules.

A fourth possibility is that Heidi might rely directly on a perception of similarity: ocelots and bears are alike when placed in residential neighborhoods. This possibility must be approached with caution, because a judgment of similarity that appears to be intuitive may in fact be based on a general rule. In other words, Heidi may, in the course of a lifetime, have internalized certain generalizations so deeply that she can act on them without bringing them consciously to mind. Rather than simply perceiving a likeness between ocelots and bears, she is calculating the implications of a general proposition about the dangers of wild animals so rapidly that she herself is unaware of all the steps in her reasoning. In this case, the operative source of Heidi's judgment is the underlying general rule, and her thought process is a process of reasoning rather than intuition: she has reasoned to her conclusion, in an abbreviated way.

Suppose, however, that it is psychologically possible for Heidi simply to perceive an important likeness between ocelots and bears, either because they evoke a similar emotional response (fear) or because Heidi's mind is wired to respond to problems through pattern recognition and metaphor.[23] Her judgment of similarity, in other words, is purely intuitive. If this is an accurate description of Heidi's decisional process, she has not *reasoned* to a conclusion.[24] Reasoning entails, at a minimum, a

---

[23] See, e.g., George Lakoff and Mark Johnson, *Philosophy in the Flesh: The Embodied Mind and Its Challenge to Western Thought* (New York: Basic Books 1999); Howard Margolis, *Patterns, Thinking, and Cognition: A Theory of Judgment* 1–6, 42–86 (1987); George Lakoff and Mark Johnson, *Metaphors We Live By* (Chicago: University of Chicago Press 1981).

[24] At least, it is not reasoning as we have defined it in reference to authoritative decision making. We stated earlier that reasoning means "conscious, language-based deliberation about reasons for the choice ultimately made"; see Chapter 1, *supra* text at note 3. See Jonathan Haidt, *The Emotional Dog and Its Rational Tail: A Social Intuitionist Approach to Moral Judgment*, 4 *Psychological Review* 814, 818 (2001). The goal of settlement that is the foundation of law as we understand it requires that authoritative decisions be reached through reasoning in this sense. Id.

Others may, of course, define reasoning more broadly for different purposes. See, e.g., Steven A. Sloman, *Two Systems of Reasoning*, in *Heuristics and Biases: The Psychology of Intuitive Judgment* 379 (Thomas Gilovich, Dale Griffin, and Daniel Kahneman, eds., Cambridge: Cambridge University Press 2002). Lakoff and Johnson, *Philosophy in the Flesh*, *supra* note 23, at 4–5.

process of thought that one can articulate to oneself and to others. A coin toss is not a form of reasoning; nor is a perceived analogy. Whatever psychological mechanism allows judges to class ocelots and bears together for purposes of residential land use, the classification is not a reasoned one unless it refers to some more general proposition that links common properties of ocelots and bears to the problem the judge is trying to solve.

At this point, the proponent of analogical decision making may say fine, what Heidi is doing is not reasoning as you define it. But it is what judges do. They manage to decide cases in this way. This is, in effect, Weinreb's argument for analogical reasoning in law.[25]

To answer this argument, we first point out that the subject under discussion is analogical reasoning as a form of constraint. Precedent outcomes are supposed to dictate, or at least to provide reasons for, parallel outcomes in cases judged to be similar. With this assumption in place, we can return to Heidi's decision and consider more closely how she might reach it.

Suppose first that Heidi looks at the precedent case involving Edward's bear and has an intuition of important similarity between Edward's bear and Karl's ocelot. She then hypothesizes a general proposition that supports her intuition: dangerous wild animals should not be kept in residential neighborhoods. If she is satisfied with this proposition as a reason for decision, and if she confirms that both ocelots and bears are dangerous wild animals, she will enter an injunction against Karl.[26]

An important current debate in the field of psychology concerns the respective roles of reason and intuition in moral judgment. See, e.g., Sloman, supra, at 380–84 (discussing associative and rule-based reasoning); Haidt, supra (taking the position that the primary cause of moral judgment is intuition; reason enters in as a source of supporting arguments to justify the initial judgment to others).

[25] See Weinreb, supra note 1, at 91–92. Levi offers the following insight: "If this is really reasoning, then by common standards, thought of in terms of closed systems, it is imperfect unless some overall rule has announced that this common and ascertainable similarity is to be decisive. But no such fixed prior rule exists. It could be suggested that reasoning is not involved at all; that is, that no new insight is arrived at through a comparison of cases. But reasoning appears to be involved; the conclusion is arrived at through a process and was not immediately apparent. It seems better to say there is reasoning, but it is imperfect." Levi, supra note 1, at 3. See also Roscoe Pound, Law Finding through Experience and Reason 45–65 (Athens: University of Georgia Press 1960) (cautioning against confusion of analogical reasoning with "reason").

[26] This is structurally similar to the form of analogical reasoning described by Scott Brewer. According to Brewer, the analogical reasoner abduces a potential rule of decision from the common facts of the precedent case and the new case (the "target"), tests the rule against a

We have no difficulty with this method of decision making, but it is not truly an analogical method. If we assume our description of Heidi's mental process is correct, the intuition of important similarity plays only a minor role, as the inspiration for a more complete process of reasoning. Nor does the outcome of Edward's case constrain Heidi's decision. The lawmaker is not the precedent judge, but Heidi, who engages in ordinary moral and deductive reasoning, with the help of intuition, to formulate a rule of decision.

Now suppose that Heidi first reasons to a tentative conclusion about Karl's case: she determines that, based on an appropriate balance of liberty and protection against harm, she should permit Karl to keep his ocelot. She then studies Edward's case and has an intuition of important similarity between Edward's case and Karl's. Next, she hypothesizes a general proposition that supports her intuition of similarity: dangerous wild animals should not be kept in residential neighborhoods. She tests this proposition with further examples (crocodiles, lions) and finds that it fits her intuitions about these cases and also seems to fit her beliefs about liberty and harm. Ultimately, she abandons her initial conclusion, applies the proposition that dangerous wild animals should not be kept in residential neighborhoods, and enters an injunction against Karl. Again, Heidi's decision is not truly analogical; her method is ordinary reasoning and Edward's case does not constrain the outcome. Heidi's intuition of important similarity between Karl's ocelot and Edward's bear simply triggered a reasoned reexamination of her original position.

Another possibility is that Heidi begins by reasoning to a conclusion in favor of Karl, based on the comparative moral value of liberty and protection against harm. She then studies Edward's case and has an intuition of important similarity between Karl's ocelot and Edward's bear. Without more, she decides to treat the two cases alike and order Karl to remove his ocelot from the neighborhood. This reconstruction

---

broader rationale, and then, if the rule proves satisfactory, deduces an outcome. *See* Brewer, *supra* note 1, at 962–65. Brewer assumes, however, that the reasoner is bound to apply a rule abduced from existing precedents. In other words, the decisional rule generated by Brewer's reasoner is a *legal* principle of the kind we reject in the next section of this chapter.

In contrast, the judge in our description searches for a morally sound rule that supports her intuition of similarity. If she cannot formulate a satisfactory rule, the intuition of similarity is unsupported and will not justify a decision.

supports the possibility of a purely analogical approach to judicial decision making, but it strikes us as implausible. There is nothing in Heidi's
unconscious and inaccessible intuition of similarity between ocelots and
bears that provides a reason capable of overriding the conclusions she has
reached through a process of moral reasoning. Only if she can construct
a justification for the intuition, as in the prior example, will she abandon
her reasoned moral judgment.

The possibility that poses the greatest difficulty for our position is
this: Heidi begins with an intuition of important similarity between
ocelots and bears. She then decides to reason no further and to decide
Karl's case as the precedent judge decided Edward's case: remove the
ocelot. If we assume that it is in fact psychologically possible for Heidi
to intuit important similarity without referring to a supporting generalization, this decision is genuinely analogical. Given Heidi's intuition, the
precedent outcome controls the outcome of Karl's case. The lawmaker
is the precedent judge, who has exercised authority by describing facts
and reaching a decision that dictates a like decision in Karl's case. This
is, however, a very impoverished view of judicial decision making, which
we are reluctant to attribute to judges adjudicating in good faith. The
intuition of important similarity on which it relies is completely opaque:
it provides no warrant – no accessible justifying reason – for Heidi's
decision. We emphasize again that the two cases are not identical; they
are only felt to be similar (why?). There is no way even to think about
whether Heidi's judgment of important similarity is right or wrong.[27]

At this point, our argument is partly a normative one. As an analytical
matter, we can say that purely intuitive analogical decision making is not
a form of reasoning. We can also say that what appears to be analogical
decision making may in fact be ordinary reasoning. Finally, we can return
to one of the basic assumptions we made in our initial discussion of
settlement as a social end and a justification for authority: the assumption
that settlement, as a social end, means reasoned settlement.[28] Members

---

[27] Brian Leiter finds support for judgments of this kind in Heidegger. *See* Brian Leiter, *Heidegger
and the Theory of Adjudication*, 106 Yale L.J. 253, 259–61, 277–78 (1996) (criteria of relevant
similarity, on which analogical decision making depends, "can never be made fully explicit";
therefore judicial decision making resists theorization or critical evaluation and is best
understood as practical wisdom).

[28] *See* Chapter 1, *supra* text at note 3.

of a community choose an authority to translate values they recognize as reasons for action into particular decisions or rules when their own judgments conflict. Whether the authority's conclusion is right or wrong, it is expected that the process of translation will be capable, at least in principle, of articulation and justification. Otherwise, the choice of an authority is no different from the flip of a coin. This leads to the normative point: judicial decision making, as an exercise of authority, ought to meet this minimal requirement, and therefore ought to entail more than blind, untested, and untestable intuition.

B. A FORTIORI CONSTRAINT

We have argued that factual similarities between cases cannot constrain judicial decision making. Similarities are infinite; therefore some rule or principle is necessary to identify important similarities. Once a court has identified such a rule or principle, the rule or principle, rather than the factual similarities themselves, determines the outcome of the pending case. Analogy alone, therefore, does not enable courts to extend the "law" of past cases into new domains.

It might be argued, however, that analogies can play a more limited role in judicial decision making by dictating outcomes "a fortiori."[29] In this version of analogical reasoning, the court compares the relative strength of two sets of facts – the facts of the precedent case and the facts of a new case now under consideration. If the facts of the new case provide support for the outcome reached in the precedent case that is stronger than the support provided by the facts of the precedent case itself, then it follows, a fortiori, that the new court should reach a parallel result.

For example, suppose Heidi is considering a nuisance claim against Felix, who has established a private zoo in a residential neighborhood. On display at the zoo are a bear, a lion, and a python. Heidi discovers a prior case in which a court ordered Edward to remove his pet bear from a residential neighborhood. A fortiori, Heidi should order Felix to close his zoo. This conclusion follows even if Heidi believes Edward's case

---

[29] See Horty, supra note 1; Larry Alexander, Constrained by Precedent, 63 S. Cal. L. Rev. 1, 29–30 (1989). See also Lamond, supra note 1 (defending what appears to be a form of a fortiori decision making).

was wrongly decided and, accordingly, would have held for Felix in the absence of Edward's case.

The a fortiori method of decision making appears more promising as a form of case-to-case reasoning than a method that relies solely on the court's sense of similarity. Here, the court compares cases and draws what appears to be a necessary conclusion about the outcome of one from the facts and outcome of another. As we shall demonstrate, however, a fortiori reasoning suffers from a number of problems that diminish the effect of the precedent case to the vanishing point. Moreover, to the extent that a fortiori comparisons do in fact dictate outcomes, the possibility of erroneous precedents grossly distorts their operation. Given the presence of even a few past mistakes, a fortiori analogies can wreak havoc with the overall body of law.

The first hurdle in a fortiori reasoning is determining what facts are in play. The present judge, Heidi, does not have access to all the facts of the precedent case (the case of Edward's bear). The parties' lawyers will have selected a subset of all the facts pertaining to Edward and his bear for presentation to the court, and the judge (or an appellate court) is likely to have culled the evidence further in composing an opinion. One possibility for Heidi is to assume that the comparison must be between the classes of facts named by the prior court and the facts of her new case. If the court in Edward's case mentioned only that Edward was keeping a "bear," then the presence of any type of bear can support a claim of nuisance.[30] This approach could result in significant constraint: a precedent court could, by design or by mistake, exert a very strong influence on future cases by casting its description of facts in general terms. At the same time, it could produce unwanted results. An opinion in Edward's case stating that Edward was keeping an *animal* would result in a great many a fortiori nuisances, not all sensible.

As a result, courts are more likely to take the view that the appropriate comparison is between particulars actually described in the prior opinion

---

[30] At this point, a fortiori decision making may appear to collapse into rule-bound decision making: all bears are nuisances. See Alexander, *supra* note 29, at 43. John Horty points out that an important difference remains. The later court could find that an additional fact, present in the later case but not in the precedent case, favors the opposite fact. In the later case, for example, the cage may be stronger or the neighborhood differently configured. See Horty, *supra* note 1, at 28–29.

and the facts of the new case.[31] If the court in Edward's case stated without further elaboration that Edward was keeping a "bear," then details about the bear in Felix's zoo might serve to distinguish the case against Felix. Once judges take this more creative approach to factual comparison of cases, however, an a fortiori effect is very easy to avoid. No two cases are perfectly identical in their facts, and the current judge need only pick out some feature of his or her case that was not mentioned in the precedent opinion and that, *if* it was not in fact present in the precedent case, tips the scales in favor of a new result. Assume that Heidi is sympathetic to Felix's zoo. If Felix's bear is declawed and kept in a sturdy cage, and if the opinion in Edward's case does not specify that Edward's bear was likewise declawed and kept in a sturdy cage, Heidi can treat these as distinguishing facts. Moreover, in any case in which the a fortiori effect of a precedent case makes a difference to the current judge's decision – that is, in any case in which the judge would otherwise reach a different result – we can assume that the judge will be tempted to manipulate factual assumptions in this way to avoid a result the judge thinks is wrong. (Even if Felix's bear is a ferocious grizzly, if Heidi is sympathetic to his zoo, she can assume that Edward's bear was an even *more* ferocious grizzly; after all, the "fact" that Edward's bear was *not* more ferocious than Felix's was *not* among the facts mentioned in Edward's case and thus, according to our hypothesis, may be assumed *not* to have been present.)

In theory, factual comparisons between cases are not infinitely manipulable. The judge must identify facts that tip the scales or, in other words, facts about the new case that, if not also present in the precedent case, make the new case a weaker case for the precedent outcome. This leads to another problem, which is how a judge can "weigh" facts in favor of one outcome or another.

To weigh the facts of two cases, the judge must first determine what outcome particular facts tend to favor and then assign a weight to that tendency.[32] The tendency of a fact may seem obvious: the large size of a

---

[31] *See* Raz, *supra* note 1, at 187; Lamond, *supra* note 1, at 16.

[32] *See* Lamond, *supra* note 1, at 15 (acknowledging that, because "cases come before courts with all of their multitudinous facts," courts must determine the relevance of certain facts); Horty, *supra* note 1, at 23–27 (using a set of equations based on the "polarities" of different facts to explain a fortiori reasoning). *See also* Burton, *supra* note 1, at 31–41 (discussing, somewhat mysteriously, the need for a "judgment of importance").

bear favors an order to remove the bear from a residential neighborhood. But this is not as simple as it first appears. The size of a bear does not *in itself* recommend an injunction. Bear size must be linked to bear removal either by an inaccessible intuition or by a process of reasoning that relies on general propositions: owners must not impose unreasonable risks on the safety of those around them, and large bears pose a greater safety risk than small bears.[33] In other words, a fortiori reasoning runs aground for the same reasons that simple similarity-based analogies run aground: facts alone have no implications for future decision making.

A further problem is that if the new case involves facts that tend both in favor of and against the outcome of the precedent case, the court must assign weight to the facts in order to determine whether the a fortiori effect of the precedent case is dispelled. This may not be possible if the tendencies of different facts depend on wholly different values. For example, Felix's zoo contains not only a bear but other animals as well, a fact that presumably favors an injunction. Suppose, however, that Felix's zoo also doubles as a breeding facility for endangered species, a fact that favors a decision for Felix. If human safety and preservation of species are incommensurable values, neither of which has lexical (or absolute) priority, it follows that there is no way to weigh them in the manner an a fortiori comparison calls for. Calculation of the relative strength of additional animals (in favor of an injunction) and a breeding program (against an injunction) requires either a ranking of values or a common metric for measurement.[34]

---

[33] *See* Lamond, *supra* note 1, at 16 (appearing to rely on the precedent court's explanation of why particular facts justified a conclusion as establishing the relevance of those facts).

[34] Horty argues that it is possible for precedents to have an a fortiori effect in the absence of a metric for comparing the weight of different facts. If a precedent case is decided for the plaintiff, and if all the facts that supported the plaintiff in the precedent case are present in a later case, *and* all the facts that support the defendant in the later case were present in the precedent case, then the later case follows a fortiori from the precedent case. Horty, *supra* note 1, at 23–24. This seems correct, but the constraint provided by the precedent is minimal. All that is needed to free the later court to decide as it believes best is a single new fact in support of the defendant.

Horty also gives the example of a case involving two precedents. In the first precedent case, a certain plaintiff-favoring fact ($f_1\pi$) outweighed a certain defendant-favoring fact ($f_1\delta$). In the second precedent case, a different plaintiff-favoring fact ($f_2\pi$) was outweighed by a different defendant-favoring fact ($f_2\delta$). If the later case involves the plaintiff-favoring facts present in both of the precedent cases and also the defendant-favoring fact that was outweighed in the first precedent case ($f_1\pi$, $f_2\pi$, and $f_1\delta$), the later case is governed a fortiori

Some moral systems, such as utilitarianism, provide a universal metric that allows, in principle, for quantitative comparison of the facts of past and present cases. Within a system of this kind, a fortiori comparisons may be logically, if not practically, possible. The consequences, however, are nonsensical. We must assume that, in any legal system, some precedent cases have been erroneously decided: if judges always decided correctly, there would be no need for precedential constraint. We must also assume that, but for the precedent case, the judge in the new case would decide the new case differently; otherwise, the precedent would have no effect. In these circumstances, a process of quantitative comparison yields results that are perverse and ultimately self-contradictory.[35]

To illustrate, suppose that homeowners have asked Heidi to enjoin Max from opening a gas station in their neighborhood.[36] After calculating potential decreases in human happiness from traffic, fumes, and aesthetic offense, as well as potential increases in happiness from financial profit, convenience, and employment, Heidi finds that the gas station is likely to cause a net loss of three units of utility (utils). Accordingly, she is inclined to grant an injunction. Max, however, points to a prior case in which Jerome was allowed to keep a crocodile in a residential neighborhood. These cases may not appear to have much in common. But assume Heidi believes the prior decision was wrong: by her calculation, Jerome's crocodile was likely (ex ante) to cause a net loss of 6 utils. Max can now argue that in any case in which a use of land will cause a net loss of six or fewer utils, Jerome's case is an a fortiori precedent for denying an injunction. In fact, if utils are the denominator for comparison, Max might be able to cite a wholly unrelated precedent – say, an erroneous decision in the field of contract law – as a reason to decide in his favor.

Alternatively, Heidi might compare potential gains and losses of utility.[37] Assume that the court in Jerome's case concluded, erroneously, that the happiness Jerome would gain from his crocodile exceeded the

---

by the precedent cases. Id. at 25. But again, a single new fact is enough to dispel the a fortiori effect.

[35] See Alexander, *supra* note 29, at 34–37.

[36] See Bortz v. Troth, 59 A.2d 93 (Pa. 1948) (holding a gas station to be a nuisance per se).

[37] Cf. Russell Hardin, *Rational Choice*, in II *Encyclopedia of Ethics* 1062, 1063–64 (Lawrence C. Becker and Charlotte B. Becker, eds., New York: Garland Publishing 1992) (discussing cardinal and ordinal utility measurement).

loss of happiness his neighbors would suffer from contemplating the risks posed by a crocodile residing nearby. Heidi believes that in Max's case, the neighbors' potential loss of happiness due to traffic, fumes, and aesthetic offense will exceed Max's and others' gains in happiness due to profits, convenience, and employment. But if she also concludes that fumes, traffic, and aesthetic loss from Max's gas station will cause a lesser loss of happiness than the proximity of Jerome's crocodile was likely to cause, and that profit, convenience, and employment from the gas station will produce more gains in happiness than Jerome's enjoyment of his crocodile, then she is again constrained, a fortiori, to deny the injunction against Max. (Heidi believes that in Max's case, fact set x outweighs fact set y; but in the precedent case, fact set b was found to outweigh fact set a; if a outweighs x and y outweighs b, then the precedent case demands that Heidi treat y as if it outweighs x.) This cannot be a sensible way to resolve the dispute.

The problem is compounded by the presence of both correct and incorrect precedents. Assume that Heidi discovers two precedents. One is Jerome's case, in which the court denied an injunction, resulting in an expected net loss of six utils at the time of decision. The other is Edward's case, in which the court ordered Edward to remove his bear. Heidi determines that Edward's case was correct and that it resulted in an expected net gain of one util. These two cases stand as precedents both for granting and for denying an injunction in Max's case (and in all other cases in which the sum of expected utils if an injunction is granted is between one and six). At this point, a fortiori reasoning yields only confusion.

A fortiori decision making has one virtue: it taps the ability of reasoners to make comparative judgments. Comparing the degree to which a certain property is present in two objects – light A is brighter than light B – is an easier task for the human mind to manage than determining an absolute value – how bright is light A?[38] Thus, judges can make a fortiori judgments about past and present cases with greater confidence

---

[38] See, e.g., William N. Dember and Joel S. Warm, *The Psychology of Perception* 113, 116–17 (2d ed., New York: Holt 1979); Daniel Kahneman and Amos Tversky, *Prospect Theory: An Analysis of Decision under Risk*, 47 *Econometrica* 263, 277 (1979); Anne Treisman, *Properties, Parts, and Objects*, in II *Handbook of Perception and Human Performance* 35–34 (Kenneth R. Boff, Lloyd Kaufman, and James P. Thomas, eds., New York: John Wiley & Sons 1986).

than they can assess present cases in isolation. Yet this does not mean that judges can reason from case to case without more. A comparison of cases is possible only by reference to a general proposition that identifies which features of the cases should be compared. To know that lights *A* and *B* should be judged on the scale of brightness, one first must have in mind a rule, "Choose the brightest light."

Perhaps a fortiori decision making can be redescribed in a way that gives guidance to courts in comparing the facts of past and present cases. Grant Lamond suggests that precedent requires later courts to assume that precedent cases were correctly decided on their facts.[39] According to Lamond's "reason-based" account of precedent, a later court must accept the *ratio* of a precedent case – the proposition supporting its outcome – as a sufficient reason for the outcome in the factual context of the precedent case.[40] Then, if the facts entailed by the *ratio* of the precedent case are present in a later case, the later court must reach a parallel result *unless* additional facts create a reason for a different outcome that is strong enough to defeat the reason given by the precedent *ratio*. If no such facts appear, the prior case is an a fortiori precedent. Lamond refers to this as a "reason-based" account of precedent because it compares the reasons that justify outcomes in the context of particular facts.[41]

For example, homeowners have asked Heidi to enjoin Max from opening a gas station. Heidi finds a precedent case in which the presiding judge stated that "businesses that significantly increase traffic in residential neighborhoods are nuisances" and enjoined construction of a Pizza Hut.[42] Heidi must grant the injunction against Max unless she concludes that the convenience of a local gas station defeats the burden of significant new traffic.

If we assume that Heidi must accept the precedent judge's statement of the *ratio* of its decision,[43] the precedent opinion appears to constrain

---

[39] *See* Lamond, *supra* note 1, at 2–4, 16–20.

[40] See id. The notion of "ratio decidendi" is discussed in A. W. B. Simpson, *The Ratio Decidendi of a Case and the Doctrine of Binding Precedent*, in *Oxford Essays in Jurisprudence* 148, 160–63 (A. G. Guest, ed., Oxford: Oxford University Press 1961).

[41] Lamond, *supra* note 1, at 2.

[42] *See* Diehl v. Lockard, 385 A.2d 550 (1978) (holding a Pizza Hut to be a nuisance per se).

[43] Lamond does not make clear whether the "reason" for the precedent outcome is the reason stated or implied by the precedent court, or a reason constructed by the later court. He says at one point that "What the precedent court decided [and therefore what the later court must

Heidi by providing a reason that must be overcome: protection of home-owners against business traffic. Suppose, however, that Heidi believes that the precedent judge's reasoning was wrong; in her view, traffic is unavoidable if the neighborhood is to have normal amenities. If so, the reason generated by the new fact (a local gas station is convenient) will always be "stronger" than the reason for the precedent outcome, from Heidi's point of view. Again, there is no real limit on what Heidi can decide.

C. DISTINGUISHING PRECEDENTS

A third form of analogical decision making, very popular among courts, is the use of *dissimilarities* to avoid the implications of precedent rules. If a new case falls within the terms of a precedent rule but includes facts that are not specifically mentioned in the rule and were not present in the precedent case in which the rule was announced, the court can "distinguish" the new case and reach a result contrary to what the rule prescribes.[44]

Distinguishing precedents can be seen as the reverse of expansion of precedents on the basis of similarity: here, the court limits the effect of precedents on the basis of dissimilarity. The process of distinguishing precedents can also be conceived of as a reverse a fortiori calculation. The new court is free to reach a new result if the facts of the new case provide weaker support for the precedent outcome than the facts of the precedent case.[45]

---

accept] was that in the context of [the precedent facts, certain facts] justified the conclusion C." Lamond, *supra* note 1, at 16. At another point he says that "the later court . . . must consider how strong the reason provided by [the facts entailed by the ratio of the precedent case] for C really is and whether it is defeated by any reason[s] based on [different facts of the later case]. Id. At yet another point, he states that "the ratio sets out the factors that ground the reason(s) in favor of the result: the later court must determine the strength of the reason in favor of the result in the precedent on the basis of those factors." Id. at 18.

[44] *See, e.g.*, Raz, *supra* note 1, at 185–87; Lamond, *supra* note 1, at 16–17. *See also* Robert S. Summers, *Precedent in the United States (New York)*, in *Interpreting Precedents: A Comparative Study* 355, 390–92 (D. Neil MacCormick and Robert S. Summers, eds., Aldershot: Dartmouth Publishing 1997) (describing the practice of distinguishing as "arguing either that the material facts were different or that the substantive rationale for the ruling does not apply to the facts of the case under consideration).

[45] *See* Lamond, *supra* note 1, at 17.

For example, Andrei is considering a nuisance claim against Herman, who is keeping a large dog in a residential neighborhood. He discovers a prior case in which Heidi ordered Karl to give up his ocelot and stated that "large animals in residential neighborhoods are nuisances." By the general terms of Heidi's rule, Herman's dog must go. According to conventional understanding, however, Andrei can distinguish the precedent rule on the ground that Herman's dog, unlike Karl's ocelot, is a domestic animal, and the rule does not say in so many words that large domestic animals are nuisances. As a consequence, the precedent rule is modified to provide that "large wild animals in residential neighborhoods are nuisances."

The first point we wish to make about the practice of distinguishing is that it is not, as is sometimes suggested, a qualified version of the rule model of precedent.[46] Andrei appears to consult a precedent rule (no large animals), identify a fact about Herman's case that is not named in the predicate of the rule, restate the rule in a modified form (no large wild animals), and apply it to the case before him. But, in fact, the precedent rule plays no role in Andrei's decision.

To see this, suppose that the new case before Andrei is the case of Jerome, who is keeping a pet crocodile in his home. Andrei is sympathetic to Jerome. Suppose further that, in the precedent case, Heidi ordered Karl to remove his ocelot from a residential neighborhood and stated a rule, "Wild animals in residential neighborhoods are nuisances." To distinguish this precedent, Andrei can point to the fact that Jerome's crocodile, unlike Karl's ocelot, has no fur. The precedent rule does not specifically mention animals without fur; therefore, Andrei is free to decide in favor of Jerome. Moreover, this type of distinction will always be possible, because no precedent rule can be specific enough to cover all the particulars of all future cases. No matter what the rule, Andrei will be able to find some fact about Jerome's case that the rule does not particularly name. It follows that the rule has no constraining effect on the outcome of the case.

---

[46] We agree with Lamond on this point. *See* id. at 17–18, 19–20. *See also* Levi, *supra* note 1, at 3 ("rules discovered in the process of determining similarities and differences"). For the common view that distinguishing creates exceptions to rules, *see, e.g.,* Eisenberg, *supra* note 12, at 66–68; Raz, *supra* note 1, 183–89; Simpson, *supra* note 40, at 158–59; Summers, *supra* note 44, at 391.

Joseph Raz has suggested that the practice of distinguishing precedents, as conventionally understood, constrains judges by limiting the
manner in which they can modify precedent rules.[47] According to Raz,
a judge seeking to distinguish a precedent rule must restate the rule in a
way that meets two conditions: the modified rule must be the precedent
rule with some further condition added, and the modified rule must support the outcome of the precedent case. He illustrates with an example
in which the precedent case involved facts *a, b, c, d,* and *e,* the result was
X, and the opinion announced a rule "If *A, B,* and *C,* then *X.*" The new
case involves facts *a, b, c, d,* and *f,* but not *e.* The court can distinguish the
new case and announce a modified rule "if *A, B, C,* and *E,* then *X,*" or a
modified rule, "If *A, B, C,* and not *F,* then *X.*" But it cannot announce a
modified rule "If *A, B, C,* and not *D,* then *X,*" because this rule does not
support the outcome of the precedent case.[48]

In our view, this constraint is illusory. Assume again that in Karl's
case, Heidi announced the rule "Wild animals in residential neighborhoods are nuisances." Andrei distinguishes Jerome's case on the ground
that Jerome's crocodile has no fur. He then announces a rule, "Furry
wild animals in residential neighborhoods are nuisances." This rule may
not be ideal, and it authorizes a result that seems contrary to the values the precedent rule was designed to protect; but it meets Raz's two
conditions: it is the precedent rule with a condition added, and it justifies the outcome of the precedent case. Nor do Raz's conditions guarantee that the modified rule will be similar in effect to the precedent
rule. Andrei could announce a rule, "Wild animals that are three-year-
old ocelots with one lame foot are nuisances," without running afoul
of the supposedly constraining conditions. But the pattern of future
nuisance decisions under the rule will be radically different from the
pattern one would have expected under Heidi's rule, "Wild animals
are nuisances."

---

[47] *See* Raz, *supra* note 1, at 1886–87.
[48] Id. Raz assumes that any fact that *might* not have been present in the precedent case – that
is, any fact not mentioned in the precedent opinion – can be a ground of distinction. If
no mention was made of fact *f* in the precedent opinion, the court in the new case can
assume that *f* is a new fact and can announce a modified rule "If *A, B, C,* and not *F,* then *X.*"
Id. at 187.

Raz alludes to a third possible condition, that the court should adopt "only that modification which will best improve the rule."[49] From the standpoint of a judge who thinks the precedent rule is misconceived, however, any narrowing of the rule is an improvement, and the narrowest version may be the best, however ungainly. A condition requiring that any modification of the precedent rule must serve the purposes of the rule, or that any modification must conform to common sense, might help to solve the problem.[50] But these conditions are too indeterminate to provide effective constraint.

Thus, when judges distinguish precedent rules, the precedent rules have no constraining effect, either on the outcomes of new cases or on the content of the rules announced by new judges. When the new court announces a "modified" rule, it is not following precedent but acting as a lawmaking authority in its own right. The new court, not the precedent court, is the author of the rule.

Beyond this, many of the observations we have already made about analogical decision making apply equally to the disanalogies used to distinguish precedents. The possibilities for factual distinction between any two cases, like the possibilities for findings of factual similarity, are infinite. Further, as in the case of a fortiori decision making, the factual descriptions provided by precedent judges place no meaningful limit on judges' ability to distinguish new cases because current judges are likely to assume that facts not actually mentioned in precedent opinions were not present.[51] The outcome of the prior case does not in itself illuminate which dissimilarities are important. Therefore, the practice of distinguishing is most plausibly and appealingly understood as a process of ordinary reasoning that refers to moral principles or rules to identify important differences among cases, rather than a decision-making method in which

---

[49] Id. at 187.
[50] Lamond, in developing his "reason-based" account of precedent, suggests that a later court's choice of distinguishing facts is limited by a requirement that "if the difference provides an argument of the same kind as a fact that has already been rejected [as a ground of distinction by a precedent court], then the argument must be a compelling one." Lamond, *supra* note 1, at 21. He adds, however, that when a court distinguishes on the basis of a fact that "is not of the same kind," this limit does not apply. Id. *See* Simpson, *supra* note 40, at 174–75 (maintaining that not all factual distinctions suffice to distinguish precedents, but only those that "justify" refusal to follow the precedent).
[51] *See* note 47 and accompanying text, *supra*.

the outcome of one case bears directly on the outcome of another. So understood, findings of dissimilarity, like findings of similarity, do not entail a form of "legal" reasoning that differs from the reasoning used in any other field.

D. SUMMARY: WHY PURELY ANALOGICAL DECISION MAKING DOES NOT EXIST

Analogical reasoning is supposed to act as a constraint on judicial decision making, either dictating parallel results a fortiori, dictating parallel results in similar cases, or determining when judges may avoid precedent rules. We hope we have shown that it does none of these things.

Analogical decision making based on factual similarity between cases is either intuitive or deductive. If the process of identifying important similarities is intuitive, the precedent case does not constrain the outcome of the new case in any predictable or even detectable way. If the process is deductive, the rules or principles that govern similarity, rather than the outcome of the precedent case, determine the result of the new case.

A precedent case cannot determine the result of a new case a fortiori because some fact about the new case can always be cited as weighing in favor of a different result and therefore dispelling the a fortiori effect of the precedent. Moreover, the notion of weighing sets of facts is problematic. To "weigh" two different sets of facts, a judge must identify a common metric for comparison. If such a metric exists at all, its application to a body of precedent that includes incorrect decisions will result in legal chaos.

Finally, distinguishing precedent rules is an open-ended process in which the precedent rules themselves have no constraining effect. Rather than applying modified precedent rules, judges in new cases exercise rule-making authority, constrained only by such limits as there may be on findings of dissimilarity. Findings of dissimilarity, however, can be limited only by independent principles or rules that establish the importance of particular facts. The prior decisions themselves ultimately are inert.

There is one possible qualification to what we have just said. We noted in our discussion of constraint by similarity that a court might base a determination of similarity not on an independent moral principle or rule but on a "legal" principle that explains precedent cases. If so, precedent cases might constrain current outcomes by restricting the content of the legal principle on which the analogy is based. We take up, and reject, this possibility in the next section.

II. Reasoning from Legal Principles

We have argued that analogical reasoning does not exist, apart from supporting general rules. To the extent that the analogies are supported by moral principles, morally justified rules, or serious precedent rules, analogical reasoning is not a special form of reasoning known to lawyers but an exercise in ordinary moral, empirical, and deductive reasoning. There remains, however, one alternative possibility, which has played a leading part in the mystification of legal reasoning: the possibility of reasoning from legal principles.

The idea that judges decide cases by reasoning from legal principles has a venerable history and a strong resonance for most lawyers and judges. According to this view of legal reasoning, a judge presiding over a dispute surveys the body of legal precedents, formulates a principle that explains them, and then applies the principle to determine the rights of the parties in the pending case.[52] Law students are taught to reason in this way, judicial opinions follow this pattern, and traditional academic commentary employs a similar method to explain the law and propose reform.[53]

---

[52] See Hart and Sacks, supra note 3, lxxix–lxxx, 545–96; Pound, An Introduction to Legal Philosophy, supra note 3, at 56; Pound, Survey of the Conference Problems, supra note 3, at 328–31. Pound also embraced the idea that judges should act as "social engineers." See Pound, supra note 25, at 42–43; Pound, An Introduction to Legal Philosophy, supra, at 47.

[53] Zenon Bankowski, Neil MacCormick, and Geoffrey Marshall aptly refer to this as a "determinative" theory of precedent. Zenon Bankowski, D. Neil MacCormick, and Geoffrey Marshall, Precedent in the United Kingdom, in Interpreting Precedents, supra note 44, at 315, 332. They explain that a theory of this kind views law as "[g]rounded in principles partly emergent from practice and custom, partly constructed out of moral or ideological elements that bring together practice and contemporary values in a coherent order. . . . Legal rules and judicial rulings on points of law are then to be understood as 'determinations' (in the Thomist sense) of background principles – neither deductions from them nor arbitrarily discretionary decisions about them, but partly discretionary decisions as to the best way of making the law determinate for a given (type of) case. . . . Precedent is authoritative because each decision is a determination of law, but no decision is absolutely defeasible." Id.

A. THE NATURE OF LEGAL PRINCIPLES

The best-known and most rigorous account of the process of reasoning from legal principles comes from Ronald Dworkin.[54] Dworkin describes legal principles as the morally best principles capable of explaining a substantial proportion of past legal decisions. More precisely, two criteria govern the formulation of legal principles: legal principles must satisfy a threshold requirement of "fit" with existing legal materials; and they must come as close as they can, given the requirement of fit, to being morally ideal.[55]

Legal principles do not dictate outcomes in the manner of rules; rather, they are "starting points" for decision making,[56] which "weigh" in favor of outcomes.[57] At the same time, legal principles are authoritative in the sense that the combination of legal principles applicable to any case determines the judge's decision. Other legal materials do not directly govern judicial decision making but serve only as data points for construction of legal principles.[58] Effectively, therefore, legal principles make up the content of the common law.

For example, Heidi must decide the case of Roscoe, who is planning to open a paintball arena in a residential neighborhood. Surrounding owners argue that a paintball arena will increase traffic and noise and should be enjoined as a nuisance. The parties refer to a number of prior nuisance cases: in one line of cases, courts enjoined defendants from keeping a bear, an ocelot, and a crocodile, respectively, in residential neighborhoods, citing danger to the safety of homeowners. In another line of cases, courts declined to enjoin a tennis club, a bowling alley, a golf course, and a rifle range. An archery range, however, was enjoined. Courts have also permitted a day care center, a halfway house serving nonviolent offenders, and a carefully managed sewage treatment plant to operate in residential neighborhoods. From these precedents, Heidi

---

[54] See Dworkin, Law's Empire, supra note 3, at 230–32, 254–58; Dworkin, Taking Rights Seriously, supra note 3, at 22–31, 115–18.

[55] See Dworkin, Law's Empire, supra note 3, at 228–32, 240–50, 254–58; Dworkin, Taking Rights Seriously, supra note 3, at 115–18.

[56] Pound, Survey of the Conference Problems, supra note 3, at 331.

[57] Dworkin, Taking Rights Seriously, supra note 3, at 26–27 ("Principles have a dimension that rules do not – the dimension of weight").

[58] See id. at 37.

abduces a legal principle: landowners in residential neighborhoods are at liberty to pursue activities that pose no significant risk to human safety or health. If Roscoe can show that the safety risks of paintball are minimal, and if no other principles are in play, Heidi will then deny the injunction and enter a judgment for Roscoe.

One use (or purported use) of legal principles is to derive solutions to new cases from past decisions. Heidi's decision in favor of Roscoe, for example, can be viewed as an extension of the line of cases permitting nondangerous recreational activities in residential neighborhoods by means of a principle that ties those cases together and explains their relation to other cases. Legal principles can also be used to avoid rules announced in past cases. Suppose, for example, that in the prior case involving an archery range, the court announced a rule, "Sports involving mechanically enhanced projectiles are nuisances in a residential neighborhood." In the sport of paintball, players use guns to shoot paint at one another; therefore, the precedent rule, treated as a serious rule, calls for an injunction. In a regime governed by legal principles, however, rules do not operate as serious rules but only as evidence of legal principles. It follows that legal principles override announced rules. Heidi can conclude that the principle that best supports both the pattern of past outcomes and the precedent rule is the principle that owners are at liberty to pursue activities that pose no significant risk to health or safety. This principle explains the outcome of the archery case and is arguably consistent with the purposes of the no-mechanically-enhanced-projectile rule; at the same time, it permits a decision for Roscoe, contrary to the terms of the rule.

Descriptions of legal principles vary as to the sources from which such principles are drawn and with which they must "fit." Some accounts suggest that, as far as the common law is concerned, only the facts and outcomes of past decisions are relevant; the current judge is free to disregard rules and other statements found in past opinions.[59] This

---

[59] Dworkin can be read in this way. He states, for example, that "[f]itting what judges did is more important than fitting what they said"; that "an interpretation [of precedent] need not be consistent with past judicial attitudes or opinions, with how past judges saw what they were doing, in order to count as an eligible interpretation of what they in fact did"; and that the ideal judge assigns "only an initial or prima facie place in his scheme of justification" to rationales offered by prior judges. Dworkin, *Law's Empire, supra* note 3, at 284; Dworkin,

description of legal principles connects them to analogical reasoning: legal principles are the generalizations drawn from past results, which judges can then use to identify relevant similarities among cases.

In other accounts, rules and principles set forth in prior opinions, as well as facts and outcomes, are pertinent to the content of legal principles.[60] But here a distinction must be drawn: a judge reasoning from legal principles treats past statements as data from which to derive a principle; disposition of the case is then governed not by the past statements but by the principle they are found to support. If the judge treats past statements as direct constraints on his or her decision, the judge is not applying a legal principle in the Dworkinian sense but is deducing an outcome from posited precedent rules.

Legal principles, therefore, are fundamentally different from legal rules. The difference is not a function of the form of the prior judge's statement but of the role it plays in the current judge's decision. If Heidi decides for Roscoe because prior judges have stated that activities that pose no significant risk to human health or safety are permissible in residential neighborhoods, she is treating past statements as rules. If she decides for Roscoe because she believes past judicial statements about safety support a principle that activities that pose no significant risk to human health or safety are permissible, she is following the method that Dworkin recommends.

Another way to put this is that a judicial rule is a norm posited by a prior judge.[61] The precedent judge acts as lawmaker, exercising authority by announcing a rule.[62] A principle is not posited but organic. Due to the dimension of fit, it changes as the body of legal decisions changes over time.[63] The lawmaker is the current judge, who defines and applies a

---

Taking Rights Seriously, supra note 3, at 118. He adds, however, that fit with judicial opinions is "one desideratum that might be outweighed by others." Dworkin, *Law's Empire, supra* note 3, at 285. *Cf.* Dworkin, *Taking Rights Seriously, supra* note 3, at 110–15 (referring to the "enactment force" and "gravitational force" of precedents).

[60] *See* Hart and Sacks, *supra* note 3, at 369; Stephen R. Perry, *Two Models of Legal Principles,* 82 *Iowa L. Rev.* 787, 807–8 (1997) (understanding Dworkinian "fit" to refer to fit with rules as well as decisions); Pound, *Survey of the Conference Problems, supra* note 3, at 330–31 (indicating that principles are formulated gradually as a series of judges explain their reasoning in opinions).

[61] *See* Chapter 2, *supra* text at note 52.

[62] *See* Chapter 2, *supra* text at notes 29–32.

[63] *See* Dworkin, *Law's Empire, supra* note 3, at 254–58.

principle that appears consistent with the decisions and statements of past judges. Future judges, however, will remake the principle as they decide the cases that come before them against the background of precedent cases as those stand at the time of their decisions. Thus, legal principles are not posited by past judges; nor are they posited by the current judge who constructs them for the purpose of deciding a case.

Rules also differ from legal principles in that they determine the results of future cases that fall within their terms. Legal principles, in contrast, are not determinative of outcomes. Instead, they are reasons for decision that have "weight" when they come in conflict with other legal principles. The outcome of any given case depends on the balance of applicable principles.[64] For example, the legal principle in Roscoe's case (landowners in residential neighborhoods are at liberty to pursue activities that pose no significant risk to human safety or health) might be restated as two principles: a principle that owners should be allowed the maximum use of their property and a competing principle that owners must not use their property in ways that pose significant health or safety risks to neighbors. If the latter proves to be of greater weight, Roscoe is enjoined.

At the same time, legal principles are not moral principles; they are principles internal to law. The dimension of fit requires that legal principles must conform to the pattern of past decisions, even if, as a consequence, the principles that result are morally flawed.[65] Legal principles need only be the morally best principles that pass the threshold of fit.

Thus, Heidi may believe that paintball has no redeeming social value that justifies the burdens of traffic and noise it imposes on surrounding owners. More generally, she may believe that the correct moral principle for nuisance cases holds that landowners may not engage in activities that pose significant burdens of any kind on surrounding property owners unless those burdens are justified by the importance of the activity as a service to the community. In Roscoe's case, however, prior decisional history appears to rule out Heidi's ideal principle. Recall that in prior

---

[64] *See* note 57 and accompanying text, *supra.*
[65] *See* Dworkin, *Law's Empire, supra* note 3, at 230–31, 255; Dworkin, *Taking Rights Seriously, supra* note 3, at 116–17.

cases, courts enjoined several owners from keeping wild animals and enjoined an owner from opening an archery range, but they permitted other owners to maintain a tennis club, a bowling alley, a golf course, a rifle range, a day care center, a halfway house, and sewage treatment plant. A perfect fit with these decisions is not required – for example, Heidi probably can disregard the rifle range case as a mistake. But three of ten other precedents permitted recreational uses that were likely to increase traffic and noise. Therefore, the threshold of fit seems to require that Heidi modify her ideal principle to allow uses that do not fill an important social need, unless those uses pose a threat to health or safety. In other words, given the inevitable fact of erroneous outcomes in the past, legal principles are the most morally attractive morally *incorrect* principles that fit the background of prior decisions.[66]

A further observation, related to the last, is that the process of for-mulating legal principles is not a process of reflective equilibrium.[67] The structure of reasoning is similar – the judge refers to particular judgments and formulates a principle to support them; but the effect is radically different. Legal principles must be consistent with a certain (undefined) percentage of the judgments with which the reasoner begins. Not all past decisions can be rejected. In the case of reflective equilibrium, the reasoner can reject any and all judgments that cannot be explained by what the reasoner holds confidently to be a morally correct principle.

A second, closely related difference between judicial formulation of legal principles and the method of reflective equilibrium is that the judgments from which the reasoner (the current judge) draws a legal principle are not moral judgments but authoritative acts by past judges. They may be morally correct or incorrect, but this does not matter; until the threshold of fit has been passed, the fact that past decisions were wrong does not alter their effect on the content of the principle. In contrast, the judgments from which a moral principle is drawn in the

---

[66] *See* Larry Alexander and Emily Sherwin, *The Rule of Rules: Morality, Rules, and the Dilemmas of Law* 147 (Durham: Duke University Press 2001); Joseph Raz, *Ethics in the Public Domain* 296 (Oxford: Oxford University Press 1996); Larry Alexander, *Precedent*, in *A Companion to Philosophy of Law and Legal Theory* 503, 509 (Dennis Patterson, ed., Cambridge, Mass.: Blackwell Publishers 1996).

[67] *See* note 19, *supra*.

process of reflective equilibrium are moral judgments, whose effect on the outcome of reasoning depends on their ability to survive reflection.

As with analogical reasoning, much of the appeal of legal principles lies in the compromise they appear to allow between unconstrained natural reasoning and serious rules that preempt reasoning.[68] Judges reasoning from legal principles are constrained by the limits that institutional history (in the form of past decisions) places on the principles' content. At the same time, judges need not set aside moral values or abstain from exercising their powers of reason when deciding cases. They must formulate and apply the most morally attractive principles that fit with institutional history; but, in doing so, they can discard at least some past mistakes.

Another part of the allure of legal principles is the promise of a body of law shaped by internal coherence.[69] Legal principles maintain consistency among past, present, and future decisions and across doctrinal boundaries. A regime of legal principles, in which coherence provides a standard for development of law, has the added advantage of providing an answer (although not necessarily a unique answer) to every dispute, which is grounded in preexisting law.[70] The right outcome in any new case is the outcome that, in the judge's view, best fits what has come before.

Or so it may seem. We do not accept the claims made for this form of decision making. As a matter of logic, we do not believe legal principles are viable as constraints on judicial reasoning. If they do constrain, we believe they are a vice, not a virtue, of legal decision making.

---

[68] See Dworkin, Law's Empire, supra note 3, at 254–58.

[69] See id. at 225, 228–32 ("The adjudicative principle of integrity instructs judges to identify legal rights and duties, so far as possible, on the assumption that they were all created by a single author – the community personified – expressing a coherent conception of justice and fairness"); Barbara Baum Levenbook, The Meaning of a Precedent, 6 Legal Theory 185, 233–34 (2000) (interpreting Dworkin's theory of precedent as a coherence theory); Kenneth J. Kress, Legal Reasoning and Coherence Theories: Dworkin's Rights Thesis, Retroactivity, and the Linear Order of Decisions, 72 Cal. L. Rev. 369, 370 (1984) (associating Dworkin with coherence theory).

[70] See Dworkin, Law's Empire, supra note 3, at 258; Dworkin, Taking Rights Seriously, supra note 3, at 81–84 (elaborating the "rights thesis"). See also Hart and Sacks, supra note 3, at 369 (referring to the common law as "a process of settlement which tries to relate the grounds of present determination in some reasoned fashion to previously established principles and policies and rules and standards).

B. FAULTY LOGIC

Working from Dworkin's description of legal principles, we can demon-strate in two ways that legal principles are incapable of constraining judicial decisions. Our first argument is based on the notion of weight: the effect of a legal principle on the outcome of any dispute is a function of its weight in competition with other principles.[71] The process by which a judge is to calculate a principle's weight, however, is mysterious.[72]

Recall that, by hypothesis, legal principles differ from morally cor-rect principles because they must be made to fit a body of decisions that is sure to contain some mistakes. It is possible that, in a given area of law, so few decisions will be mistaken that the legal principle sug-gested by past cases will correspond to a correct moral principle. But it is equally possible, and probably more likely, that the legal principle suggested by past decisions in an area of law will not pass the threshold of fit unless it conforms to a significant number of past errors. The best legal principle will then be morally incorrect. Further, if both morally correct and morally incorrect legal principles are immanent in existing legal materials, it must be the case that morally incorrect legal principles will sometimes outweigh morally correct legal principles; otherwise, all outcomes would follow from morally correct principles, and past out-comes would have no practical effect on present decisions. Given these assumptions, the question for the judge becomes, what weight should a morally incorrect legal principle have in competition with other correct and incorrect principles?

There is nothing in the past decisions themselves that can determine the weight of the legal principle they support. The judge might count the number of decisions that support a particular legal principle, but the number of supporting decisions does not tell the judge what weight the erroneous legal principle has as a reason for decision in the current case. Nor can the judge refer to correct moral principles to assign weight to an incorrect legal principle, because correct moral principles will always dictate that incorrect principles should have no weight at all. In

---

[71] *See* note 57 and accompanying text, *supra*.
[72] The following paragraphs track the argument set out in Larry Alexander and Ken Kress, *Against Legal Principles,* in *Law and Interpretation: Essays in Legal Philosophy* 301–6 (Andrei Marmor, ed., Oxford: Clarendon Press 1995).

other words, there is no possible standard for determining the weight of incorrect legal principles: their weight must be a matter of unregulated intuition or discretion. Therefore, legal principles cannot control what the judge ultimately decides.[73]

Our second argument to show that legal principles cannot constrain judicial decision making is based on the requirement of fit with past decisions. An initial difficulty is that the necessary degree of fit cannot be specified in a nonarbitrary way. We know only that a legal principle must fit well enough with past decisions to meet the objective of coherence and that it must fit some number of mistaken decisions if it is to be distinguished from natural reasoning. Beyond this, nothing in the idea of a legal principle tells where the threshold of fit lies and how many recalcitrant decisions the judge can ignore.[74]

But suppose we assume that judges can interpret the threshold of fit in a reasonably determinate way. This brings us to our main point, which is that the requirement of fit is not a real constraint: a judge can always devise a legal principle that fits perfectly with past cases and also applies a correct moral principle to present and future cases. To do this, the judge simply states the applicable moral principle and adds an exception describing past outcomes.[75]

For example, assume that the correct moral principle governing land use in residential neighborhoods is that landowners may not engage in activities that pose significant burdens on surrounding owners unless those burdens are justified by the activity's importance as a service to the community. Heidi believes that, based on this principle, she should enjoin Roscoe from opening his paintball arena; however, she also believes that the correct moral principle is at odds with past decisions allowing a tennis club, a bowling alley, and a golf course to operate in residential neighborhoods (decisions X, Y, and Z). To escape this bind, she can

---

[73] For an effort to systematize the process of weighing principles, see S. L. Hurley, Coherence, Hypothetical Cases, and Precedent, 10 Oxford J. of Legal Stud. 221 (1990) (suggesting that settled cases, actual and hypothetical, provide guidance about the relative weight of principles in particular factual settings).

[74] See Dworkin, Law's Empire, supra note 3, at 255 ("different judges will set [the threshold of fit] differently").

[75] See Alexander and Kress, supra note 72, at 304–6. Thus, if P_C is the correct moral principle, and P_L is the best legal principle in terms of fit and moral attractiveness, and there are N incorrect past cases, C_N, then P_L is $P_C - C_N$. Id.

formulate a legal principle, "Landowners may not engage in activities that impose significant burdens on surrounding owners unless those burdens are justified by the activity's importance as a service to the community; *except* that they may operate the specific tennis clubs, bowling alleys, or golf courses permitted in past cases X, Y, and Z." This principle supports all past decisions but favors an injunction against Roscoe. Given that the past cases are past, and that X, Y, and Z can never recur, the principle also favors morally correct outcomes in all future cases. In its prospective effect, Heidi's legal principle is indistinguishable from the correct moral principle. In practice, therefore, the "legal" component of the principle is inert.

If judicial maneuvering of this kind seems implausible, recall that the only cases in which legal principles constrain natural reasoning are cases in which the judge believes the outcome indicated by the legal principle is morally wrong. The moral superiority of a principle that applies correct moral principles with an exception for past mistakes may well counteract its ungainly ad hoc formulation. In fact, if we take Dworkin's criteria for legal principles literally, it appears that Heidi must formulate her legal principle this way, in order to achieve the maximum of both fit and moral attractiveness.

We have addressed our arguments so far to Dworkin's account of legal principles, in which a judge constructs a legal principle from the data of past decisions to resolve a current dispute. Suppose instead that we take a conventional view of legal principles: legal principles are the decisional principles generally agreed upon within the legal profession.[76] Could such a principle constrain judicial decision making? We do not think so.

We note, first, that to count as legal principles, conventional legal principles must operate as legal principles, not as rules. They must be organic rather than posited, changing as the body of professional opinion changes. Their content must be governed at least in part by coherence with past decisions. They must influence future decisions by exerting weight, rather than determine future decisions by prescribing results.[77]

---

[76] *See* Owen Fiss, *Objectivity and Interpretation*, 34 *Stan. L. Rev.* 739, 744–50 (1982).

[77] *See* text at notes 55–58, 61–63, *supra*.

The weight of a conventional legal principle, as well as its content, is established by professional agreement. There are two ways to conceive of legal principles as products of convention. First, legal professionals might agree on the principles themselves: legal principles, and their weights, are constituted by professional agreement. We can reject this understanding quickly. If legal principles are *posited* by the profession – for example, in judicial opinions or legal texts – they count not as legal principles but as posited rules. If, on the other hand, they arise out of agreement alone, they are self-referential. Professional agreement cannot create a preexisting principle, and if the principle does not predate professional agreement, the profession cannot be *agreeing upon* the principle but, rather, must be generating it. If the profession generates the principle, it is, once again, a posited rule, not something distinct.

Alternatively, legal professionals might agree not directly about the content of legal principles but about how particular cases should be decided. In that case, legal principles might be conceived of as the best principles that conform to particularized professional judgments. The main difficulty with this account of legal principles is that it depends on the unlikely event of broad professional consensus. To the extent that professionals disagree about outcomes, there are no legal principles. A further problem is that when professionals do agree on particular outcomes, it is not at all clear that their agreement on outcomes reflects an agreement on legal principles and their comparative weights. Consensus about outcomes might just as well follow from agreement on an unstated moral rule. In other words, professional judgment about outcomes might be shaped not by institutional history (in the manner of a legal principle) but by moral principles, including principles that give moral weight to past decisions.

C. PERNICIOUS EFFECTS

We have argued that judges cannot reason from legal principles: legal principles are logically incapable of imposing constraint. At this point, we suspend logic and assume both that past decisions shape legal principles and that legal principles affect the outcome of current decisions. Our argument here is that legal principles, if in fact they are effective, can seriously impair the quality of decision making.

Our basic argument is simple. Legal principles incorporate moral error into law without the compensating benefits of serious rules. We have already explained that legal principles are imperfect from a moral point of view because they must conform to past decisions, some of which will be moral mistakes. As a result, they are inferior to ideal natural reasoning, which perfectly reflects moral ideals.[78]

Rules, too, are morally imperfect. They are based on moral principles, but to guide decisions, they must generalize in ways that lead to morally mistaken outcomes in some cases. They may also fall short of moral standards due to obsolescence or faulty design. Rules, however, compensate in several ways for the moral mistakes they produce. They settle moral controversy, preempt errors by individual decision makers, provide coordination, and make decision making more efficient.[79]

Legal principles provide none of these benefits. Principles whose content is determined by a standard of coherence with past decisions may yield answers to legal questions, but they will not yield unique answers because more than one principle may satisfy the requirement of coherence. Further, even if we assume that morally incorrect legal principles can have weight and that judges will not circumvent the requirement of fit through creative use of exceptions, judges have considerable freedom in reasoning from legal principles. To formulate and apply a legal principle, a judge must draw tentative principles from past cases, determine which among eligible principles is morally best, and assign weight to competing principles. The risk that judges will err as they proceed through these steps is at least as great as the risk of error in natural reasoning. The process of decision making under legal principles is just as complex as natural reasoning, if not more so. Because judges may vary in the legal principles they extrapolate from precedents and the moral values that guide them in selecting principles and assigning them weight,[80] legal principles cannot provide the benefits of coordination and will thus lead to further moral costs beyond their incorporation of past errors.

Not only do legal principles fail to provide the benefits of serious rules; they also override rules. According to some descriptions at least,

[78] *See* text at note 65, *supra*.
[79] *See* Chapter 2, *supra* text at notes 31–39.
[80] *See* Dworkin, *Law's Empire, supra* note 3, at 255–57.

rules announced in prior opinions are among the legal materials with which legal principles must be made to fit.[81] Once the threshold of fit has been passed, however, rules can be discarded; and, in any event, precedent rules do not prescribe results but only help to shape legal principles. In a regime of legal principles, therefore, there can be no serious rules.

D. THE FAILURE OF PROPOSED JUSTIFICATIONS FOR LEGAL PRINCIPLES

Various normative arguments have been made on behalf of legal principles; in our view, none succeed. One such argument is that reasoning from legal principles promotes equality or "integrity." The requirement of fit with past decisions means that past and present litigants who are similarly situated (as defined by the legal principle itself) will be treated alike.[82] More generally, legal principles drawn from past decisions provide judges with a comprehensive set of decisional standards that unite the body of law and reflect a "coherent conception of justice and fairness" applicable to all parties in all cases.[83]

We have already explained why we reject like treatment of litigants over time as a moral ideal.[84] Legal cases are never identical, and past opinions offer limited factual descriptions that can filter out important differences. More substantively, aside from the effects of justified reliance, morally incorrect decisions in the past do not justify morally incorrect decisions in the present and future. Equality is theory-dependent: it requires, if anything, that any given moral principle be applied equally to all. A lapse in the past is a cause for regret but not for additional moral wrongs.

For those who are convinced that equal treatment among litigants is a moral good even when governing moral principles are misapplied, we suggest that legal principles are not a reliable source of consistency in judicial decision making. Given the variability of legal principles among

---

[81] *See* note 60 and accompanying text, *supra*.

[82] *See* Dworkin, *Taking Rights Seriously, supra* note 3, at 112–15; Michael S. Moore, *Legal Principles Revisited*, 82 *Iowa L. Rev.* 867, 872–89 (1997).

[83] Dworkin, *Law's Empire, supra* note 3, at 225. This is the ideal Dworkin refers to as "integrity" in law. Id. For a detailed refutation of Dworkin's claim that reasoning from legal principles leads to "integrity," *see* Alexander and Kress, *supra* note 72, at 310–26.

[84] *See* Chapter 2, *supra* text at notes 11–13.

judges and the changeability of legal principles over time, past and present litigants may not in fact be treated alike. Serious rules at least guarantee like treatment of all cases that fall within the classes defined by a rule; legal principles are too unstable to guarantee a similar level of consistency. And, as we have noted, legal principles make serious rules impossible.

A second, related claim on behalf of legal principles is that they avoid retroactivity.[85] Natural and rule-based models of law allow judges to reach decisions that are not dictated by preexisting law, in the manner of legislatures. Natural reasoning does not rely on predefined standards of decision, and legal rules apply only to the classes of cases that fall within their terms; in any other case, the judge must decide what is best, all things considered, or formulate a new rule and apply it to events that occurred before the announcement of the rule. Legal principles, in contrast, "exist" prior to their application to particular cases, as the morally best principles that explain the body of decisions to date. They are capable of resolving all possible disputes, because coherence with the past supplies a decisional standard for new cases. It follows, according to this claim, that when judges decide cases on the basis of legal principles, they are enforcing preexisting rights of the parties.

This argument for legal principle fails on several grounds. First, natural decision making, including natural decision making in the interstices of legal rules, takes account of the moral concerns that make retroactivity a problem. Judges who reason naturally can and must consider the effects of their decisions on justified expectations of the parties and other actors.[86] Second, it is not so clear that legal principles preexist particular decisions in a way that matters morally. As we explained in comparing legal principles with rules, legal principles are indeterminate in several ways.[87] Indeterminacy means, in turn, that the prior "existence" of legal principles is no guaranty against unfair surprise.

Moreover, as Ken Kress has shown, the content of legal principles changes over time.[88] Legal principles, at least as defined by Dworkin, are the morally best principles that pass a threshold of fit with prior

---

[85] See Dworkin, *Taking Rights Seriously, supra* note 3, at 30, 85–86, 110–15, 335–38.
[86] See Chapter 2, *supra* text at notes 7–9.
[87] See text at notes 71–74, *supra*.
[88] See Kress, *supra* note 69, at 377–88; Alexander and Kress, *supra* note 72, at 296–97.

decisions. If we assume that judges do not simply combine correct moral principles with exceptions for past cases, and that the set of past decisions includes some mistakes, the best available legal principle will always be a principle that fits the minimum allowable number of past decisions. Beyond this threshold, judges will discard mistaken precedents in order to formulate morally preferable principles. Meanwhile, new decisions are constantly entering the body of law. As this occurs, judges will discard more past mistakes, new mistakes will need to be accounted for, and legal principles will change accordingly. Legal principles, in other words, are organic rather than fixed, and it is impossible to predict with confidence their content at any time. As Kress demonstrates, they may even change between the time of the disputed transaction and the time the dispute is adjudicated, thus resulting in retroactivity. In other words, reasoning from legal principles may be less rather than more capable of avoiding pernicious retroactivity than natural reasoning on the rule model.

E. SUMMARY: WHY LEGAL PRINCIPLES DO NOT AND SHOULD NOT HAVE A ROLE IN JUDICIAL DECISION MAKING

For many lawyers, the idea of legal principles seems to capture an important part of legal reasoning. As a matter of logic, however, legal principles cannot operate in the way their proponents suggest, as a medium by which past decisions constrain the outcome of natural reasoning in current cases. The notion of weight is too elusive, and the criterion of fit with prior decisions is too malleable to sustain the argument that legal principles guide judges in reaching decisions.

Perhaps if judges took the requirement of fit very seriously – legal principles must explain all prior decisions without resort to awkward exceptions – past decisions would exert some (vague) power over current outcomes. The effect, however, would be pernicious: legal principles would entrench past errors without securing the benefits associated with legal rules. In any event, coherence would eventually break down under a strict standard of fit. Not surprisingly, therefore, proponents of legal principles do not support a standard of this kind.

Accordingly, we eliminate from our account of legal reasoning the entire apparatus of legal principles. To the extent that analogical reasoning rests on similarities identified by reference to legal principles, we also exclude analogical reasoning from our account. In the next chapter, we suggest that the process of drawing analogies and searching past decisions for evidence of principles may have a practical function for judges. But legal principles, and analogies based on legal principles, do not determine the outcomes of cases. Judges who purport to reason on this basis are either reasoning naturally under the guise of legal principles or reasoning deductively from informally posited rules.

IV

Common-Law Practice

In our analysis of the common law, we have argued that judges resolving legal disputes reason in the ways that all decision makers reason. They reason naturally, drawing moral and empirical conclusions through induction and the method of reflective equilibrium, and they reason deductively from authoritative rules. Natural reasoning is unconstrained by law; deductive reasoning is constrained by legal rules that preempt natural reasoning. Other methods of decision making popularly attributed to judges, including analogical reasoning from case to case and reasoning from legal principles, are illusory. Judges may appear to do these things, but analogies and legal principles impose no actual constraint on judicial reasoning. The outcome of purportedly analogical processes rests in fact on natural or deductive reasoning.

We have also suggested that the common law will be most effective, both in correctly resolving particular disputes and in settling future controversies, if current judges treat rules established by prior judges as binding in a preemptive sense. This model of judicial decision making, which we have called the rule model, entails that judges have rule-making authority. In Chapter 2, we addressed some of the theoretical questions that arise when judges act as rule makers, including the scope of their rule-making authority, preconditions for establishment of binding precedent rules, and overruling of precedent rules.[1] In the present chapter, we consider some practical objections to the rule model, both as a prescription for judicial decision making and as a description of judicial practice.

The most significant difficulty facing the rule model as a prescription for decision making is that judges may not be good rule makers. Our argument for the superiority of the rule model of judicial decision making over unconstrained natural reasoning depends on the quality of judicial rules. Deduction from precedent rules can improve on natural reasoning only if rules prevent more error by preempting faulty reasoning, coordinating conduct, and simplifying decision making than they cause by prescribing the wrong result in particular cases.

Precedent rules can be faulty in several ways. Most obviously, rules may be substantively misconceived: they may serve inappropriate ends, or the means they select may be inapt. Alternatively, rules may be formally defective. Rules may be so blunt that errors of overinclusiveness exceed the errors that would result from unconstrained reasoning and lack of coordination. Overinclusiveness is an unavoidable by-product of the qualities of generality and determinateness that make rules effective; at some point, however, it goes too far.[2] Precedent rules may also be overly complex: if rules are too confusing, judges and actors may err so frequently in applying them that actual outcomes will not be superior to the outcomes of natural reasoning.[3] Another possibility is that rules

---

[1] *See* Chapter 2, *supra* text at notes 41–61.

[2] On the possibility of optimal but over- and underinclusive rules, *see* Frederick Schauer, *Playing by the Rules: A Philosophical Examination of Rule-Based Decision-Making in Life and Law* 47–52 (Oxford: Clarendon Press 1991). An overinclusive rule may be justified in the sense that it prevents more errors than it causes, but suboptimal because another rule would do a better job of reducing error. Conversely, precedent rules may be suboptimal because they are underinclusive. An underinclusive rule may be justified in terms of error reduction, but suboptimal because a broader rule would provide greater settlement value.

[3] *See* Larry Alexander and Emily Sherwin, *The Rule of Rules: Morality, Rules, and the Dilemmas of Law* 31 (Durham: Duke University Press 2001).

may be too vague and indeterminate to preempt natural reasoning, or they may generate interpretive controversies that are just as costly as the moral controversies the rules were designed to settle.[4]

Whether any given judicial rule meets the standard of net error reduction is, ultimately, an empirical question. Certain features of the environment in which judges announce rules, however, give cause for concern about the quality of judicial rules. Under the rule model of judicial decision making, judges are not only rule makers but also adjudicators. For reasons we outline later in this chapter, the demands and distractions of adjudication create a special risk of suboptimal rules.

Our argument for the rule model of judicial decision making can also be challenged on descriptive grounds: judges and lawyers behave in ways that appear to contradict both the rule model of decision making and our more general conclusion that judicial reasoning consists of nothing more than ordinary moral, inductive, and deductive reasoning. The rule model assumes that judicial decisions are constrained only by posited rules; yet judges claim to be guided by factual analogies to prior cases, and lawyers regularly present analogies to judges as a source of persuasion.[5] The rule model assumes that judges have plenary authority to make rules; yet, to the extent judges announce rules at all, they typically confine themselves to narrow rules tailored to the dispute before them.[6] When precedent judges do issue rules that go beyond the needs of adjudication, future judges may disregard the rules as dicta.[7] The rule model permits overruling but does not recognize the practice of distinguishing rules; in contrast, judges typically are reluctant to overrule precedents but frequently claim to distinguish precedent rules.[8]

---

[4] *See* id. at 30–31.
[5] *See* Lloyd L. Weinreb, *Legal Reason: The Use of Analogy in Legal Argument* 44–45 (Cambridge: Cambridge University Press 2005).
[6] *See, e.g.,* Cass R. Sunstein, *One Case at a Time* 4 (Cambridge, Mass.: Harvard University Press 1999); A. W. B. Simpson, *The Ratio Decidendi of Case and the Doctrine of Binding Precedent,* in *Oxford Essays in Jurisprudence* 148, 160–61, 167 (A. G. Guest, ed., London: Oxford University Press 1961).
[7] *See* Steven J. Burton, *An Introduction to Law and Legal Reasoning* 37–38, 60 (Boston: Little, Brown 1995); Simpson, *supra* note 6, at 160–61; Karl N. Llewellyn, *The Common Law Tradition: Deciding Appeals* 86 (Boston: Little, Brown 1960).
[8] *See, e.g.,* Joseph Raz, *The Authority of Law* 183–91 (Oxford: Clarendon Press 1979); Grant Lamond, *Do Precedents Create Rules?,* 11 *Legal Theory* 1, 12 (2005); Robert S. Summers, *Precedent in the United States (New York),* in *Interpreting Precedents: A Comparative Study* 355,

In the sections that follow, we raise the possibility that various conventions traditionally associated with the common law may help to counteract the disadvantages judges face as rule makers. The conventions we consider do not ensure that judges will adopt sound precedent rules, but they serve, indirectly, to neutralize some predictable sources of error. If, in fact, conventional practices can improve the quality of judicial rules, they place the rule model on a sounder practical footing. Further, the possibility that conventional practices assist judges in designing sound rules helps to explain the descriptive gaps between the rule model and actual judicial behavior. Practices that appear to contradict the rule model of decision making may have developed in response to the special problems that arise when a single authority must both resolve a particular dispute and announce rules for a broader class of future cases.

The picture of common law in action we present in this chapter is far from ideal. The practices we describe are not direct, rational responses to the deficiencies of judicial rule making but rather are customary practices that counteract those deficiencies in a rough and indirect way. Because they depend on professional custom, they are also potentially unstable. Yet the capacity of these practices to improve the quality of judicial rules may explain why seemingly illogical methods of decision and argumentation occupy a central place in legal training and convention and also why the common law appears to have evolved more sensibly over time than its circumstances might predict.

I. Judges as Rule Makers

The rule model of the common law, in which precedent rules are binding on later judges, is defensible only if precedent rules prevent more error than they cause. Judicial rules need not perfectly translate moral principles into concrete prescriptions, but they must be sufficiently well designed that judges will do a better job of implementing moral principles by following precedent rules than by reasoning without constraint.[9]

390–92, 394–97 (D. Neil MacCormick and Robert S. Summers, eds., Aldershot: Dartmouth Publishing 1997).
[9] *See* Chapter 2, *supra* text following note 25.

All rules – judicial or legislative – must meet this standard to be justified as rules. Judges, however, must combine the task of rule making with the task of adjudication. As a result, they face special difficulties in designing rules that will bring about a net reduction in error.

A. INATTENTION

The first impediment to sound judicial rule making is that judges tend to treat rule making as incidental to adjudication. For much of the history of English and American common law, judges were reluctant to acknowledge their role as lawmakers. Creating law was the province of legislatures; the role of judges was to resolve disputes according to previously established law.[10] In the absence of positive (legislated) law, judicial decisions were governed by the common law, but the common law was viewed as an independent body of norms located in custom and "reason" rather than judicial opinions.[11] Because judges were both learned in legal custom and experienced in the application of reason, their statements and decisions served as evidence of law. But they had no personal authority to make law by announcing rules; they merely discovered and applied the law.[12]

This view of the matter did not deter early courts from developing a comprehensive body of law, but it prevented them from acknowledging lawmaking as an equal part of their work.[13] Modern judges, recognizing

---

[10] See J. W. Tubbs, *The Common Law Mind: Medieval and Early Modern Conceptions* 182 (Baltimore: Johns Hopkins University Press 2000); Sir Matthew Hale, *The History of the Common Law of England* 45 (1713) (Charles M. Gary, ed., Chicago: University of Chicago Press 1971); A. W. B Simpson, *The Common Law and Legal Theory*, in *Oxford Essays in Jurisprudence* 77, 84–86 (2d ser., A. W. B. Simpson, ed., Oxford: Clarendon Press 1973); 1 William Blackstone, *Commentaries on the Laws of England* 69–70 (Oxford: Clarendon Press 1765); Gerald J. Postema, *Classical Common Law Jurisprudence, Part I*, 2 *Oxford U. Commonwealth L.J.* 155, 166–67 (2002).

[11] On the role of "reason" in early common law, see Sir Edward Coke, *The First Part of the Institutes of the Law of England*, §138, ¶97B (1628), reprinted in II *The Selected Writings of Sir Edward Coke* 577, 701 (Steve Sheppard, ed., Indianapolis: Liberty Fund 2003); Tubbs, *supra* note 10, at 45–52, 148–68; Postema, *supra* note 10, at 176–80; Gerald J. Postema, *Classical Common Law Tradition, Part II*, 3 *Oxford U. Commonwealth L.J.* 1, 1–11 (2003); Introduction, *supra* note 2; Part 2, introductory paragraphs, *supra* note 6.

[12] This view continues to be influential. *See* Weinreb, *supra* note 5, at 147–52; Ronald Dworkin, *Taking Rights Seriously* 82 (Cambridge, Mass.: Harvard University Press 1977).

[13] *See* David Lieberman, *The Province of Legislation Determined* 86–87, 122–43 (Cambridge: Cambridge University Press 1989); Postema, *supra* note 10, at 162.

that their opinions affect conduct, are quicker to admit that they can and do create law, and some are quite explicit about announcing rules to govern future cases.[14] Yet, for most courts, rule making continues to be a secondary concern; the immediate need is to resolve a dispute.

As a result, judges are not as well situated as legislatures are to attend to the full range of consequences of the rules they announce. Heidi, drafting an opinion in the case of Edward's bear, might state that "wild animals in residential neighborhoods are nuisances"; therefore, the bear must go. Because her attention is focused on explaining why she has decided against Edward, she may not pause to consider the breadth of the rule, which by its terms bans not only bears but also field mice and other odd but harmless pets.

Of course, Heidi's statement may not in fact amount to a rule. As we understand the nature of authoritative rules, if Heidi did not intend to announce a rule, no precedent rule exists.[15] In that case, no harm is done. Yet it is also possible that Heidi meant to state a rule justifying her decision but formulated the rule in haste without thinking systematically about future cases. If so, the result is an authoritative but suboptimal rule.

This is not to suggest that legislatures are impeccable rule makers. For a variety of reasons, they too are capable of enacting poor rules. Legislatures, however, are at least more likely to view future governance as a central part of their project.

B. COGNITIVE BIAS

A second difficulty is that even when judges turn their full attention to rule making, the facts of the dispute before them may distort their reasoning about rules. In the developing field of behavioral decision theory, cognitive psychologists have demonstrated that human decision makers rely on a variety of "heuristics" – cognitive shortcuts – to reach empirical conclusions.[16] These heuristics are useful because they allow people to

---

[14] See Peter M. Tiersma, *The Textualization of Precedent*, 52–69, available from *Social Science Research Network*, http://ssrn.com/abstract=680901 (2005) (citing explicit holdings and "tests," especially in Supreme Court opinions, as evidence of the "textualization" of the common law).

[15] On the requirement that precedent rules must be posited, *see* Chapter 2, *supra* text at notes 50–51.

[16] See generally Thomas Gilovich and Dale Griffin, *Introduction – Heuristics and Biases: Then and Now*, in *Heuristics and Biases: The Psychology of Intuitive Judgment* (Thomas Gilovich,

form judgments with confidence under conditions of complexity and uncertainty. Yet, because cognitive heuristics replace full unbiased reasoning with simpler, indirect decisional strategies, they can also lead the reasoner into error.[17]

Judges, like all human reasoners, are subject to errors of this kind. Cognitive heuristics can affect the accuracy of judicial fact finding. For example, well-documented biases can lead judges (and juries) to err in calculating probabilities,[18] determining causation and responsibility,[19] judging the foreseeability of past events,[20] fixing damage awards,[21] evaluating settlements,[22] estimating the chance of reversal on appeal,[23] and assessing the merits of appeals.[24]

Dale Griffin, and Daniel Kahneman, eds., Cambridge: Cambridge University Press 2002); Scott Plous, *The Psychology of Judgment and Decision Making* (Philadelphia: Temple University Press 1993); Amos Tversky and Daniel Kahneman, *Availability: A Heuristic for Judging Frequency and Probability*, in *Judgment under Uncertainty: Heuristics and Biases* 163 (Daniel Kahneman, Paul Slovic, and Amos Tversky, eds., Cambridge: Cambridge University Press 1982); *Symposium: The Behavioral Analysis of Legal Institutions: Possibilities, Limitations, and New Directions*, 32 *Fla. St. L. Rev.* 315 (2005).

[17] *See* Gilovich and Griffin, *supra* note 16, at 1; Plous, *supra* note 16, at 109; Amos Tversky and Daniel Kahneman, *Judgment under Uncertainty: Heuristics and Biases*, in *Judgment under Uncertainty: Heuristics and Biases*, *supra* note 16, at 3, 4–14; Chris Guthrie, Jeffrey J. Rachlinski, and Andrew J. Wistrich, *Inside the Judicial Mind*, 86 *Cornell L. Rev.* 777, 780 (2001).

[18] *See* Guthrie, Rachlinski, and Wistrich, *supra* note 17, at 807 (discussing representativeness biases in assessment of forensic evidence); Jeffrey J. Rachlinski, *Heuristics and Biases in the Courts: Ignorance and Adaptation*, 79 *Ore. L. Rev.* 61, 85–86 (2000) (same).

[19] *See* Jeffrey J. Rachlinski, *Bottom-Up and Top-Down Decisionmaking*, 73 *U. Chi. L. Rev.* 933, 947–49 (2006) (discussing attribution biases); Guthrie, Rachlinski, and Wistrich, *supra* note 17, at 808–11 (studying the effects of representativeness bias on findings of negligence).

[20] *See* Guthrie, Rachlinski, and Wistrich, *supra* note 17, at 799–805 (studying the effects of hindsight on judicial assessment of the likelihood of appeal); Jeffrey J. Rachlinski, *A Positive Psychological Theory of Judging in Hindsight*, 65 *U. Chi. L. Rev.* 571 (1998) (discussing hindsight biases and legal mechanisms developed in response).

[21] *See* Keith Sharfman, *Judicial Valuation Behavior: Some Evidence from Bankruptcy*, 32 *Fla. St. L. Rev.* 387 (2005) (studying the effects of loss aversion bias on valuations in bankruptcy); Guthrie, Rachlinski, and Wistrich, *supra* note 17, at 790–94 (studying the effects of anchoring on damages). *See also* Cass R. Sunstein, Daniel Kahneman, David Schkade, and Ilana Ritov, *Predictably Incoherent Judgments*, 54 *Stan. L. Rev.* 1153 (2002) (studying contrast effects on punitive damages assessment).

[22] *See* Guthrie, Rachlinski, and Wistrich, *supra* note 17, at 796–94 (studying the effects of framing on settlement supervision).

[23] *See* id. at 814–16 (studying the effects of egocentric bias on trial court assessments of appeal prospects).

[24] *See* Chris Guthrie and Tracey E. George, *The Futility of Appeal: Disciplinary Insights into the "Affirmance Effect" on the United States Courts of Appeals*, 32 *Fla. St. L. Rev.* 357 (2005) (studying affirmance effects).

More important for our purposes, cognitive biases can affect the design of judicial rules. When the facts of a particular dispute are prominent in a rule maker's mind, certain heuristics are especially likely to come into play and to cause the rule maker to miscalculate the future effects of rules. Accordingly, as Frederick Schauer has observed, there is reason to doubt the common assumption that judicial rules benefit from the concrete factual settings in which judges work.[25] Concrete facts may give judges a sense of rules in action, but they also can distort judicial analysis of the consequences of rules across the range of cases to which they apply.

The cognitive heuristic that bears most directly on the rule making in the context of adjudication is "availability."[26] In judging the frequency or probability of events, decision makers tend to assume that the events that come most easily to mind are also the most likely to occur. This assumption can work fairly well as a time-saving rule of thumb, but it can also lead the reasoner to overlook statistical probabilities.

When a judge formulates a rule for future cases, the facts of the case currently pending are easy to recall, while other potential applications of the rule are distant and possibly unknown to the judge. As a result, the current case may appear more representative than it is of the class of cases covered by the rule, and the court may announce a faulty rule. For example, Heidi is considering the case of Martha, whose mean-tempered pit bull recently attacked a neighbor. With Martha's pit bull in mind, Heidi formulates a rule, "Pit bulls in residential neighborhoods are nuisances." Martha's dog, however, may not be typical. If, in fact, most pit bulls are docile, this rule may cause more errors that it prevents.

---

[25] *See* Alexander and Sherwin, *supra* note 3, at 132–33 (noting the possibility of cognitive bias in judicial rule making); Frederick Schauer, *Do Cases Make Bad Law?*, 73 *U. Chi. L. Rev.* 833, 893–906 (2006); Emily Sherwin, *A Defense of Analogical Reasoning in Law*, 66 *U. Chi. L. Rev.* 1179, 1192 (1999) (same); Emily Sherwin, *Rules and Judicial Review*, 6 *Legal Theory* 299, 315 (1999) (same).

[26] *See, e.g., Plous, supra* note 16, at 121–30; Tversky and Kahneman, *Availability: A Heuristic for Judging Frequency and Probability, supra* note 16, at 163; Schauer, *supra* note 25, at 894–95; Rachlinski, *supra* note 19, at 942–43; Norbert Schwarz and Leigh Ann Vaughn, *The Availability Heuristic Revisited: Ease of Recall and Content of Recall as Distinct Source of Information*, in *Heuristics and Biases, supra* note 16, at 103. *See also* Cass R. Sunstein, *What's Available?: Social Influences and Behavioral Economics*, 97 *Nw. U. L. Rev.* 1295 (2003) (discussing legislation); Timur Kuran and Cass R. Sunstein, *Availability Cascades and Risk Regulation*, 51 *Stan. L. Rev.* 683 (1999) (same).

Another heuristic likely to influence judges in their dual capacity as rule makers and adjudicators is "affect."[27] Particular images may evoke positive or negative emotions in reasoners, based on the reasoner's experience. As a cognitive heuristic, affect manifests itself in a number of ways. The most pertinent for our purposes is that decision makers give more weight to information that translates easily into emotionally charged images than to information that does not produce a ready affective response. Thus, people take risks more seriously when the risk is presented as a frequency (1 in 10) than when it is presented as a probability (10 percent). The reason for this, presumably, is that frequency information refers to instances and is therefore more likely to raise specific images in the decision maker's mind. When risk information is presented in narrative form, the response is stronger still.[28]

Like the availability heuristic, the affect heuristic suggests that, in formulating rules, judges may give greater weight to the facts of the cases they are currently adjudicating than to other cases that might fall within the terms of the rule. The case at hand provides a ready-made set of images, often presented in a manner calculated to invoke the adjudicator's emotions. As a result, it may command the judge's attention in a way that statistical information about the class of cases governed by the rule does not. The picture of Martha's pit bull mauling a child may lead Heidi to adopt the wrong nuisance rule. Legislators can be influenced by affect and availability as well, as when they act in response to events that have engaged public emotions. In the case of judges, however, vivid images that are likely to provoke an affective response are a regular feature of the rule-making environment.

Another possibly relevant heuristic is "anchoring."[29] In assessing value or probability, decision makers may be influenced by particular

---

[27] See, e.g., Paul Slovic, Melissa Finucane, Ellen Peters, and Donald G. MacGregor, *The Affect Heuristic*, in *Heuristics and Biases, supra* note 16, at 397; Rachlinski, *supra* note 19, at 942.

[28] See Slovic, Finucane, Peters, and MacGregor, *supra* note 27, at 413–14. When the affective association is very strong, people may ignore probability altogether. *See id.* at 409.

[29] See, e.g., Amos Tversky and Daniel Kahneman, *Judgment under Uncertainty: Heuristics and Biases*, 185 *Science* 1124, 1128–30 (1974); Guthrie, Rachlinski, and Wistrich, *supra* note 17, at 787–94; Gretchen B. Chapman and Eric J. Johnson, *Incorporating the Irrelevant: Anchors in Judgments of Belief and Value*, in *Heuristics and Biases, supra* note 16, at 120, 121–23.

numbers or instances that have been brought to their attention, even if those numbers or instances are not typical. For example, Heidi is considering whether to announce a rule that pit bulls in residential neighborhoods are nuisances. A pertinent question is what percentage of pit bulls are dangerously aggressive. The plaintiffs in Martha's case have shown that Martha owns four pet pit bulls, two of which have attacked children or dogs in the neighborhood (50 percent). Heidi knows that Martha trained her dogs to act as watch dogs and that she should, accordingly, adjust her estimate of the general aggressiveness of pit bulls downward from 50 percent. Yet, in the absence of further evidence (which neither party has much reason to present), the anchoring heuristic suggests that Heidi will not adjust sufficiently from the initial figure suggested by the facts.

There are other possibilities. Research suggests that decision makers handle statistical calculations more accurately when they understand that they are assessing a series of cases (how often do pit bulls bite?) than when they focus on a single event (how likely was it that Martha's pit bull would bite?).[30] Perceptions may be distorted by a sense of contrast when decision makers begin with a single observation (compared to Martha's pit bull, Airedales may appear safer than they are).[31] Decision makers who observe the actions of others, as judges do in deciding cases, are prone to commit the *fundamental attribution error* – that is, they tend to attribute causal responsibility to personal traits of the actor rather than background conditions, because the actor is more salient. A pit bull may appear aggressive when in fact it is suffering from indigestion.[32]

Adjudication may have some positive effects on judicial cognition as well. Affect and examples appear to facilitate and clarify decision making

---

[30] *See* Rachlinski, *supra* note 19, at 946. In the example we give in the text, bias hindsight is a problem as well. If Heidi focuses on Martha's pit bull rather than pit bulls generally, her reasoning about ex ante probability will be affected by her knowledge that, in fact, the dog did bite. *See* materials cited in note 20, *supra*.

[31] For discussion of "contrast effects," *see* Plous, *supra* note 16, at 38–41; Rachlinski, *supra* note 19, at 945–46; Sunstein, Kahneman, Schkade, and Ritov, *supra* note 21.

[32] For discussion of the "fundamental attribution error," *see* Plous, *supra* note 16, at 180–82; Lee D. Ross, *The Intuitive Psychologist and His Shortcomings: Distortions in the Attribution Process*, in 10 *Advances in Experimental Social Psychology* 174 (Leonard Berkowitz, ed., New York: Academic Press 1977); Rachlinski, *supra* note 19, at 947–48.

in some situations.[33] Focusing on a specific set of facts may also lead judges to announce narrower rules, which, while not necessarily optimal, will at least cause less damage if they turn out to have been misconceived.[34] Overall, however, the special salience of a pending dispute in the mind of the judge seems likely to interfere with, rather than enhance, the reasoning needed to design sound rules for future cases.[35]

C. OVERRULING PROBLEMS

The rule model of judicial decision making assumes that judges have authority not only to make precedent rules but also to overrule them.[36] At the same time, the rule model does not and cannot distinguish between overruling precedent rules and modifying or "distinguishing" them.[37] When a judge makes an exception to a rule to accommodate a particular

---

[33] See Rachlinski, *supra* note 19, at 954–55 (noting that the "multiple frames" courts encounter in developing common law may improve the quality of judicial rules); Slovic, Finucane, Peters, and MacGregor, *supra* note 27, at 406, 413–14 (noting instances in which affective associations increase the accuracy of prediction).

[34] *Cf.* Rachlinski, *supra* note 19, at 953–54 (suggesting that the decentralization of courts provides opportunities for "experimentation and error correction").

Narrow judicial rulings may be connected to the "representativeness" heuristic, in the following way. Representativeness comes into play when decision makers rely on resemblance rather than probability to determine causal connections or membership in a class. *See* Guthrie, Rachlinski, and Wistrich, *supra* note 17, at 805–6; Rachlinski, *supra* note 18, at 82–83; Plous, *supra* note 16, at 109–12, 115–16; Tversky and Kahneman, *supra* note 17, at 4–9; Maya Bar-Hillel, *Studies of Representativeness*, in *Judgment under Uncertainty*, *supra* note 16, at 69; Amos Tversky and Daniel Kahneman, *Judgments of and by Representativeness*, in *Judgment under Uncertainty*, *supra* note 16, at 84. One manifestation of this heuristic is the conjunction fallacy, in which the decision maker perceives a specific factual description (pit bull bites child) to be more probable than a more general description (dog bites child). *See* Amos Tversky and Daniel Kahneman, *Extensional versus Intuitive Reasoning: The Conjunction Fallacy in Probability Judgment*, in *Heuristics and Biases*, *supra* note 16, at 19, 26–32. The detailed description more closely resembles the decision maker's expectations, although the general description is more probable. This suggests that judges who have in mind a particular instance of a problem may deem that instance to be particularly likely, and therefore tailor their rules to address the instance rather than the general problem. Thus, Heidi, having in mind the case of Martha's pit bull, might be more likely to announce the rule "Pit bulls are nuisances" than the rule "Dogs are nuisances," because she views pit bull bites as more likely than dog bites.

[35] *Cf.* Rachlinski, *supra* note 19, at 951–63 (confirming that courts may be misled by the context of adjudication, but reaching a mixed conclusion about the comparative rule-making aptitude of courts and legislatures).

[36] *See* Chapter 2, *supra* text at note 57.

[37] *See* Chapter 2, *supra* text at note 56; Chapter 2, *supra* text at notes 46–49.

case, the judge is effectively eliminating the precedent rule and announcing a new rule in its place.

As we explained in Chapter 2, judges ideally should overrule precedent rules only when they are unjustified or suboptimal *as rules*. More precisely, judges should overrule *either* when, due to obsolescence or poor design, a precedent rule is likely to cause more erroneous results than it prevents over the range of cases to which it applies, *or* when an alternative rule would prevent more error or cause less error than the precedent rule, *and* the likely benefits from error reduction exceed the costs of the disruption likely to follow from overruling the precedent. The costs of overruling a rule include harm to expectations based on the particular rule and also more general destabilizing effects on the practice of rule following. At the same time, judges must bear in mind that rules can be both justified and optimal *as rules* – likely to reduce the sum of error over the range of their application and preferable to any alternative – and yet prescribe the wrong result in certain cases. When a generally sound rule appears to require an erroneous result, courts should not overrule; they should treat the rule as a serious rule and follow it without second-guessing what it prescribes.[38]

As Schauer points out, judges may not succeed in overruling precedent rules when and only when they should.[39] One problem is the overruling standard itself. The rule model requires that, as adjudicators, judges must follow precedent rules without regard to the moral justification of the results those rules prescribe in particular cases. As makers and abrogators of rules, however, judges can and should evaluate the overall moral justification of rules before determining whether to retain them or to overrule them. This is a fine line for judges to walk. If they fail to make the distinction between erroneous outcomes and unjustified or suboptimal rules, they may either upset settlements by overruling sound rules to accommodate the supposed "equities" of particular cases or entrench error by retaining defective rules.

The first problem – precipitous overruling – is aggravated by the same cognitive heuristics that affect the design of precedent rules, particularly

---

[38] *See* Chapter 2, *supra* text following notes 57–58.

[39] *See* Schauer, *supra* note 25, at 906–12. Schauer refers to this as the "dynamic" aspect of judicial rule making.

the tendency to assume that readily recalled facts or affectively charged images are representative of the larger classes to which they belong.[40] For example, Heidi is considering the case of Sally, who keeps a well-trained, amiable pit bull in her home. In a previous nuisance case, a judge announced the rule, "Pit bulls in residential neighborhoods are nuisances." Assume this rule is sound: a rule excluding all pit bulls will produce more correct decisions overall, and greater coordination benefits, than case-by-case prediction of the probable behavior of particular pit bulls. When Heidi assesses this rule, however, the picture most likely to come to mind is Sally's well-mannered dog. Particularly if the image of Sally and her pet evokes a positive emotional response, the facts of the case are likely to have a greater effect on Heidi's deliberations than more abstract information, such as the statistical likelihood of pit bull attacks and the coordination value of an unqualified no-pit-bull rule.[41] As a result, Heidi may be tempted to overrule the precedent rule or modify it to allow owners of well-trained pit bulls to keep their pets. If the rule in its existing form is the best rule for future pit bull disputes, this will be an error: cognitive bias triggered by the adjudicatory setting will have led Heidi to mistake a single regrettable outcome for lack of overall justification for the rule.

As Schauer has noted, the second problem – failure to overrule rules that are suboptimal or unjustified as rules – is exacerbated by case selection effects.[42] Judges address precedent rules only when the rules are challenged by parties to a dispute. When the law governing a dispute is clear, however, parties are likely to settle rather than bring their case to court.[43] It follows that judges may not often preside over cases that involve core applications of a precedent rule. Trials and appeals become more likely when the rule's application to particular facts is indeterminate.[44] In cases of indeterminacy, however, the judge can avoid allegedly infelicitous

---

[40] See id. at 907–8.
[41] See notes 26–28 and accompanying text, supra.
[42] See Schauer, supra note 25, at 909–12.
[43] See George L. Priest and Benjamin Klein, The Selection of Disputes for Litigation, 13 J. Legal Stud. 1, 9–15 (1984) (explaining the selection effect).
[44] The rule model requires judges to treat rules as serious rules, but parties may calculate that they will not always do so, either because it is not rational for the judge to follow the rule when the judge believes the result it describes is wrong or because the judge mistakenly believes the rule itself, as opposed to the result, is unjustified.

applications of the rule by interpreting the rule narrowly so as to avoid those applications, leaving the rule as so interpreted fully in effect. Thus, judges may have few opportunities to assess the everyday application of rules that are obsolete or misconceived. A particularly harsh application may give the party opposing the rule hope for an exception, but, as we have noted, a harsh application does not necessarily indicate that the rule itself is unsound.

D. SUMMARY: WHY JUDGES ARE POOR RULE MAKERS

The rule model of judicial decision making casts judges as both rule makers and adjudicators. The dual role that judges perform in the legal process is likely to affect the quality of judicial rules in several ways. The demands of adjudication, together with traditions and political pressures that relegate rule making to a secondary position, can lead judges to pay less attention than they should to the potential consequences of their rules. Cognitive heuristics, triggered by attention to particular facts, can lead to miscalculation or disregard of the consequences of rules. Adjudication may also have adverse effects on judicial oversight of precedent rules.

This is not to say that legislation is clearly superior to common law as a source of settlement. Moral and empirical deliberation by elected representatives is notoriously subject to interest group politics and collective action problems, in addition to cognitive biases and ordinary reasoning errors.[45] We are not equipped to undertake a full comparison of judicial and legislative rule making; we note only that there is reason to believe Schauer is correct in his observation that the need to resolve a particular dispute hinders rather than helps judges in producing sound precedent rules. As Schauer suggests, not only hard cases but adjudication in general can result in imperfect law: "Cases make bad rules."[46]

---

[45] *See* Rachlinski, *supra* note 19, at 951–63 (noting cognitive biases affecting legislation); Schauer, *supra* note 25, at 912–13 (noting legislative pathologies and avoiding speculation about the comparative virtues of courts and legislatures as rule makers). *See also* Sunstein, *supra* note 26 (discussing availability biases in legislation); Kuran and Sunstein, *supra* note 26 (same).

[46] Schauer, *supra* note 25. Schauer is obviously playing off the old saw that hard cases make bad law.

II. Correctives to Judicial Rule Making

Because judges announce rules in the course of resolving particular disputes, they face impediments in designing sound rules. The risk of poor-
quality rules challenges the key assumption of the rule model of judicial
decision making – the assumption that following precedent rules will
reduce the sum of error. The prospects for effective common law, however, may not be as bleak as our analysis so far suggests. In the sections
that follow, we suggest that some aspects of traditional common-law
decision making – practices and norms that we find difficult to explain
on any other ground – may work to improve the quality of judicial rules.
We make this suggestion cautiously: the practices we have in mind do not
address the problems of judicial rule making directly, and the correctives
they provide are partial at best.

A. THE METHOD OF ANALOGY

We have argued that so-called analogical reasoning does not contribute in
a meaningful way to judicial decision making.[47] The outcome of one case,
without more, carries no logical implications for the outcome of another
case. Nor do past decisions constrain decision making through the device
of "legal principles."[48] Our analysis of the notion of legal principles (in
its best-known and most attractive form) suggests that past decisions
do not generate legal principles and that, if they could, legal principles
would in any event have no real impact on current decisions. Further, if
past decisions could constrain the content of legal principles, and if legal
principles could constrain the outcome of current cases, they would do
so only at the cost of entrenching error. If we are correct that analogical
reasoning and reasoning from legal principles are spurious constraints,
it follows that the only viable forms of legal reasoning are natural moral
and empirical reasoning and deduction from rules.

The analogical methods practiced by judges and lawyers may nevertheless have a positive influence on legal rules. The most serious impediment to sound judicial rule making is the possibility that a particular set

---

[47] *See* Chapter 3, *supra* text at notes 4–51.
[48] *See* id., text at notes 52–88, *infra*.

of facts will have inordinate influence on the judge's deliberations about rules.[49] Reacting to evidence that Martha's pit bull recently attacked a child, Heidi may respond too quickly with a rule: "Pit bulls in residential neighborhoods are nuisances."

Seeking analogies in prior cases widens the judge's perspective by bringing alternative sets of facts to mind. This in turn reduces the risk of bias in rule making. If the judge proceeds to formulate a rule, exposure to additional facts makes it less likely that the judge will assume the pending case is representative of the larger class of cases covered by the rule.[50]

Thus, in the case of Martha's pit bull, Heidi, aided by lawyers, will pause to review past nuisance cases involving dogs. Assume she finds two cases in which courts allowed owners to keep docile pit bulls, one in which a court ordered an owner to give up a German shepherd that bit a landscaper, and another in which the court allowed an owner to keep a very large sheepdog with no history of aggressive behavior. After consulting these cases, Heidi may adjust her position and conclude that breeds are not the most accurate criteria for judging when dogs are nuisances. She may choose instead to issue a narrower rule ("Attack-trained pit bulls are nuisances"), a different rule ("Dogs that have previously engaged in aggressive behavior are nuisances"), or no rule at all.

The benefits of analogical methodology are indirect. Analogies to past decisions do not constrain the content of judicial rules, any more than they constrain the outcome of adjudication. Instead, the process of searching for analogies and comparing cases dilutes the impact of the pending dispute and places the judges in a better position to seek reflective equilibrium before announcing a rule. After scanning an array of factual settings, the judge is in a better position to test the application of possible rules. Actual evidence in the pending case may be more vivid than descriptions of facts in past opinions, but the images it presents are no longer unopposed.

Ideally, the notion of analogy would not be necessary. In the course of natural reasoning about rules, judges would test potential rules against examples drawn from past cases and from other legal and extralegal

---

[49] *See* text at notes 26–32, *supra.*
[50] *See* Emily Sherwin, *Judges as Rulemakers,* 73 U. Chi. L. Rev. 919, 927–29 (2006); Sherwin, *A Defense of Analogical Reasoning in Law, supra* note 25.

sources as well, including hypothetical cases.[51] Analogy enters in because, in practice, time pressure and preoccupation with the task of adjudication are likely to cut the process of deliberation short. The widely accepted belief that analogies can and should guide judicial decision making leads judges to study a broader array of factual possibilities than they otherwise likely would.

To some extent, the rule model of decision making itself may enlarge the perspective of judges. Judges operating under the rule model will come into contact with past decisions as they search for precedent rules. Analogical methods, however, are likely to be more effective because they require the judge to engage with the facts of prior cases, make comparisons, and formulate rules that explain the importance or unimportance of common facts. Analogical techniques are also broader in scope. All cases are potentially "governed" by analogy, whereas precedent rules cover only those cases that fall within their stated terms. Accordingly, the search for analogies continues even if the court is satisfied that no rule applies.

Analogical methods are not without risks. A judge who believes that analogies in themselves provide a ground for decision may decide on the basis of an unexplained intuition of similarity.[52] Thus, Heidi might conclude that Martha's pit bull is "like" a German shepherd. Alternatively, the judge may construct a "legal principle" based largely on fit with prior cases and, in doing so, entrench past mistakes.[53] If Martha's pit bull, unlike the pit bulls in prior cases, is a French pit bull, Heidi might decide according to the principle, "European guard dogs are nuisances in residential neighborhoods."

B. RESTRICTIONS ON THE SCOPE OF PRECEDENT RULES

If judges are not good rule makers, it follows that they should be cautious in announcing rules. Ideally, they should avoid rule making only when bias affects their judgment; but cognitive bias, by its nature, is difficult for the reasoner to detect and cure. As a fallback, the safest course for judges

---

[51] *See* Chapter 2, *supra* text at note 4.
[52] *See* Chapter 3, *supra* text at notes 23, 27–28.
[53] *See* id., text at notes 78–81, *infra.*

may be to minimize the impact of unsound precedent rules by limiting the scope of all precedent rules, leaving a large domain ungoverned by precedent rules and subject only to the natural model's case-by-case, all-things-considered, particularistic moral reasoning.

Established conventions restrict judicial rule making in several ways. We noted in Chapter 2 that, in announcing precedent rules, judges typically confine themselves to rules that provide an answer to the dispute before the court.[54] In a dispute over Edward's bear, Heidi will stop short of announcing a rule about lawn mowing in residential neighborhoods, even if her research on the subject of nuisances has convinced her that a lawn-mowing rule would be beneficial. Judicial restraint in promulgating rules is reinforced by prevailing methods of interpreting prior opinions. Later judges typically characterize statements that are not necessary to explain the result of the prior case as nonbinding dicta, even if they take the form of rules.[55] Thus, if Heidi states in her opinion in Edward's case that residential landowners must mow their lawns on Saturday, future judges will feel free to regard her statement as a stray remark or at best a suggestion.

These limits on judicial rule making are not entailed by the rule model, which confers rule-making authority on judges without qualification.[56] Limits of this kind, however, may be sensible responses to the problems judicial rule-making encounters. A self-imposed restraint against rule making on subjects that are unrelated to the dispute at hand tends to result in narrow rules and cautious development of common law.

Analogical methods can have a similar conservative effect on judicial rules. We have argued that *reasoning* by analogy (as opposed to purely intuitive analogical decision making) amounts to formulating and applying rules that support like treatment of cases.[57] Connections between the facts of past and present cases are easiest to see and articulate at a low level of generality; therefore, analogy-warranting rules tend to be modest and concrete.[58] For example, suppose Heidi determines that Karl's

---

[54] *See* sources cited in note 6, *supra.*
[55] *See* sources cited in note 7, *supra.*
[56] We defend this view in Chapter 3, *supra* text at notes 45–47.
[57] *See* Chapter 2, *supra* text at notes 12–28.
[58] *See* Cass R. Sunstein, *Legal Reasoning and Political Conflict* 63, 68–69 (New York: Oxford University Press 1996).

ocelot is importantly similar to Edward's bear, which a prior judge held
to be a nuisance. She explains the likeness of the cases by reference to
a rule: "Dangerous wild animals in residential neighborhoods are nuisances." The same moral principles that justify this rule might also justify
a broader rule: "Potentially dangerous agents that are difficult to control are nuisances when maintained in an area where they might cause
serious personal injury." This rule, however, does not capture the link
between Karl's ocelot and Edward's bear as effectively as the narrower
dangerous-wild-animal rule. The broader rule also calls for a much wider
search of prior cases to test the rule against outcomes within its range.[59]
Therefore, Heidi is likely to choose the narrower form. If the resulting
rule is unsound, the harm it causes will be correspondingly small.

C. DISTINGUISHING AND OVERRULING

The rule model of judicial decision making has no conceptual room for
the practice of distinguishing rules. Precedent rules are serious rules,
meaning that judges must either follow them according to their terms,
without reference to the underlying moral principles they are designed
to implement, or overrule them. At the same time, the rule model
itself does not limit the power to overrule: judges have authority to
make rules, and therefore judges have authority to replace or eliminate
rules. Ideally, judges will overrule precedent rules only when the existing rule is either unjustified or suboptimal *as a rule* – that is, when it
causes more error than it prevents or performs less well than an alternative rule – and only when the harm to expectations and coordination from overruling or the prospect of overruling does not militate in
favor of retaining a suboptimal rule.[60] When sound rules appear to prescribe mistaken results, judges should leave them in place and decide as
they require.

As we have noted, however, the ideal standard for overruling, as just
described, is difficult if not impossible for judges to apply. Unjustified

---

[59] Past outcomes, in our view, do not determine either current outcomes or the content of newly
announced rules. Judges practicing the method of analogy, however, must at least consider
decisions that are inconsistent with the analogy-warranting rules on which they rely and, if
the inconsistency cannot be resolved, discard either the rule or the inconsistent decisions.
[60] *See* Chapter 2, *supra* text at notes 57–61.

rules are logically distinct from justified rules that produce erroneous outcomes; psychologically, however, it is hard to separate the two. Cognitive heuristics exacerbate the problem: the availability and affective power of live parties and narrative facts will illuminate an unappealing outcome in the case before the court and obscure the more abstract benefits of upholding a sound rule.[61] An artificial presumption in favor of rule following might counteract the effects of compelling facts, although applying such a presumption is not a fully rational response. Why should a judge follow a precedent rule when the judge believes the balance favors overruling?

The stance that judges traditionally have taken toward precedent rules is rather different from what the rule model recommends. Judges tend to be cautious in overruling precedent rules; at least, they do not repeal rules at will in the manner of a legislature. On the other hand, they commonly distinguish precedent rules, carving out exceptions based on factual differences between the current case and past cases in which the rule was applied.[62]

As we have said, distinguishing is not a form of partial rule following. For the reasons outlined in the preceding chapter, when a judge distinguishes a precedent rule, that rule has no impact on the outcome of the pending case or the content of the "modified" rule. Nor do the facts of prior cases applying the rule constrain the outcome of the pending case. Distinguishing is based on factual disanalogies that, like analogies, have no independent rational force. Either disanalogies are purely intuitive, or they stem from a rule that identifies important differences among cases. Ultimately, therefore, there is no constraint on the ability of judges to distinguish rules if distinguishing is permitted: distinguishing rules is logically equivalent to repealing rules at will.[63]

As a practice, however, distinguishing differs in one important way from simple overruling of precedent rules. Before distinguishing a rule, the judge studies and compares the facts of past cases applying the rule. In the process, the judge is likely to encounter at least one and probably more than one concrete example in which the rule performed well. Just

---

[61] *See* text at notes 26–28, *supra.*
[62] *See* sources cited in note 8, *supra.*
[63] *See* Chapter 3, *supra,* text at notes 46–49.

as seeking analogies helps judges assess the consequences of rules beyond a single case, the practice of distinguishing may enable judges to perceive more easily the benefits of adhering to precedent rules.

For example, Heidi is considering the case of Edward's bear. A prior opinion, in a nuisance suit against Walter, announced the rule, "Bears in residential neighborhoods are nuisances." Heidi believes that the purposes of this rule do not apply to Edward's bear, a gentle retired circus animal that has lived uneventfully in Edward's home for years. So she sets about distinguishing Edward's case. To do this, she reads descriptions of facts provided by the judge in Walter's case: Walter's pet bear escaped and wandered into a school cafeteria, frightening children and teachers. She also consults the description of facts in a later case that applied the no-bear rule in a nuisance action against Charles: Charles's bear, which had previously been well behaved, clawed a representative of a charitable organization canvassing door-to-door. At this point, Heidi is still free to distinguish Edward's case: Edward may keep his bear in an especially sturdy cage, and Walter's and Charles's bears may never have worked in the circus. But the facts of the prior cases provide competing narratives that demonstrate the value of an unqualified no-bear rule in a manner that is more likely to influence Heidi's deliberations than abstract arguments about error prevention and coordination. As a result, Heidi may be less tempted to distinguish (and thereby overrule) the rule.

The practice of distinguishing precedent rules is dangerous to the stability of rules because it creates an illusion of modesty. Judges may intervene more often when they believe they are merely modifying, rather than overruling, established rules. This belief is mistaken because modifying or distinguishing precedent rules just *is* overruling them. Yet, if judges cannot reliably separate faulty rules from regrettable outcomes, a set of conventions by which judges hesitate to "overrule" rules but are willing to "distinguish" rules based on factual dissimilarities between cases may be the next-best solution. Erroneous rules are not permanently entrenched, but judges normally will not overrule rules without first consulting examples that counteract the tendency to overrule in response to the engaging facts of the disputes before them.

D. SUMMARY: CORRECTIVE PRACTICES

Judges traditionally have engaged in a number of practices that are not required by the rule model of the common law and in some cases appear to contradict either the rule model itself or the related assumption that judicial reasoning is nothing other than ordinary moral and empirical reasoning and deduction from rules. Judges seek analogies; they avoid rules that are not necessary to the outcome of a pending case and dismiss unnecessary rules as dicta; they purport to distinguish precedent rules based on factual differences among cases. In our view, these practices do not embody a special form of legal reasoning: apart from their effect in narrowing the pool of eligible precedent rules, they do not determine the outcomes of judicial decision making. They become more understandable, however, when viewed as indirect strategies that counteract the disadvantages of judges as rule makers. The task of adjudication can lead judges to formulate rules infelicitously; the practices we have described may serve, partially and imperfectly, to correct the effects of adjudication on rule making.

We offer this suggestion cautiously. The potential benefits we have attributed to otherwise mysterious judicial practices are possibilities, not empirically verified and not without accompanying risks to the stability of precedent rules. If our speculations are correct, however, the relationship between these practices and judicial rule making helps to reconcile the rule model of decision making with the conventional behavior of lawyers and judges.

III. Rationality and Sustainability of Judicial Practice

Certain conventional judicial practices – seeking analogies with past decisions, avoiding or disregarding rules that are not necessary to the outcome of a pending case, and distinguishing precedent rules – may help to improve the quality of judicial rules or limit the damage done by rules that are infelicitous. We have already noted several concerns about these practices. Analogical methods invite intuitive judgment and, to the extent they constrain judicial decision making, can entrench error. Restrictions on the scope of precedent rules limit the opportunity for settlement. Distinguishing precedent rules, which is really overruling precedent rules, can undermine the settlement value of existing rules.

Apart from these potential adverse consequences, the conventional practices we have mentioned suffer from two problems of a deeper kind. First, judges do not consciously adopt these methods as indirect strategies for reducing error; instead, they draw analogies, announce narrow rules, and distinguish precedent rules because they believe this is the right way to decide cases. In other words, judges have, in a sense, tricked themselves into adopting what might well be good rule-making habits. This state of affairs is hard to reconcile with the ideal of legal decision making as a publicly accessible process based on reason.

The element of unreason is most evident in the case of analogical decision making: judges deciding by analogy purport to resolve disputes on grounds that are logically unavailable. Conventions that restrict judicial rule making to rules that explain the outcome of adjudication are more straightforward, but they treat a cautionary strategy as a limit on judicial power. The practice of distinguishing precedent rules disguises overruling as something more modest. In each case, the practice in question is justifiable, if at all, for reasons of which practitioners are unaware.

Indirection and self-deception are common enough in law.[64] Rules themselves illustrate this point. As we noted in Chapter 1, legal rules serve moral values indirectly. Rules reduce the errors of natural reasoning by prescribing answers in a form that will sometimes yield the wrong results. As a consequence, following rules means acting against the balance of reasons in some cases. Acting against the balance of reasons is not rational. Therefore, to accept the authority of rules, one must convince oneself that following the rule is the right thing to do in every case, even though it is not.[65] Self-deception of this kind allows rules to perform the morally valuable function of settling controversy, but it is nevertheless disturbing.

---

[64] See Larry Alexander, *Pursuing the Good – Indirectly*, 95 *Ethics* 315 (1985). On the ethical and practical problems of indirection and deception, including self-deception, *see, e.g.*, Alexander and Sherwin, *supra* note 3, at 89–91; Thomas Schelling, *The Strategy of Conflict* (Cambridge, Mass.: Harvard University Press 1980); Larry Alexander and Emily Sherwin, *The Deceptive Nature of Rules*, 142 *U. Pa. L. Rev.* 1191, 1211–25; Gregory Kavka, *The Toxin Puzzle*, 43 *Analysis* 33 (1983); Gregory Kavka, *Some Paradoxes of Deterrence*, 75 *J. Phil.* 285 (1978).

[65] See Alexander and Sherwin, *supra* note 3, at 553–95; Schauer, *supra* note 2, at 128–34; Chapter 1, *supra*, text at notes 18–25.

Any departure from reasoned decision making, even if justifiable on reasoned grounds, is a cause for regret.

The second problem is a practical one. Because the conventional judicial practices we have described involve self-deception and irrationality, they are also unstable. If lawyers and judges come to understand that conventional practices are not rationally defensible on their own terms, they may cease to accept those practices, and whatever benefits conventional practices hold for rule making will be lost. Analogical reasoning appears to be firmly established at present: our critical analysis of analogical methods is not likely to prevail over pervasive legal training and professional acceptance. Careful factual comparisons, however, may eventually give way to quicker word-based searches for applicable rules.[66] Judicial diffidence in rule making may be more vulnerable, as judges come to accept that they possess a full complement of rule-making power. There are also indications that courts have become more comfortable with direct overruling of precedent rules, and therefore may be less likely to search past cases for distinguishing facts.[67]

The common law, therefore, stands on movable ground. The rule model of judicial decision making, which allows the common law to function as law and to settle controversy, is defensible only when judicial rules are justified as rules, and only when judicial rules are generally followed. Rule following depends on the willingness of judges and actors to apply rules even when the results the rules prescribe conflict with their own best judgment. To the extent that practices we have discussed in this chapter are important to the quality of judicial rules, the justification of precedent rules also depends in part on conventional attitudes and practices of judges. It follows that perfect rationality can subvert the conditions for sound and effective common law.

---

[66] See Helen Hershkoff, State Courts and the "Passive Virtues": Rethinking the Judicial Function, 114 Harv. L. Rev. 1833, 1844–52 (2001) (discussing advisory opinions in state courts); Tiersma, supra note 14, at 56–61, 66–68 (tracing an increase in explicit judicial "holdings").

[67] See Zenon Bankowski, D. Neil MacCormick, and Geoffrey Marshall, Precedent in the United Kingdom, in Interpreting Precedents, supra note 8, at 315, 342 (discussing English practice); Tiersma, supra note 14, at 61–62 (noting an increase in explicit overruling by American courts).

PART THREE

Reasoning from Canonical Legal Texts

I n the previous part we have focused on common-law reasoning by judges and have concluded that there is nothing special about it. In cases unconstrained by precedent, judges use ordinary moral reasoning – the method of reflective equilibrium – and ordinary empirical reasoning to decide controversies and to craft precedent rules for future cases. In cases that are constrained by precedential rules, judges use ordinary deductive reasoning. Reasoning from results in precedent cases rather than from rules, reasoning by analogy from precedent cases, and reasoning from legal principles that emerge from precedent cases have all been shown to be illusory as forms of legal reasoning. The results of such special forms of "reasoning" – special in that they are deemed uniquely emblematic of the legal craft – lack rational force. They are some combination of indeterminate, incoherent, and normatively unattractive. In a limited sense, what appear to be such types of "reasoning" may reflect some useful heuristics for judicial decision making in certain kinds of cases. But they do not qualify as forms of reasoning themselves. Legal reasoning in common-law cases, to the extent it is reasoning at all, is nothing more than ordinary moral, empirical, and deductive reasoning. Legal training is not required to do it, or to do it well.

In this part we turn our attention to another precinct of legal reasoning, that of interpreting canonical authoritative rules promulgated by lawmakers of various types. The lawmakers can be legislators enacting statutes, administrators promulgating rules under either their delegated or their inherent authority to do so, or judges establishing precedent rules under the rule model of precedent. The lawmakers whose rules are in question can be solitary natural persons – the president or the mayor, for example – or they may be multimembered institutions such as legislatures, administrative agencies, and appellate courts. (We deal with constitutions and those who "enact" constitutions in a chapter devoted just to those topics and therefore ignore them here.)

Governing society by rules requires not only that lawmakers promulgate rules but also that those rules be understood by those who will be guided by them, including lawyers helping clients navigate the corpus juris and representing them in legal disputes, and judges adjudicating cases arising under the rules. Ideally, the meaning of the rules would be clear to all concerned. After all, as we have said, clear guidance is the rules' raison d'être. Realistically, that will never be the case universally. The meaning of some rules will be unclear to some people. Moreover, even when the meaning of the rules is clear, it is worth reflecting upon how one determines what a promulgated rule means. When a rule's meaning is clear, what makes it so? And when a rule's meaning is unclear, how do we clarify it? It is to these topics that we now turn.

V

Interpreting Statutes and Other Posited Rules

What kind of "reasoning" or methodology is employed when judges, lawyers, administrators, and ordinary citizens interpret statutes or other humanly authored and promulgated (posited) laws? Is the interpretation of laws a special form of reasoning, a methodology learned only in law schools?

The reader will not be surprised that we do not regard legal interpretation as some special technique that imbues the notion of legal reasoning with a mystique. Our view is the commonsense, person-on-the-street view: posited laws are nothing more or less than communications from lawmakers to others regarding what the lawmakers have determined the others should do. If, for example, the legislature passes a statute that states, "No property owner shall keep a bear within one thousand feet of a private residence," the statute represents the legislature's determination of what property owners should do regarding any bears they might possess and probably what sheriffs, judges, and others should or may do if property owners do not act accordingly.

Our starting point, therefore, is that, aside from the irrelevancy that it makes a demand rather than a request, such a statute is fundamentally no different from a letter written by Mom requesting that you put out the dog the next time she comes to visit, or a note signed by your two kids asking you to rent a movie on your way home. The statute, Mom's letter, and the kids' note all refer to some behavior that is either demanded or requested. And each may pose identical problems of interpretation.

I. The Goal of Legal Interpretation: The Lawmaker's Intended Meaning

In the cases of Mom's letter and the kids' note, what are we seeking when we interpret? When the meaning is clear, what makes it so? When the meaning is unclear, what clarifies it? The answer seems obvious. What we want to know is what is the meaning that Mom or the kids *intended* to convey[1] – what is called the *speaker's meaning.*[2]

Now a moment's reflection will reveal that most of us, even without legal training, are pretty good at divining speakers' meanings. We are constantly doing it after all. Of course, in probably a majority of instances we are aided by the fact that those whose intended meanings we are seeking express their intended meanings felicitously: they choose apt words or other signs and array them in an apt syntactical and grammatical manner. But even when they express their intended meanings infelicitously, we are usually pretty adept at figuring out what meaning they intended. We know something about them and about the context in which they are writing or speaking.

---

[1] See Stanley Fish, *There Is No Textualist Position,* 42 *San Diego L. Review* 629 (2005); Steven Knapp and Walter Benn Michaels, *Not a Matter of Interpretation,* 42 *San Diego L. Rev.* 651 (2005); Larry Alexander and Saikrishna Prakash, *"Is That English You're Speaking?" Why Intention Free Interpretation Is an Impossibility,* 41 *San Diego L. Rev.* 967 (2004); Larry Alexander, *All or Nothing at All? The Intentions of Authorities and the Authority of Intentions,* in *Law and Interpretation: Essays in Legal Interpretation* 357–404 (A. Marmor, ed., Oxford: Clarendon Press 1995). *See generally* Larry Alexander and Emily Sherwin, *The Rule of Rules: Morality, Rules, and the Dilemmas of Law* Ch. 5 (Durham: Duke University Press 2001).
[2] Paul Grice, *Studies in the Way of Words* 86–137 (Cambridge, Mass.: Harvard University Press 1991).

Consider Mom's request to put out the dog. Given what you know about Mom – that she is an English speaker, who is somewhat afraid of dogs but loathes cruelty toward them – you would know that you were not honoring her request if instead of sending Rover to the backyard when Mom arrived, you teased Rover to the point of frustration (you "put out" Rover). Similarly with the kids' request: you would know that you were not honoring it were you to stop by Blockbuster, slash a DVD with a knife, and then proceed home (although you did "rent" a movie). You know in both cases that you are not honoring the requests because you know the speakers' intended meanings. If, on the other hand, your Mom relished cruelty to animals, and your kids were rental movie terrorists, you might well have been honoring their requests.

Or suppose Mom has never mastered the distinction between autobahn and ottoman, and she leaves you a note requesting that you pull up the "autobahn" next to the sofa when she comes to visit. You surely know what to do, and it isn't to run a German highway through your den.[3] We are good at gleaning intended meanings despite infelicities in diction, spelling, grammar, punctuation, and syntax. The reason why the sign outside the church – "In despair and seeking to end it all? Let the church help" – is funny is because we know the meaning that was intended. Similarly, we know the ratifiers of the Seventeenth Amendment did not intend that it expire in six years, despite the comma that would otherwise signal that meaning.[4] And we know the Arkansas legislators, in enacting an obscure statute, did not intend that "all laws . . . [be] hereby repealed."[5]

Our point is the banal one that just as we do with requests or demands from Mom, the kids, and others in daily life, we seek the speaker's intended meaning when we wish to interpret a legally authoritative communication in the form of a statute or an administrative or judicial rule or order. Interpretation in law as in life is a search for speaker's meaning.[6]

---

[3] *See* Alexander and Prakash, *supra* note 1.
[4] "The Senate of the United States shall be composed of two Senators from each state, elected by the people thereof, for six years. . . ." U.S. Const. amend. XVII.
[5] *See* Cernauskas v. Fletcher, 201 S.W.2d 999 (1997) (holding that law containing the fractured boilerplate "all laws . . . are hereby repealed" did not in fact repeal all of Arkansas's laws).
[6] *See* Fish, *supra* note 1.

This position is often objected to on the ground that it unjustifi-
ably elevates speaker's meaning above utterance meaning. The distinction between speaker's meaning and utterance meaning goes like this:
speaker's meaning is the meaning a speaker intends to convey by a word
or words (or other signifiers) on a particular occasion, whereas utterance
meaning is what those words or signs conventionally mean (in various syntactical and grammatical contexts but apart from any particular
instance of their use).[7] Mom may have meant ottoman by autobahn, but
that is *not* what autobahn means.[8] We know that because the dictionaries
and grammars tell us so. And it begs the question, so this objection goes,
for us to insist that proper interpretation of legal rules turns on speaker's
meaning – the intended meaning of the rules' promulgators – rather than
on utterance meaning.

This objection misses the mark. A moment's reflection will reveal
that utterance meaning is wholly derivative of speaker's meaning and
merely reports what most speakers mean by a certain string of marks
or sounds. When enough speakers use a particular sign, that sign will
appear in a dictionary along with its definition, which is nothing more
than what most speakers who use that sign intend to signify by it. And
when a lot of speakers begin using the sign to signify something else –
their intended meaning diverges from the utterance meaning – the dictionaries will report that fact, by either adding a new definition or, if
the old definition has fallen into sufficient disuse, replacing it with the
new one. In either case, utterance meaning is changed to bring it in line
with speaker's meaning. Speaker's meaning – what speakers intend to
convey by the sign – is always the independent variable, whereas utterance meaning, being merely a report of speakers' meanings, is always the
dependent variable.

Sometimes – indeed, often – an individual speaker will mean something quite different from the utterance meaning. It may be because the
speaker is ignorant of the utterance meaning – Mom and autobahn, for
example – or it may be because the speaker is being ironic or is punning.
Of course, if enough speakers start using a word ironically – for example,
using "bad" to mean "really good" – dictionaries will pick up this usage,

---

[7] *See* Grice, *supra* note 2.
[8] *See* Michael S. Moore, *A Natural Law Theory of Interpretation*, 58 So. Cal. L. Rev. 277 (1985).

so that the ironic meaning becomes one of the listed utterance meanings. Moreover, even with Mom, it is somewhat arbitrary whether we say she used "autobahn" mistakenly, even if she was not using it ironically or facetiously; for it is arbitrary to say she is speaking English (mistakenly) rather than Mom-English (Menglish), a language very much like English, except that in Menglish, autobahn means a type of footstool.[9]

Languages and their relations between signs and meanings cannot be pried apart from speakers' intended meanings. Indeed, we cannot identify what language is being used without reference to the intent of the user.[10] You, the reader of this book, are undoubtedly assuming that we are communicating to you in standard English (although if any minor solecisms have slipped past us and our copy editor, we trust you will be able to discern our intended meanings through circumstantial clues). You are assuming as well that the black marks on the pages, and not the white spaces between them, are the relevant signs. But if you were to discover that we were speakers of Esperanto, not English, or members of an exotic culture whose alphabet was represented by the white spaces and

---

[9] *See* Alexander and Prakash, *supra* note 1.

[10] *See, e.g.,* id.; Keith E. Whittington, *Constitutional Interpretation: Textual Meaning, Original Intent, and Judicial Review* 94–99 (Lawrence: University Press of Kansas 1999) (asserting the ontological identity of text and authorial intent and the semantic meaninglessness of unauthored "signs"); Laurence H. Tribe, *Comment,* in Antonin Scalia, *A Matter of Interpretation: Federal Courts and the Law* 65, 76–77 (Princeton: Princeton University Press 1997) (pointing out that even "this text is to be read with the aid of the Oxford English Dictionary" may not mean what we think it does if *it* is not intended to be in English); Timothy A. O. Endicott, *Linguistic Indeterminacy,* 16 *Oxford J. Legal Stud.* 667, 682–85 (1996) (demonstrating the semantic meaninglessness of unauthored "signs"); Alexander, *supra* note 1, at 361–62 (arguing that the meaningfulness of a text requires an author who intends to communicate meaning in a particular language); Fish, *supra* note 1 (same); Knapp and Michaels, *supra* note 1 (same); Steven Knapp and Walter Benn Michaels, *Intention, Identity, and the Constitution: A Response to David Hoy,* in *Legal Hermeneutics: History, Theory, and Practice* 187, 190 (G. Leyh, ed., Berkeley: University of California Press 1992) (same); Richard S. Kay, *Original Intentions, Standard Meanings, and the Legal Character of the Constitution,* 6 *Const. Commentary* 39, 40–45 (1989) (same); E. D. Hirsch Jr., *Counterfactuals in Interpretation,* in *Interpreting Law and Literature: A Hermeneutic Reader* 57 (Sanford Levinson and Steven Mailloux, eds., Evanston, Ill.: Northwestern University Press 1988) (same); Steven Knapp and Walter Benn Michaels, *Against Theory 2: Hermeneutics and Deconstruction,* 14 *Critical Theory* 49, 54, 60 (1987) (same); Steven Knapp and Walter Benn Michaels, *Against Theory,* 8 *Critical Theory* 723, 725–30 (1982) (same); Stanley Fish, *Play of Surfaces: Theory and the Law,* in *Legal Hermeneutics, supra,* at 297, 299–300 (endorsing authorial intention as central to interpretation); Paul Campos, *Against Constitutional Theory,* 4 *Yale J. L. & Human.* 270, 301–2 (1992) (same); Jorge J. E. Garcia, *Can There Be Texts without Historical Authors?,* 31 *Amer. Phil. Q.* 245, 251–52 (1994) (same).

not the black marks, your understanding of our message would change. For it is what *we* mean – not what others could have meant by these marks and spaces – that you are presumably seeking to discover when you read this book.

Someone still might resist. The marks on the page can mean something even if it is not what you meant by those marks, or so they might argue.

This response is true in a limited sense: the marks could have been made by another author intending to convey a different meaning from the meaning we intend to convey, even though they were not.[11] Thus, the very same marks could have meant something different from what they do mean. But that does not make the meaning of the marks autonomous from the intended meaning of their author. Rather, it merely shows that any sign can be used to signify anything. "Autobahn," when used by someone other than Mom, could mean German highway. But it could also mean "firefly," "zip up your pants," or anything else. And when Mom uses it, it refers to a footstool that standard English dictionaries and the speakers' usages they reflect would call an "ottoman."

Thus, signs signify whatever their users intend to signify; however, when the "signs" are created in the absence of any intent to signify something, they are not signs at all, even if they look like signs. If an observer believes that a cloud formation that looks like a *C*, an *A*, and a *T* is not a message from God but is rather the result of natural processes, it would be odd for him to express puzzlement over whether the cloud formation means "domestic cat" as opposed to "all felines," or whether the cloud formation is in English or in French.[12] In the absence of a speaker with an intended meaning to convey through them, the clouds are just clouds, however much they resemble letters.

For the same reason that recourse to speaker's meaning is necessary for identifying the particular language being used or whether a language is being used at all, recourse to speaker's meaning is necessary for resolving ambiguities. Even if we know that the speaker is intending to convey a meaning, is intending to convey it in standard English, and is a competent user of standard English, if the speaker uses, say, the word "cat," reference

[11] *See* Alexander and Prakash, *supra* note 1, at 977–78 n. 26.
[12] *See* id. at 977.

to the speaker's intended meaning is necessary for determining whether "cat" means "domestic tabby," "any feline," or "jazz musician." Because the utterance has several meanings, *its* meaning can be resolved only by reference to the speaker's meaning.[13] And, as stated, the speaker's meaning is not tethered to *any* of the utterance meanings, much less any one in particular. The speaker might have meant "alligator" or "paintbrush" by "cat."

Now, it is possible to imagine a regime of legal interpretation in which interpreters – judges, administrators, lawyers, and ordinary citizens – were instructed to interpret the legal rule in question as if it had been authored by a hypothetical person or body with certain characteristics.[14] For example, the interpreter might be instructed to assume that the

---

[13] *See, e.g.,* id.; Jeffrey Goldsworthy, *Marmor on Meaning, Interpretation, and Legislative Intention,* 1 *Legal Theory* 439, 454–56, 460–63 (1995) (showing the impoverished nature of literal meaning and the dependence of sentence meaning on context and background assumptions); John R. Searle, *The Construction of Social Reality* 129–37 (New York: Free Press 1995) (same); Whittington *supra* note 10, at 95–96 (same); John R. Searle, *Literal Meaning,* in *Expression and Meaning: Studies in the Theory of Speech Acts* 117, 127 (J. Searle, ed., Oxford: Clarendon Press 1979) (same); Kent Greenawalt, *Legislation: Statutory Interpretation: 20 Questions* 38–39 (New York: Foundation Press 1999) (same, and illustrating by comparing "Keep off the grass" uttered by a park custodian and with the same command uttered by a drug counselor); Abner S. Greene, *The Work of Knowledge,* 72 *Notre Dame L. Rev.* 1479, 1486–89 (1997) (arguing that meaning depends on authorial intent); Alexander *supra* note 10 (pointing out that ambiguities in "text" produced by the proverbial thousand monkeys are in principle unresolvable).

[14] *See* Alexander and Prakash, *supra* note 1, at 971. Noël Carroll distinguishes actual intentionalism from hypothetical intentionalism. The latter looks to the actual speaker's intent only for the purpose of determining which standard language he is speaking in, but then relies on utterance meanings. As Carroll points out, utterance meaning cannot resolve ambiguities (e.g., "rent" a DVD). Nor does invoking an idealized hypothetical reader help, because what such a reader would conclude the speaker meant would always be relative to whatever contextual evidence of the actual speaker's intent we ascribe to the hypothetical reader. Carroll endorses actual intentionalism, though he would constrain it by the text itself. He accuses actual intentionalists like us who do not constrain their actual intentionalism of "Humpty Dumptyism." We accept the charge. If Mom says autobahn, her actual intended meaning is what standard English would deem an "ottoman." If she had said "put out the cat," and we know she confuses cats and dogs, we will put out Rover. Indeed, it seems arbitrary to deem her to be speaking English rather than Menglish, the language in which autobahn means footstool and the cat refers to Rover. The distinctions between a language, a dialect of that language (*e.g.,* Appalachian English), and an idiolect (Mom's version of English, Menglish) are surely matters of degree and not kind.

We return to Carroll's approach in Chapter 7 in our discussion of textualism as merely intentionalism with certain evidence of authorial intent excluded from consideration. Noël Carroll, *Interpretation and Intention: The Debate between Hypothetical and Actual Intentionalism,* 31 *Metaphilosophy* 75 (2000).

author(s) of the legal rules in question spoke standard English (as set forth in a particular dictionary), complied with the orthodox rules of grammar (again, as set forth in a particular book on style and usage), and, where the dictionary gave a word two or more meanings, always adopted the first meaning listed. Because the actual lawmakers – the real legal authorities – would know that their rules would be interpreted this way, they would try to craft them so that the interpretation would reflect *their* intended meaning. Nonetheless, whenever they failed, the law would instruct interpreters to ignore the actual lawmakers' intended meaning in favor of the meaning the hypothetical author would have intended. In the case of the Seventeenth Amendment, for example, if the hypothetical author used standard punctuation, then the change to direct election of senators expired six years after ratification. Or, in the case of Arkansas's scrivener's error, its entire legal system was repealed through enactment of a minor law.

An interpretive norm such as the one just described functions as a higher-order norm compared to the norms whose interpretation is at issue.[15] It tells lawmakers that their laws will be interpreted on the basis not of their intended meanings but of the signs they use and the dictionaries, grammars, and so forth through which those signs are filtered. If the norms to be interpreted are ordinary laws, then the interpretive norm is a higher-order, constitutional law. If the norms to be interpreted are constitutional norms, then the interpretive norm is metaconstitutional.

We shall have more to say on authoritative norms governing inter-pretation later.[16] One point that should be stressed here, however, is that when an interpreter employs an "interpretive" norm such as the one just described, the result is *not* an *interpretation* of the lawmaker's rule. Rather, the interpreter is *constructing* a rule out of materials provided by the original lawmaker and, in doing so, is acting as a lawmaker in

---

[15] *See* Larry Alexander and Emily Sherwin, *Interpreting Rules: The Nature and Limits of Inchoate Intentions*, in *Legal Interpretation in Democratic States* 1, 18–21 (Jeffrey Goldsworthy and Tom Campbell, eds., Aldershot: Ashgate 2002); Alexander, *supra* note 1, at 384–86. That is why the higher-order norm cannot itself be imposed by an authority who is not superior to the authority whose interpretation the higher-order norm is meant to constrain. *See, e.g.,* Larry Alexander and Saikrishna Prakash, *Mother, May I? Imposing Mandatory Prospective Rules of Statutory Interpretation*, 20 *Const. Comm.* 97, 103–6 (2003).

[16] *See* Chapter 6.

his or her own right.[17] If one is interpreting, one is seeking the author's intended meaning. When one is constructing a meaning that may not be the meaning intended by the author of the signs in question, one is not interpreting but establishing a rule. If you were to hold Mom to an "interpretive" norm that seeks not her intended meaning but the intended meaning of a hypothetical speaker with perfect command of English, you would indeed present her with a highway, not a footstool. And she would be quite correct to accuse you of failing to interpret her request correctly.

Why does this distinction between interpreting – finding the actual speaker's intended meaning – and constructing a meaning based on what a hypothetical speaker would have intended matter? It matters for the same reason it does with your Mom and your kids. In all these cases, we care what the actual speakers intend that we do. If all we were interested in were coordination, then the interpretive norm described here might be preferable to actual interpretation – that is, to seeking the lawmaker's intended meaning. But coordination is not the only benefit we seek from vesting lawmakers with the authority to determine what ought to be done. We also seek expertise. Any determinate rule will facilitate coordination. But only some rules will be morally preferable to leaving matters unsettled. We select legislators, administrators, and judges in large part based on our assessment of their moral expertise, that is, their ability to craft rules that represent moral improvements over the status quo ante. (Or, in the case of legislators at least, we select them because they hold the values that we hold.)

Thus, when the legislature enacts the prohibition on property owners' keeping bears within one thousand feet of other's property, we want to know what *it* meant by "bears," "private residences," and so forth, not what its signs mean in Swahili, Esperanto, or French, or even what a hypothetical author using standard English would have meant by those signs, except insofar as this is *evidence* of what the actual legislature did mean by them.[18] If we know that the lawmakers use nonstandard English,

[17] *See* authorities cited in note 15 *supra*.
[18] *See, e.g.*, Saikrishna B. Prakash, *Unoriginalism's Law without Meaning*, 15 *Const. Comment.* 529, 541–46 (1998) (arguing that because the author of a legal text is the lawmaker – the person with authority to prescribe what ought to be done – we will want to know what he intended by his words, and that when we accept a text as law, we accept the meaning that

or are prone to malapropisms, we will discount the evidentiary weight of standard English meanings.[19]

It may be useful to imagine that our lawmakers are like a famous chef who has written a cookbook. Because we wish to take advantage of the chef's culinary expertise, when we read her recipes we are seeking to discover what she meant by the marks on the pages. If, for example, she mentions "salt" as an ingredient in a recipe, we will want to know whether she meant ordinary salt or kosher salt. If she intended for us to take her to mean ordinary salt, then the fact that the same marks could have been made by a chef who intended for us to use kosher salt is irrelevant to following the recipe correctly. If it is *her* recipe that we want, then we want to know what *she* intended.[20]

Likewise with the lawmakers' rule about property owners and bears. The lawmakers and their subjects are engaged in an attempt to achieve a common understanding. The lawmakers intend for certain actions to be taken, and they want to communicate that intention to those whose actions are at issue. The latter in turn want to know what the lawmakers intend for them to do. Both the lawmakers and their addressees will employ semantic and pragmatic conventions to achieve their mutual communicative goal of having the addressees understand what the lawmakers intend for them to understand through their communication of the rule in its canonical formulation.

If, then, the lawmakers' expertise is important to morally successful settlement of what ought to be done, the settlement must be what the

the lawmaker intended it to carry); Gary Lawson, *On Reading Recipes . . . and Constitutions*, 85 *Geo. L.J.* 1823 (1997) (analogizing constitutional interpretation to the reading of a recipe); Jeffrey Goldsworthy, *Marmor on Meaning, Interpretation, and Legislative Intention*, 1 *Legal Theory* 439, 448 (1995).

[19] *See, e.g.*, Whittington, *supra* note 10, at 60 (pointing out that all communications occur within a context that provides information for deciphering authorial intent); Searle, *supra* note 13 (same); Greenawalt, *supra* note 13, at 46–49, 51–54, 57, 66 n. 82, 93, 162–66 (discussing slips, unintended meanings, etc.); Goldsworthy, *supra* note 18, at 456–58 (arguing that speaker's meaning is partially inferred from contextual implications); Hirsch, *supra* note 10, at 66–67 (discussing slips of the tongue); Peter Jeremy Smith, *Commas, Constitutional Grammar, and the Straight-Face Test: What If Conan the Grammarian Were a Strict Textualist?*, 16 *Const. Comment.* 7 (1999) (demonstrating that we frequently disregard some evidence of speaker's meaning – such as the rules of grammar and punctuation and dictionary definitions – whenever the contextual evidence of grammatical, punctuation, or dictation errors outweighs it); Alexander, *supra* note 1, at 364, 403–4 (discussing nonstandard or idiosyncratic meanings and malapropisms).

[20] *See, e.g.*, Lawson, *supra* note 18 (analogizing legal rules to recipes).

relevant lawmaker – the one given the authority to effect the settlement – has deliberately chosen it to be. This in turn implies that if the lawmaker settles what ought to be done by promulgating authoritative rules, the relevant meaning of those rules, the meaning that their interpretation seeks, must be the meaning intended by the lawmaker. Thus, the meaning legal interpretation seeks is not to be equated with the dictionary-plus-grammar meaning of the rule (the utterance meaning). Likewise, it is not to be equated with the real nature of the things to which the rule's terms refer, or to the way in which various hypothetical readers with stipulated deficits of information would understand the rule. Nor is it to be equated with the more general moral purposes the rule is intended to further, or the overall moral judgment of whoever is called on to apply the rule, or some combination of these. The objective of authoritative settlement dictates that the only meaning that should count and that should guide legal interpretation is the meaning the lawmaker intended to convey through his rule.

II. What Is the State of Mind That Constitutes the Lawmaker's Intended Meaning?

We have spoken to this point of the lawmaker's intended meaning of his rule and argued that interpretation of his rule is nothing more or less than an attempt to discern that intended meaning, just as it is whenever we wish to comply with requests from Mom or the kids. But just what kind of fact is an intended meaning? What thing in the world makes it true that such-and-such was so-and-so's intended meaning? Is an attribution of a particular intended meaning made true by a mental state that the lawmaker possessed at the time he enacted the law; and if so, what mental state?

We assume that the interpreter is in search of the lawmaker's mental state at the time of enactment, just as we are concerned with what Mom has in mind when she asks us to put out the dog. But obviously the content of both the lawmaker's and Mom's minds at the times in question is quite limited. The lawmaker might have a mental picture of a ferocious grizzly bear at the time he promulgates the "no bear" rule. Mom might picture Rover as he looked last time she visited. Nonetheless, despite the quite limited nature of the mental states in question, we do believe that the intended meanings extend well beyond the particular images contained in those mental states. The lawmaker may never have seen or even heard of Malaysian sun bears, for example, or spectacled bears. Nevertheless, both he and his audience can be quite certain that he intended to include them within his rule's prohibition. This does not mean that we are concerned with utterance meanings rather than intended ones. The lawmaker may have used the word "cat," which we know he uses when he means "bear." Whether or not he uses the word "bear," if his intended meaning is "bears," it probably covers bears that he has never heard of, much less pictured, at the time of enactment.

Moreover, sometimes an example comes within the intended meaning even if it does not come within the purpose that the rule is meant to accomplish.[21] For instance, suppose a property owner possesses a declawed, defanged, quite gentle, and much-beloved-by-all-children black bear, which he keeps in a very secure cage. This bear presents no danger whatsoever to adjoining property owners. Indeed, it actually benefits them. Yet for all that, it may be true that this bear falls within the intended prohibition for either of two reasons. Confronted with the situation, the lawmaker might think, "I did intend to prohibit all bears, but I was mistaken not to have carved out an exception for bears like this one." Alternatively, the lawmaker might think, "I intended a broad and blunt rule prohibiting all bears, and I was well aware that there would be cases like this under the rule. I resisted making such an exception in favor of determinateness, learnability, and so forth, believing that the benefits of the broad, blunt rule would outweigh the costs presented by instances such as this one."

Both of these examples illustrate the possibility that a lawmaker's intended meaning can extend to things that he did not envision at the

---

[21] See, e.g., Kent Greenawalt, *The Nature of Rules and the Meaning of Meaning*, 72 Notre Dame L. Rev. 1449, 1462–68 (1997) (arguing that having context and purpose supply meaning to rules does not undermine their ruleness); Greenawalt, *supra* note 13, at 40–43, 66, 69 (same); Tom D. Campbell, *The Legal Theory of Ethical Positivism* 141–42 (Aldershot: Dartmouth Publishing 1996) (same). *See also* Goldsworthy, *supra* note 18, at 454–55 (giving examples of cases where purpose behind a rule contributes to a rule's meaning); Frederick Schauer, *Formalism*, 97 Yale L.J. 509, 526–28 (1988) (showing how a rule's meaning can be a function of its purpose without being reducible to or necessarily consistent with that purpose).

moment of enactment and that also do not fall within the purpose his rule is designed to accomplish. Moreover, a lawmaker's intended meaning can be completely at odds with his purpose for enacting the rule. Perhaps, for some reason, allowing landowners to possess bears would actually increase the safety and welfare of adjoining landowners. (They may, for example, be able to take effective and relatively costless precautions against bear attacks and at the same time learn how to profit from bears' proximity; or statistics may show that crime decreases in neighborhoods with bears.) It may turn out then that prohibiting bears within one thousand feet of residences is a colossal legislative mistake. Nonetheless, it may be quite clear to both the lawmaker and his audience that such a prohibition, however ill-advised, was his intended meaning.[22] It is, therefore, the meaning of the rule.

On the other hand, there may be some cases of "bears within one thousand feet" that the lawmaker clearly did not intend to include within his prohibition. Suppose our hypothetical landowner with the declawed, defanged, lovable black bear is faced with an oncoming forest fire or flood and escapes with his pet bear by a route on his property within one thousand feet of a neighbor. The lawmaker may very well say, correctly, "I didn't intend my prohibition to apply to *that* case, and it would be absurd for anyone to imagine I did."[23] It follows that the case is not covered by

---

[22] *See* Alexander and Sherwin, *supra* note 1, at 115; Alexander, *supra* note 1, at 376 (request for curry powder not satisfied by alfalfa sprouts even if it is true the purpose behind the request was, at the most general level, well-being, and that in the long term more well-being will be derived from developing a preference for the latter over the former). *See also* Alexander and Prakash, *supra* note 1, at 994–95 (pointing out that the intended meaning of a directive can diverge from what its author intended it to accomplish; Mom may believe the ottoman – her "autobahn" – will make her comfortable when it in fact will not do so, but it is still her intended meaning that the ottoman be pulled next to the sofa).

[23] *See* Alexander and Sherwin, *supra* note 1, at 114–15. For some other examples like this in literature, *see* Cass R. Sunstein, *One Case at a Time* 219–21 (Cambridge, Mass.: Harvard University Press 1999) (discussing the case of Church of the Holy Trinity v. United States, 143 U.S. 457 [1892], in which the question was whether a ban on the importation of laborers included a ban on a church's hiring a minister from abroad, and concluding that there are times when the context of legislation reveals that some literal application was not intended); Kent Greenawalt, *Law and Objectivity* 16–18 (New York: Oxford University Press 1992) (discussing Sam's [a superior's] request to Beth [a subordinate] to shut Sam's office door, and suggesting that the request does not require shutting the door in the face of the company president, who, unbeknownst to Sam, is about to enter Sam's office); Ludwig Wittgenstein, *Philosophical Investigations* § 203 (Oxford: Blackwell 1997) ("Someone says to me: 'Shew the children a game.' I teach them gaming with dice, and the other says, 'I didn't mean that

the rule. Likewise, Mom might say the same if the question is whether, in order to comply with her request, Rover should be put out on a cold evening if he is suffering from pneumonia. He should not.

Finally, however odd this may seem, there may be some cases where the lawmaker himself will not be able to determine what he intended. Suppose the lawmaker had no idea the gentle panda was indeed a species of bear. Or suppose a new bear species is discovered whose members are the size of a Lhasa Apso and quite shy and docile. The lawmaker himself might be quite perplexed over whether he did or did not prohibit possession of that species of bear.[24] (The line between indeterminate rules – where the rule maker himself would be perplexed over what meaning he intended – and determinate but infelicitous rules [rules the rule maker would regret] will itself be an uncertain line. Nonetheless,

sort of game.' Must the exclusion of the game with dice have come before his mind when he gave me the order to make this last statement true?"); Bernard W. Bell, *"No Motor Vehicles in the Park": Reviving the Hart-Fuller Debate to Introduce Statutory Construction*, 48 *J. Legal Educ.* 88, 97 (1998) (giving the example of a "No vehicles in the park" rule as applied to an ambulance that enters to pick up a heart attack victim); William N. Eskridge, *Textualism, The Unknown Ideal?*, 96 *Mich. L. Rev.* 1509, 1553 (1998) (arguing that the NBA rule forbidding players from leaving the bench during a fight should not be read to forbid a player's going to the restroom or coming to the aid of a player about to be killed); Kent Greenawalt, *From the Bottom Up*, 82 *Corn. L. Rev.* 994 (1997) (arguing that an order from a basketball coach to his team, which has a three-point lead with twenty-four seconds remaining, not to take a shot, but to try to run out the clock, does not mean that if a player finds herself unguarded under the basket, she cannot take a shot that she is virtually certain to make); Alexander, *supra* note 1, at 376–77 (giving example of handing a friend your checkbook and asking him to purchase some curry powder for a dinner party you are giving, only to have him return with a bottle of curry powder and a \$2,500 deduction from your checkbook occasioned by curry powder's being in short supply); Goldsworthy, *supra* note 13, at 454–55 (discussing such cases as the ordering of a hamburger in a restaurant, in response to which the waiter brings a hamburger encased in a cube of hard plastic); id. at 456–57 (discussing how certain meanings are implied *in* statements on the basis of context and background assumptions, which meanings are different from the more general worldview implied *by* statements).

For some other examples of cases where the rule maker might plausibly say that his rule does not apply, *see* Kent Greenawalt, *From the Bottom Up, supra*. He gives the example of an easy slam dunk that a basketball player takes after being told by the coach that in order to protect a three-point lead in the last seconds of the game, the team should dribble out the clock and not shoot. Greenawalt argues that the "don't shoot" instruction can plausibly be understood as inapplicable to the uncontested slam dunk.

[24] *See* Cass R. Sunstein, *Justice Scalia's Formalism*, 107 *Yale L.J.* 529, 544 (1997) ("Because of the inevitable limitations of human foresight, even the most carefully chosen words can become unclear because and not in spite of their generality"). Sunstein cites H. L. A. Hart's famous passage in which Hart attributes penumbral uncertainty in the meaning of all rules to "relative indeterminacy of aim." H. L. A. Hart, *The Concept of Law* 125 (Oxford: Clarendon Press 1961).

over a substantial range of cases, the rule maker's intended meaning will be determinate even if infelicitous.)

We believe it is possible for a rule subject to advert in a limited way to the rule maker's purposes in order to grasp what the latter intended to do by enacting a rule, without at the same time equating the rule's meaning with those purposes. Nevertheless, we briefly take up several analyses that raise questions about this distinction and hence about whether intent can serve as the basis of determinate rules.

III. Some Challenges to the Determinacy of Intended Meanings

A. THE MULTIPLICITY OF THE RULE MAKER'S INTENTIONS

The first analysis of the determinacy of intended meanings that we consider, which comes from Gregory Bassham, suggests that when the rule maker issues his rule "No bears are allowed within one thousand feet of private residences," he has not one intention regarding what ought to be done, but several. Moreover, these various intentions can conflict.[25] Bassham distinguishes between, on the one hand, the rule-making authority's beliefs about the binding effects of what he has authored and, on the other hand, other changes in the world that the rule maker expects or hopes will be accomplished by those binding effects.[26] For example, suppose that the rule maker believes that if the "No bear" rule is enacted and enforced, land values will increase, or the rule maker will be reelected as the authority. Neither of these beliefs, even if mistaken, affects the binding effects of the rule maker's rule.[27]

Within the former category of rule maker's beliefs – his beliefs about the legally binding effects of his enactment – Bassham distinguishes among scope beliefs, counterfactual scope beliefs, and semantic intentions.[28] Scope beliefs are the actual occurrent beliefs that the rule maker

---

[25] The text from this point through the paragraph after note 42 is taken substantially from Alexander, *supra* note 1, at 367–75.

[26] Gregory Bassham, *Original Intent and the Constitution* 28–34, 69–71 (Savage, Md.: Rowman & Littlefield 1992).

[27] Bassham calls these latter intentions nonbinding intentions and includes among them such things as the authorities' intentions regarding their own authority. Id.

[28] Id. at 29.

holds at the time of enactment about the legally binding effects of that enactment.[29] Put differently, they are the rule maker's actual beliefs about what changes he has adverted to and determined should be implemented. ("No ferocious grizzly bears . . .")

Counterfactual scope beliefs are the beliefs about such binding effects that the rule maker would have held, had he considered the particular application (of his text) in question.[30] ("No Malaysian sun bears . . .") Bassham gives as an example of a counterfactual scope belief the belief the framers of the United States Constitution would have held on whether skyjacking is an "infamous" crime within the meaning of the grand jury clause of the Fifth Amendment.[31] Obviously, the framers would not have had actual beliefs about skyjacking in 1791. Nonetheless, Bassham considers it meaningful and sensible to ask what beliefs they would have held on the legal status of skyjacking under the Fifth Amendment, had they considered skyjacking. Strict intentionalists are, for Bassham, all who would interpret legal texts solely according to scope and counterfactual scope beliefs, although the strictest of strict intentionalists look only to scope beliefs.

The rule makers' semantic intentions are their intentions regarding the *meaning* of their legal texts.[32] Now this in itself is quite unhelpful because scope beliefs and counterfactual beliefs could be the exclusive determinants of the texts' *meaning*, in which case semantic intentions would merely be intentions to effectuate scope and counterfactual scope beliefs. Bassham points out, however, that a legislature that bans toxic substances may have in mind a particular concept of toxicity, or a particular definition or description of toxicity – semantic intentions – as well as some particular examples of toxic substances that they believed they were banning (scope beliefs).[33] It may turn out that the particular examples of toxic substances may not in fact be toxic according to the contemplated definition of toxicity. Or it may turn out that both the particular examples of toxic substances *and* the contemplated definition

[29] Id.
[30] Id.
[31] Id.
[32] Id.
[33] Id. at 32.

of toxicity are inconsistent with the best theory of the nature of toxicity as a concept. (In the case of bears, it may be that some of the exemplars the rule maker has in mind do not fall within the definition of "bear" he is employing; and his definition of "bear" may be at odds with the best scientific account of what defines bears as a particular family – Ursidae – of mammals.)

Bassham labels as "modern intentionalists" those who would follow the authorities' semantic intentions when these conflict with the scope and counterfactual scope intentions.[34] And within the category of semantic intentions, he distinguishes "spare," realist semantic intentions (intentions to use terms consistently with the true nature of the terms' referents) from "rich," conventionalist semantic intentions (intentions to use the terms according to the definitions or descriptions the authorities have in mind).[35] He concludes that the most defensible form of intentionalism in constitutional interpretation is moderate intentionalism in which the framers' rich semantic intentions trump their scope and counterfactual scope intentions.[36]

Although Bassham would deal with these various types of authorities' intentions – scope; counterfactual scope; and semantic, rich and spare – by choosing which one should be dispositive,[37] we suggest that the question is not one of the interpreter's choice. The question is, What did the authorities intend to communicate that they had determined ought to be done? In our view, that is a datum about the world, not a matter of choice.

[34] Id.
[35] Bassham suggests that the intentions of the framers of the U.S. Constitution were usually rich, not spare. Id. at 79. They may not always have been rich, however. Bassham gives the example of a question that can arise under the Twenty-fifth Amendment, namely, whether a president who suffered cessation of brain activity but not respiration or circulation is "dead." Here, the framers arguably intended their realist intentions to trump their conventionalist intentions. Id. at 82.
There are indications that on the question which semantic intentions should dominate – rich or spare – Bassham would follow the framers' own intentions. If a legislature discovered that its definition of toxicity was inconsistent with toxicity's true nature, it presumably would want true toxicity to control. On the other hand, Bassham suggests that the framers of the Constitution generally wanted their rich semantic intentions to control. See id. at 32, 80–82. But cf. id. at 51, 68–71 (preferring not to treat "interpretive intentions" as dispositive).
[36] Id. at 51–56.
[37] Id. at 68–71.

Choosing which one of Bassham's categories of intentions should be the basis of interpretation appears artificial for two reasons. First, whenever the various intentions conflict, there is no reason not to ask which intentions the authorities would wish to dominate in such a case. If semantic intentions conflict with scope intentions, there is no reason to choose semantic intentions as what the authorities "intended" if the authorities would have chosen their scope intentions to dominate their semantic ones.

Second, we believe that Bassham's distinctions – and other analogous ones – ultimately collapse. Consider, for example, the distinction he makes between sense and reference within semantic intentions. Ultimately, what a term refers to – its reference – cannot be determined without a definition or description (its sense). But definitions and descriptions purport to be *of* something.[38] (We would not know the thing that "death" refers to without some description of it, though likewise we think that death can be misdescribed.) Moreover, the distinction between semantic intentions and more particular scope beliefs and counterfactual scope intentions breaks down. Our definitions and descriptions can be fallible generalizations from particulars, and the particulars can be fallible inferences from generalizations.

In the end, we see no reason why a broad notion of intended meanings cannot subsume all of Bassham's categories of rule makers' intentions. What we want to know – given some fact situation, the rule makers' semantic understandings, the true nature of that to which their terms refer, and so on – is what rule makers determined the binding effect of their action should be. Because the rule makers' exemplars may be inconsistent with the definitions of the terms they employ, and the definitions may be inconsistent with the true nature of the terms' referents, the

---

[38] *See generally* Ralph Shain, *Mill, Quine, and Natural Kinds,* 24 *Metaphilosophy* 275–92 (1993) (discussing problems with the concept of "natural kinds"). *See also* Andrei Marmor, *Interpretation and Legal Theory* 144–45 (Oxford: Clarendon Press 1992); Michael Steven Green, *Dworkin's Fallacy, or What the Philosophy of Language Can't Teach Us about the Law,* 89 *Va. L. Rev.* 1897, 1907–8 n. 29 (2003). Without getting too deep in controversial philosophical waters, imagine that in the distant past A sees a yellow, glittering stone and dubs it "gold." And suppose that stone has the atomic structure Ag. Later, A sees other yellow, glittering stones and calls them "gold," but they are not Ag but pyrite. Has A made a mistake? How do we know if A's dubbing was of Ag rather than of all yellow, glittering stones? Why is Ag a "natural kind," but "pyrold" (pyrite plus some gold) is not?

question is, Which did they intend to dominate in cases of such inconsistency?[39] In some cases, perhaps, referents will dominate definitions and exemplars.[40] In other cases, definitions or exemplars will dominate.[41]

Our proposal is akin to Bassham's notion of counterfactual scope beliefs and intentions but broader and, as we explained earlier, not strictly

[39] Bear in mind that we believe that exemplars, definitions, and referents ultimately are interrelated and cannot be neatly opposed.

For an analysis of how the various types and levels of generality of intentions should be reconciled that is similar to ours, see Whittington, *supra* note 10, at 184–87; Keith E. Whittington, *Dworkin's "Originalism": The Role of Intentions in Constitutional Interpretation,* 62 *Rev. of Pol.* 197, 215–25 (2000). *See also* Greenawalt, *supra* note 13, at 131, 140–41 (arguing that legislator's dominant intention is what his rule means where his specific and general intentions conflict); Nicos Stavropoulos, *Objectivity in Law* 189–95 (1996) (dealing with conflicts of legislative intentions); M. B. W. Sinclair, *Legislative Intent: Fact or Fabrication?,* 41 *N.Y.L. Sch. L. Rev.* 1329, 1363–64, 1370 (1997) (same); Hirsch, *supra* note 10 (discussing speakers' dominant intentions); Michael W. McConnell, *The Importance of Humility in Judicial Review: A Comment on Ronald Dworkin's "Moral Reading" of the Constitution,* 65 *Fordham L. Rev.* 1269, 1280–84 (1997) (arguing that "[a] genuine commitment to the semantic intentions of the [lawmakers] requires the interpreter to seek the level of generality at which the particular language was understood by [them]").

For an excellent analysis of interpretation that correctly effaces any bright line between semantics and pragmatics, or among exemplars, definitions, and referents, see Troy L. Booher, *Putting Meaning in Its Place: Originalism and Philosophy of Language,* 25 *Law and Phil.* 387 (2006).

[40] Note that because the role of authorities is to determine what ought to be done – to make moral principles concrete enough to guide citizens and officials – when the authorities intend the true nature of the referents of the terms they employ to dominate their own inconsistent definitions and exemplars, they are in some sense defaulting their role. In making binding effects of enactment turn on the true nature of moral terms, whatever that nature happens to be, the authorities have failed to give moral guidance; and in making those efforts turn on the true nature of natural kinds, they have left a good deal to the unknown (which is why we believe that reference cannot completely take leave of sense).

[41] The best discussion of why interpretation should not be tied to the true nature of things to which the legal text's words refer is found in Stephen R. Munzer, *Realistic Limits on Realist Interpretation,* 58 *S. Cal. L. Rev.* 459 (1985). Munzer, replying to Michael Moore's realist theory of legal interpretation, points out that many words do not name "kinds" of any type (id. at 461–62), that words that name "functional kinds" do not presuppose an underlying true nature of these kinds (id. at 466–68), that moral terms and natural-kind terms may not map onto reality in any neat way (id. at 462, 464), and, finally, that, for many legal texts, conventional understandings should dominate the true nature of terms' referents (id. at 468–70). In the latter category, Munzer places a statute limiting the harvest of "fish" written at a time when whales were thought to be fish. Given certain purposes for the statute, it should be read to include whales (id.). *See also* Anthony Dardis, *How the Radically Interpreted Make Mistakes,* 33 *Dialogue* 415, 423–25 (1994) (discussing malapropisms, classic instances where semantic intentions come apart, not in terms of referent versus definition, but in terms of word chosen versus word meant). And there may be some cases where what dominates is indeterminate – even to the rule maker. That is, the rule maker will be uncertain what he intended in those cases.

"counterfactual."[42] What the rule makers mean by an enactment is what they intend its binding effects to be over a range of circumstances, not all of which – indeed, hardly any of which – they have adverted to. If the enactment is a prohibition of some behavior ("No bears . . ."), its meaning is the rule maker's intended binding effects – prohibition or no prohibition – in the circumstances in question. If the rule maker had in mind particular tokens of keeping bears near private residences when he enacted his rule, but would reply affirmatively if asked whether his rule prohibits other tokens that were not in his mind at the time, his intended meaning, and thus the meaning of his rule, is that those latter tokens of keeping bears are prohibited.

B. LEVELS OF GENERALITY OF INTENTIONS

Another point relates to what we have said about Bassham's distinctions. Our conclusion that the meaning of the rule maker's rules should be equated with the rule maker's intended legally binding effects raises another question: at what level of generality should intent be defined for purposes of interpretation? The rule maker's intent about what should be done can be understood as referring to particular cases, categories of cases, immediate ends, or ultimate ends. Thus, his intent in issuing the rule, "No bears . . . ," can be described as intent to prevent an imagined scene of a ferocious grizzly being near a home with several small children, an intent to prevent bear injuries more generally, an intent to promote safe and secure residences, an intent to promote well-being, an intent to govern well, or an intent to do what is right. Each of these is, in a sense, a true description of what the rule maker intends. Moreover, they are

---

[42] We thus do not require, in order to unpack an authority's intended meaning, an excursion into the vague and perhaps unknowable domain of "possible worlds" analysis. In our view, the authority's intention with respect to a matter to which he did not advert, and about which he might well have been misinformed or ignorant, can be quite determinate and does not require answering such counterfactuals as what would the authority have intended had he adverted to this situation or had he been more informed about it. Regardless of what the authority would have intended had he adverted to the existence of Malaysian sun bears, he can quite confidently say that he intended his "no bears" rule to include them, and to do so even if they have characteristics that make the "no bears" rule infelicitous as to them. For this reason, we disagree with the claim by Natalie Stoljar that intentionalism plunges us into the world of counterfactuals. *See* Natalie Stoljar, *Vagueness, Counterfactual Intentions, and Legal Interpretation*, 7 *Legal Theory* 447 (2001).

only some of the points along a continuum of generality, with an infinite number of gradations in between.

We have already concluded that the relevant intent must be something more than intent to govern the particular cases to which the rule maker adverted. At the other end of the continuum, our account of the functions performed by the rule maker and his rules places important limits on the extent to which the interpreter can refer to the full range of the rule maker's intentions in issuing a rule. Rules cannot be equated with the more general ends they serve without losing the benefits of their form.

For this purpose, there is a difference between interpretation of rules and interpretation of vague standards (such as "equal protection" or "due process of law"). In the case of a standard, the role of the rule maker is to identify ends and values to be pursued while saying very little about the means of pursuing them. In other words, the rule maker is not attempting a complete settlement of controversy. Accordingly, until more determinate rules have been issued to give content to the standards, there is no reason to limit the range of interpretive inquiry into the rule maker's intent. Indeed, insofar as a legal norm is a standard, it has delegated authority to its subjects and its interpreters. It is they who must translate values into determinate actions. The rule maker's intended meaning is to delegate, and any other intention of his is quite immaterial. There is really nothing to "interpret" once one has determined that a legal norm is a standard.

Our principal concern in this chapter, however, is with interpretation of determinate rules – rules that are designed to settle disputes and curtail consideration of the best means for promoting certain values or ends. Rules work by restating moral principles in concrete terms, so as to reduce the uncertainty, error, and controversy that result when individuals follow their own unconstrained moral judgment. If the meaning of rules is derived from the moral principles that the rules are designed to serve, there are, in effect, no rules and no means for curbing moral error. Another way to put this is that an important part of what the rule maker intends in issuing a rule is that it be a serious rule and not just an expression or reminder of the principles that motivated him to issue it. Thus, the rule maker's rules must have, and must be intended to have, a meaning that is independent of the rule maker's intent at its highest level of generality.

If, for example, the rule maker has issued a rule, "No bears . . . ,"
in order to promote safety, it is not open to "interpret" the rule to forbid
jaguars near residences, no matter how great a threat they pose to safety.
Nor can one conclude that a particular bear is permitted because it
causes no offense to the purpose (safety) that led the rule maker to issue
the rule. These may be instances in which the rule is underinclusive or
overinclusive when measured against the underlying moral principles,
but underinclusiveness and overinclusiveness do not affect the rule's
meaning: they are simply consequences of the rule maker's deliberate
choice to use a rule.

We would be overstating our case, however, if we insisted that the
interpreter must never refer to the purposes underlying the rule maker's
rules. We have already noted that the basic process by which people grasp
the meaning of others' words involves some reference to the speaker's
purpose(s) in using the words. At the least, to make sense of a rule, the
interpreter must learn enough about the rule maker and his purposes
to know that the rule maker intends to communicate, in a particular
language, an instruction to be followed by those who are subject to his
authority. And to interpret the rule correctly, other aspects of the rule
maker's purposes must be grasped. That is how the interpreter might
know that the rule maker did not intend his "no bears" rule to prohibit
escaping a fire with a pet bear by a route less than one thousand feet
from a residence.[43] But none of this means that the rule maker's intended
meaning for his rule is synonymous with his more general purposes, the
most general of which is always the Spike Lee purpose – "Do the right
thing."[44] A rule's purpose informs its intended meaning but is *not* its
intended meaning.

C. "TRANSLATING" THE RULE MAKER'S RULE IN LIGHT OF HIS MISTAKES

We are at this juncture in the argument. The meaning of the rule maker's
rules must comport with the rule maker's role as a governing authority.
That role is to determine what ought to be done, and his determination

---

[43] *See supra* note 23.
[44] *See* Alexander, *supra* note 1, at 376 (arguing that a request for curry powder is not satisfied
by alfalfa sprouts, even if cultivating a taste for alfalfa sprouts will ultimately lead to more
pleasure in life, which is the most general purpose behind the original request).

is what he intends to communicate to citizens and officials through his rules. The meaning of the rules, therefore, just is what the rule maker wishes to communicate through them. And although various inconsistent beliefs and intentions may be embodied in the rule maker's rules, when that is the case, the meanings of the rules are still what binding effects the rule maker would declare the rules to have when confronted with such conflicts and inconsistencies. The binding effects of a rule just are what the rule maker intends the rule to mean at the time he promulgates it.

Searching for the rule maker's intended meanings – which intended meanings, we have argued, are the key to interpreting legal texts – leads to the further problem of distinguishing between translations and corrections of the rule maker's intent. In imagining what the rule maker would say about the binding effects of his rules, we can, as we have said, envision his conceding that "I meant X, but I now see that X was a mistake." In our view, this should not alter the conclusion that the rule means X. But it raises the following issue: is it possible to distinguish between (1) what the rule maker *did determine* with respect to a factual situation that he was not adverting to at the time he authored his communication about what ought to be done, and (2) what the rule maker *should have determined* with respect to such a situation? In other words, can we distinguish between the rule maker's intended meanings and what appear from the subjects' perspective to be the meanings that should have been intended? We have insisted on this possibility, but are we correct?

Consider one of the most carefully argued and persuasive attempts to describe proper interpretation in circumstances not envisioned by the authoring authorities. In "Fidelity in Translation," Lawrence Lessig equates interpretation in such circumstances to translation.[45] Translation, says Lessig, requires two steps.[46] The first step is to read the text for the meaning it carries in its original context – how the authorities envisioned their determination would operate. The second step is to translate that meaning into the current context of application. Interpretation as translation requires that the meaning of a text be preserved as the contexts of application change. So long as the text's meaning in application

---

[45] Lawrence Lessig, *Fidelity in Translation,* 71 *Tex. L. Rev.* 1165 (1993).
[46] Id. at 1211.

is preserved through contextual change, the interpreters can be said to be carrying out what the authorities determined and communicated ought to be done rather than acting on their (the interpreters') own view of what ought to be done.

Lessig then goes on to describe translation of legal texts – how meaning in application is preserved through contextual changes.[47] The original context from which meaning is derived consists of the presuppositions of the rule makers.[48] These, categorized broadly, consist of presuppositions about matters of fact, presuppositions about matters of law, and presuppositions about values. For example, the framers of the Fifth Amendment posited a privilege against self-incrimination in a factual setting in which there were no police forces and police interrogators such as those we find today.[49] Therefore, even if the framers envisioned the clause's application to be restricted to interrogations at or before trial by magistrates or prosecutors, their meaning for the clause is preserved by applying it to the modern context of interrogation – namely, custodial interrogation of the defendant by the police. A difference in factual presuppositions between 1791 and today gets us from the Fifth Amendment to *Miranda v. Arizona*[50] (requiring a recital of rights before a custodial interrogation), such that we can say that the *Miranda* decision is what the framers of the Fifth Amendment determined. In Lessig's terms, *Miranda* is a faithful translation of the Fifth Amendment's privilege against self-incrimination.

Lessig gives as an example of a change in legal presuppositions the case where a legal text is implicitly premised on the existence of other legal doctrines, doctrines that in the interim between the promulgation of the text and the application in question are judicially overruled or legislatively repealed.[51] As an example of a change in legal presuppositions that arguably requires a change in application, Lessig points to the expansion of federal power under modern judicial interpretations of the commerce clause, a change in legal presuppositions that arguably affects whether the Tenth Amendment, reserving to the states all powers not

---

[47] Id. at 1211 et seq.
[48] Id. at 1213–14.
[49] Id. at 1234–36.
[50] 384 U.S. 436 (1966).
[51] Lessig, *supra* note 45, 1224–28.

delegated to the federal government,[52] which might originally have been nothing but a legal truism, now has some affirmative legal bite in order to preserve a meaningful domain of state sovereignty.[53]

The problem with Lessig's approach, as Lessig himself recognizes, is that it threatens to efface the distinction between interpretation – fidelity in translating the rule makers' determinations – and emendation, correcting those determinations that are, from the interpreter's point of view, mistakes.[54] In cases of interpretation, the rule makers' role to determine what ought to be done is respected. In emendation, that role is usurped by the interpreter, who becomes the ultimate rule maker.

To see why this is so, imagine any case in which the interpreter has a view on what ought to be done, a view that superficially conflicts with what the authorities have determined. To take one of Lessig's examples,[55] consider that in 1864 Congress wrote a provision into the United States Code limiting the fee that a veteran could pay an attorney for representation in a veterans' benefit suit to ten dollars. In 1864 ten dollars could purchase adequate legal services. Congress's intention was merely to limit what attorneys could charge veterans, not to exclude attorneys from veterans' benefits proceedings altogether. Today, however, because of over a century of inflation, the ten-dollar limitation would operate to exclude legal representation. The question then is, Does fidelity in translation require us to read "ten dollars" to mean the cost of the amount of legal service that ten dollars would have bought in 1864?

Lessig is aware of the importance of this question, and he addresses it in the context of setting limits to his model of translation.[56] The important limit for our purposes is what Lessig calls "structural humility."[57] Humility in translation requires that the translator not improve the original text, that is, not correct mistakes that the text contains. The translator's job is to find equivalence in meaning between contexts, not to improve the meaning.

---

[52] U.S. Const. amend. X.
[53] Lessig, *supra* note 45, 1224–28.
[54] Id. at 1251.
[55] Id. at 1176–77.
[56] Id. at 1251 et seq.
[57] Id. at 1252–61.

Not all improvements are inappropriate, however, but only improvements that affect the task for which we hold the text's authors responsible.[58] Thus, it is okay for a translator of poetry to improve the poet's handwriting but not his poetry. We do not judge the poet by her handwriting. On the other hand, it is not okay to improve the handwriting in a child's paper if penmanship is part of the child's work to be evaluated. Lessig summarizes the point: "What humility requires, then, is a claim about the background understanding of what it is the author is being held responsible for. Against this background, humility counsels the translator to stay clear of presuppositions that touch the author's responsibility."[59]

Of what presuppositions of legal rule makers must legal interpreters stay clear? Lessig answers that they must stay clear of "political" or value presuppositions but not factual or legal ones.[60] In other words, the interpreter, in faithfully translating a legal text, may correct for factual and legal presuppositions that turn out to be false, but not for value presuppositions with which the interpreter disagrees.

How does Lessig's analysis operate in the context of Congress's ten-dollar cap on attorneys' fees? Remember, the important questions for Lessig are whether there has been change in presuppositions (a change that would have resulted in a different text), and whether the changed presuppositions are factual or evaluative. The presupposition at issue that Lessig attributes to the 1864 Congress – that ten dollars will purchase adequate legal representation – surely appears to be a factual one in Lessig's schema. Therefore, the faithful interpreter, who holds Congress responsible for its value choices but not its factual beliefs, would "interpret" ten dollars to mean whatever dollar amount is now necessary to purchase what ten dollars would have purchased in attorneys' services in 1864. Moreover, one would suppose that similar results might be in order for the constitutional requirement that the president be thirty-five and serve four-year terms, and that senators serve six-year terms, or even that posted speed limits are to be taken literally.

[58] Id. at 1253–54.
[59] Id.
[60] Id. at 1254–55.

Lessig does not justify his conclusion that we should hold authoring legal rule makers responsible for their value presuppositions but not for their factual and legal presuppositions. Lessig realizes that correcting for all now-perceived-as-erroneous presuppositions of the authoring legal rule makers in effect makes the interpreters, not the authoring legal rule makers, responsible for governance.[61] Thus, he attempts to cabin such corrections by distinguishing between correcting erroneous value beliefs and correcting erroneous factual beliefs. Lessig's distinction, however, is unsatisfactory, both because the relation of fact and value is too messy, and because – as the attorneys' fees example suggests – we wish to make the authoring rule makers responsible for factual determinations.

To take the latter point first, many disagreements that interpreters have with the rule makers whose laws they must interpret are disagreements about matters of fact. Does the fifty-five-mile-per-hour speed limit save lives? Will congressional term limits increase political accountability? Will ceilings on insurance rates actually work as they are forecast to do? And although Lessig's examples of fidelity in translation involve correcting factual and legal presuppositions that were correct when made but became incorrect over (a relatively long) time, there is no reason in principle that we can see why Lessig would not want interpreters to correct factual and legal presuppositions that were erroneous when made. Or, conversely, if we hold legal rule makers responsible for failure accurately to assay the present, why should we not hold them responsible for failing accurately to predict the future?

In Lessig's scheme, it turns out to be impossible for the legal rule makers to say that the law they enacted was premised on a factual or legal error that should cause it to be repealed. For, faithfully interpreted, the law's factual and legal presuppositions are all corrected; repeals because of factual or legal error are never necessary. Because, however, we believe that such repeals are often necessary, there must be something amiss in Lessig's view of interpretation. Put differently, we think there is frequently a gap between what the authoring rule makers *did determine* ought to be done and what, *in light of the facts*, they *should have determined*.

---

[61] Id. at 1253.

Lessig's model of fidelity in translation, however, renders such a gap a conceptual impossibility.[62]

Lessig's distinction between factual and legal presuppositions, which can be corrected by the interpreter, and value presuppositions, which cannot be corrected, is also problematic. It seriously underestimates the number of value disagreements that ultimately can be reduced to disagreements about facts or to mistakes in reasoning. For example, Lessig argues that something has gone amiss if we correct as erroneous

---

[62] Lessig could be read as endorsing a counterfactual test for determining the intentions of authorities – for example, their intentions are what they should have enacted had they realized the conflict between their specific and their more general or abstract purposes. David Brink endorses just such a test, although he realizes that because authorities would always resolve such conflict between levels of generality of purposes in favor of the more abstract level, the approach threatens to make all laws into an injunction, "Do the right thing," which would not be an authoritative determination or in any way constrain interpreters. David O. Brink, *Legal Theory, Legal Interpretation, and Judicial Review*, 17 *Phil. and Pub. Aff.* 105, 126–29 (1988). *See also* Michael J. Klarman, *Antifidelity*, 70 *S. Cal. L. Rev.* 381 (1997) (arguing against Lessig's theory of translation on the ground that it reduces the meaning of the law to how the subjects would resolve the problem to which the law is addressed); Greenawalt, *supra* note 13, at 133 (same). *But see* Marmor, *supra* note 38, at 171–72 (advocating reliance on the highest-level purposes of the authorities). Marmor believes that giving precedence to how legislators intend their law to apply in given circumstances over what they intend to accomplish through such applications is incoherent. It seems to us, however, that we can intend to ban the bomb in order to promote peace and, without any incoherence, maintain that banning the bomb is what we intended even when confronted with arguments that peace is better maintained through nuclear arms. *See also* Ronald Dworkin, *Life's Dominion: An Argument about Abortion, Euthanasia, and Individual Freedom* 136–37 (New York: Knopf 1993). The problem with such a counterfactual test is that it ultimately cannot distinguish two things that must be distinguished if authorities are to play their role: what the authorities *did* and what the authorities *would have done* (had they not made various mistakes). *See* Win-Chiat Lee, *Statutory Interpretation and the Counterfactual Test for Legislative Intention*, 8 *Law and Phil.* 383, 397–401, 403–4 (1989).

With respect to factual and legal errors, Lessig's approach ultimately collapses the distinction between what is implied *in* a statute and what is implied *by* a statute. Many things about the world are implied by statutes but are not in them, in the sense that they are legally operative. A law criminalizing prostitution may imply that the legislature holds a view of the world such that refusing to enforce contracts entered into by prostitutes would be desirable. Nonetheless, it does not follow without more from this implication about the world that the law criminalizing prostitution itself renders prostitutes' contract unenforceable. Or a law imposing a duty regarding sex discrimination may imply that the legislature would view a private right of action to enforce that duty as a good idea, were it to consider the question. In order to find such a private right of action to be implied *in* the law imposing the duty, however, it has to be such a good idea that we can infer that the legislature actually determined that it existed.

For an excellent discussion of how changed circumstances can affect the meaning of a directive, *see* Greenawalt, *From the Bottom Up, supra* note 23, at 1017–26.

the constitutional framers' presupposition that bicameralism is a "better" form of government than unicameralism.[63] That presupposition was a value judgment for which the framers should be deemed responsible. It is hard to imagine, however, how that "value" judgment is anything other than a judgment about facts – that is, about how efficient, liberty-protective, and responsive the two types of government will be. And the value presuppositions behind the preference for the superior form of government in terms of efficiency, liberty-protection, and responsiveness have arguably not changed a bit since the constitutional framing.

Lessig himself admits that the line between value and factual presuppositions will not be a clear or even a stable one.[64] Ultimately, the important question is, For what do we hold the authoring legal rule makers responsible? Unfortunately for Lessig's analysis, he makes no case for the presupposition that we should hold authoring legal rule makers responsible for their values but not their factual beliefs. Indeed, if the legal rule makers' role is to make shared abstract moral notions much more determinate, the role of rule makers in determining factual matters is in some sense more important than their role in determining values.

We began this discussion of Lessig by asking whether it is possible to distinguish between what the rule makers did determine and what the rule makers should have determined with respect to factual situations to which they did not advert. Lessig fails to distinguish between two different situations: when what the authors determined changes with the context of application, and when what they determined is shown to be mistaken by the context of application. Lessig's fidelity in translation effaces that distinction with respect to factual distinctions and assumes it with respect to value determinations.

Yet, if we are correct about the existence of intended meanings, the distinction between rule makers' actual intended meanings and what they should have intended is possible in principle. The obstacle that remains is whether the inquiry into intended meanings is sufficiently determinate to support a set of meaningful rules.

[63] Lessig, *supra* note 45, at 1253.
[64] Id. at 1255.

D. THE DETERMINACY OF INTENDED MEANING:
THE "KRIPKENSTEIN" CRITIQUE

We come now to an argument that expresses skepticism about inferring intended meanings from the quite limited content of a mental state, namely, the rule maker's mental state at the time he enacts the rule. Presumably, the content of that mental state is supposed to be normative for the interpreters of the rule, including the rule maker himself. For example, the content of the rule maker's mind when he promulgates the "no bear" rule is supposed to make it true that he intended to prohibit Malaysian sun bears or the declawed black bear even if these were not in his mind at the time. Yet how can such a momentary and limited mental state be normative for such ascriptions of intention?

What we are raising is what is labeled the "Kripkenstein" critique of determinate intentions because it is based on Saul Kripke's interpretation of Wittgenstein.[65] Basically, the Kripkenstein critique stems from recognition that no mental state content, present or past, can *by itself* ever make it true that by uttering certain words, one has intended some future act. For example, when we issue the rule "Add 68 and 57," what makes it the case that by "add" we intend that arithmetic operation that will produce the answer 125? According to the critique, nothing in our past uses of "add" precludes the possibility that we might now mean an arithmetic operation that produces the answer 5. For what we did in the past is, for example, consistent with a meaning of "add" that produces the result "125 for every day before today, 5 for every day thereafter."[66]

The conclusion to draw from the Kripkenstein critique is not the skeptical one that determinate intentions and rules are an impossibility because there are no mental facts that can anchor determinacy.[67] Rather,

---

[65] *See* Jules L. Coleman and Brian Leiter, *Determinacy, Objectivity, and Authority,* 142 *U. Pa. L. Rev.* 549, 568–72 (1992). Kripke's interpretation of Wittgenstein is found in Saul A. Kripke, *Wittgenstein on Rules and Private Language: An Elementary Exposition* 55–113 (Cambridge, Mass.: Harvard University Press 1982). The primary passages in Wittgenstein that serve as a basis for the skeptical argument are in Wittgenstein, *supra* note 23, at § 203.

[66] Coleman and Leiter, *supra* note 65, at 569–70. *See also* Scott Hershovitz, *Wittgenstein on Rules: The Phantom Menace,* 22 *Oxford J. Legal Stud.* 619, 620–23 (2002).

[67] *See* John A. Humphrey, *Quine, Kripke's Wittgenstein, and Sceptical Solutions,* 37 *S.J. Phil.* 43, 46 (1999) (denying the existence of "meaning facts"); Alex Byrne, *On Misinterpreting Kripke's Wittgenstein,* 56 *Phil. and Phenomenological Res.* 339 (1996) (denying that any fact

the conclusion to draw – and that is almost universally drawn, though by differing routes – is that determinate intentions and rules are matters of *knowing how* rather than *knowing that.*[68] We learn through interaction with others how to follow rules, including those we set for ourselves.[69] When we "interpret" what we have intended with respect to situations to which we have not fully adverted – which situations exist for all intentions – we do not look for mental facts in addition to those we call the intention; rather, we just grasp, as we have learned to do, the full range of what we intended in light of the actual mental state and its

can determine meaning); Charles M. Yablon, *Law and Metaphysics,* 96 *Yale L.J.* 613, 627 (1987) (same); Thomas Nagel, *The Last Word* 45–46 (New York: Oxford University Press 1997) (same).

[68] *See* Andrei Marmor, *The Separation Thesis and the Limits of Interpretation,* 12 *Canadian J.L. and Jurisprudence* 135, 136–41 (1999) (understanding linguistic rules is learning how to engage in a complex practice); Yablon, *supra* note 67, at 631–32 (same); Christian Zapf and Eben Moglen, *Linguistic Indeterminacy and the Rule of Law: On the Perils of Misunderstanding Wittgenstein,* 84 *Geo. L.J.* 485, 500–6 (1996) (correct application of a rule is the product of training rather than reflection); Arthur Ripstein, *Law, Language, and Interpretation,* 46 *U. Toronto L.J.* 335, 338–39 (1996) (understanding rules is a matter of skill rather than intellectual fact).

[69] *See, e.g.,* Yablon, *supra* note 67, at 629–30 (rule following is learned in a community); Lawrence B. Solum, *On the Indeterminacy Crisis: Critiquing Critical Dogma,* 54 *U. Chi. L. Rev.* 462, 477–80 (1987) (same); Michael Robertson, *Picking Positivism Apart: Stanley Fish on Epistemology and Law,* 8 *S. Cal. Interdisc. L.J.* 401, 437–41 (1999) (attributing to Stanley Fish the view that clear meanings of rules come from "seeing" them with eyes shaped by a common embeddedness in the training, practices, beliefs, goals, and categories of a community); Byrne, *supra* note 67, at 343 (arguing that the meaning of a rule is in its use in a form of life); Onora O'Neill, *Toward Justice and Virtue: A Constructive Account of Practical Reasoning* 83–84 (Cambridge: Cambridge University Press 1996) (same); Gary Ebbs, *Rule Following and Realism* 296–98, 300–3 (1997) (arguing that the meaning of a rule is derived from social practices of rule following); Anthony J. Sebok, *Finding Wittgenstein at the Core of the Rule of Recognition,* 52 *S.M.U. L. Rev.* 75, 92 et seq. (1999) (same); Nagel, *supra* note 67, at 52–53 (same); Stavropoulos, *supra* note 39, at 147–55 (same); Theo van Willigenburg, *Shareability and Actual Sharing: Korsgaard's Position on the Publicity of Reasons,* 25 *Phil. Invest.* 176–77 (2002); Hershovitz, *supra* note 66, at 622–30; Philip Pettit, *Rules, Reasons, and Norms* Ch. 1 (Oxford: Oxford University Press 2002); Stefano Bertea, *Remarks on a Legal Positivist Misuse of Wittgenstein's Later Philosophy,* 22 *Law and Phil.* 513, 530–35 (2003). For a response to Pettit, see Paul A. Boghossian, *Rules, Meaning and Intention,* 124 *Phil. Stud.* 185 (2005). Despite the way we have phrased this, we do not rule out rule following by solitary Robinson Crusoes. Their intrapersonal interactions may establish the normativity of rule following just as interpersonal ones do. And just as solitary individuals can correctly follow – or disobey – their own rules, so too can entire communities. *See, e.g.,* Jussi Haukioja, *Is Solitary Rule-Following Possible?,* 32 *Philosophia* 131 (2005); William Max Knorpp, *How to Talk to Yourself, or Kripke's Wittgenstein's Solitary Language Argument and Why It Fails,* 84 *Pac. Phil. Q.* 215 (2003). *See also* Pettit, *supra;* Claudine Verheggen, *Wittgenstein's Rule-Following Paradox and the Objectivity of Meaning,* 26 *Phil. Investigations* 285, 304–7 (2003).

context.[70] Assertions about intentions are not like assertions about the speed of light, true or false independently of our social reality. Rather, assertions about intentions and their products, such as rules, are anchored in part beyond the world of social practices (in actual mental states) and in part within the world of social practices. And this is as much true of those whose intentions are in question as it is of those who seek to discover those intentions.

Indeed, the Kripkenstein critique of determinacy is bound to fail because we experience determinacy of intentions and communication daily. We follow rules correctly, be they mathematical or linguistic, and with many rules, we rarely disagree about what they require.[71] Whether we are Marxists or monarchists, we stop at stop signs, put commas after introductory dependent clauses, and get 125 when we add 67 and 58. Determinate rules are an everyday fact of life. What the Kripkenstein critique accomplishes is not the undermining of determinacy; rather, at most it forces us to seek the ground of determinacy not in mental states alone but in mental states coupled with skills learned as part of forms of life.

The issue, we believe, that lies at the core of the controversies about interpretation is not the shopworn question of how transparent intentions are toward their objects (If I intend x, and x entails y, do I intend y?), an issue that seems to be one of how to use the term "intention" and not one of what intentions are like in the world. The basic issue rather lies within the realm of transparency itself. If we say that in intending to ban

[70] See, e.g., Frederick Schauer, *Playing by the Rules: A Philosophical Examination of Rule-Based Decision-Making in Law and Life* 207–8 (Oxford: Clarendon Press 1991) (asserting that in ordinary cases, we just "grasp" what a rule means); Ripstein, *supra* note 68, at 338–39 (commenting on how we just "grasp" the meaning of many rules).

[71] See, e.g., Schauer, *supra* note 70, at 66–68 (noting how, despite the skepticism traceable to the interpretation of Wittgenstein under consideration, we *do* understand and follow rules; Yablon, *supra* note 67, at 628–33 (same); Greenawalt, *Law and Objectivity, supra* note 23, at 72–73 (same); Tomogi Shogenji, *The Problem of the Criterion in Rule-Following*, 60 *Phil. & Phenom. Res.* 501 (2000) (expressing skepticism about whether the claim that we understood rules can be justified); Richard S. Kay, *American Constitutionalism*, in *Constitutionalism: Philosophy Foundations* 28–29 (Larry Alexander, ed., Cambridge: Cambridge University Press 1998) (noting that the claim that all rules are indeterminate is operationally self-refuting); Coleman and Leiter, *supra* note 65, at 571–72 (pointing out that the absence of "meaning facts" does not undermine the determinacy of rules); Endicott, *supra* note 10, at 690–91 (same).

bears, with a grizzly as our exemplar, we intended to outlaw Malaysian sun bears, which we did not have in mind and may never have seen, heard of, or imagined, are we reporting a fact about the world, or are we applying certain norms of interpretation to our own past act, norms that are derived from values?[72]

We believe it is in part doubts about the *facticity* of intentions regarding noncontemplated applications that lead theorists to abandon authorial intentions as the key to interpretation. Intention skeptics ultimately reject any distinction between "What *did* you intend regarding unadverted-to situation S?" and "What would you have intended regarding S had you adverted to it?" The latter question has no single answer, however, because what you would have determined regarding S had you adverted to it depends upon what you would have believed about S. And because you could have believed any number of things about S, anything from what we believe about S to very different beliefs, there is no fact of the matter about what you would have determined. And because what you did determine regarding S is what you would have determined, there is no fact of the matter about what you did determine.

To be a skeptic about the facticity of intentions regarding situations not adverted to, however, makes one a skeptic about the facticity of all intentions.[73] Intentions are future-directed, yet that future, no matter how accurately imagined at the time of intending, will frequently, if not almost always, at the time of consummation be somewhat

---

[72] This issue regarding the facticity of intentions has been noted by others. *See, e.g.,* E. D. Hirsch Jr., *Counterfactuals in Interpretation,* in *Interpreting Law and Literature: A Hermeneutic Reader* 55, 66–68 (Sanford Levinson and Steven Mailloux, eds., Evanston, Ill.: Northwestern University Press 1988) (asking whether, given that the world of the future, into which intentions project, will be different from the author's world, we can say that the author's intentions survive in that world). Some theorists are quite insistent that the content of intentions is a matter of fact. *See, e.g.,* Andre Marmor, *Interpretation and Legal Theory* 120 (2d ed., Oxford: Hart Pub. 2005); Steven Knapp and Walter Benn Michaels, *Intention, Identity, and the Constitution: A Response to David Hoy,* in *Legal Hermeneutics: History, Theory, and Practice, supra* note 10, at 187, 192–93. Others deny this. *See* Fish, *supra* note 10, at 297, 300; Stanley Fish, *Wrong Again,* in *Doing What Comes Naturally* 99 (Durham: Duke University Press 1989).

There is some relation between the issue of opacity-transparency of intent and the issue of whether there is a metaphysical fact of the matter about intentions. Those who deny the latter – intention skeptics – would claim that intentions are totally opaque to all unforeseen circumstances and thus cannot have any future applications, that is, any applications whatsoever. *See generally* Michael E. Bratman, *Intentions, Plans, and Practical Reason* (Cambridge, Mass.: Harvard University Press 1987).

[73] *See* Fish, *supra* note 72, at 99 (on our need to interpret even our own intentions).

different in relevant ways. More importantly, the set of intentions regarding situations not adverted to contains all intentions about which we think the authorities were mistaken (because mistakes always indicate a failure to advert at some level of analysis). Therefore, skepticism about the facticity of intentions regarding situations not adverted to leads to a denial that there is a fact of the matter about the authorities' intentions in any case in which those intentions could restrict us from doing what is right by our own lights. Such skepticism completely undermines the role of a rule-making authority.

Yet even the intention skeptics should be loath to see all intentions fall into the category of norm-governed interpretations about which there is no fact of the matter. Not only must we say that, although the role of legal authorities is to determine what ought to be done in the future, there is never any fact of the matter about what they determine; we must also deny the legal authorities even the more limited roles that most theorists would grant them, such as determining the words to be interpreted, or the language of those words. If there is no fact of the matter about intentions regarding situations not adverted to, then there is no fact of the matter about, say, in what language the U.S. Constitution is written. For to say it is written in English normally means that that is the language its authors intended to use. And if English turns out to be in any relevant way different from what the authors contemplated, with respect to either sense or reference – as it almost always will[74] – so that there is no fact of the matter whether the authors intended *that* English, then there will be no fact of the matter about the language of the Constitution.[75]

---

[74] For related problems, *see* Shain, *supra* note 38, at 275–92 (discussing problems in classifying objects as natural kinds); Dardis, *supra* note 41, at 415, 424, 428 (1994) (discussing malapropisms); Thomas S. Kuhn, *Commensurability, Comparability, Communicability,* 2 *Phil. of Science Assoc.* 669 (1982) (discussing translation of languages with embedded mistakes about the world).

[75] Paul Campos has some useful things to say about this. *See, e.g.,* Campos, supra note 10, at 279, 283–84. Michael Moore, in *A Natural Law Theory of Interpretation, supra* note 8, gets caught in this predicament. Moore does not want to deny the facticity of intentions altogether. For example, he thinks there is a fact of the matter about whether legal authorities intend their marks or sounds to be a legal text and intend their text to be read in English. On the other hand, he denies that there is a fact of the matter about whether someone who bans bears near residences while picturing a grizzly has a like intention regarding black bears (id. at 342–43). Moore, having used the authorities' intentions to establish that the text in question is indeed a legal text in English (*see* id. at 355–57), dispenses with those intentions thereafter.

We are left then in the following predicament. The facticity of intentions is problematic. There are surely cases where even the one whose intention is in question cannot answer confidently that he did or did not intend *that*.[76] And even when he is confident that he did or did not intend *that*, it is not at all clear on what such confidence is based. On the other hand, we are confident in most cases about what we intended, including cases where we believe we should have intended something different. And the price of denying the facticity of intentions is quite high. If the author's intention cannot extend beyond his world as he sees it at the moment of authoring, there is nothing but the norms and beliefs of the interpreter to determine what ought to be done at any later time, norms and beliefs that themselves cannot be projected authoritatively into the future.

We ourselves are not skeptics about the facticity of intentions. We believe that there are real, not hypothetical, intentions about matters not specifically adverted to, and that whether or not a rule that bans bears in residential neighborhoods applies to a species of bear of which the rule makers were unaware is a question of fact.

IV. Conclusion

We have argued that when interpreters, whether they be ordinary citizens or officials, are faced with a canonical legal text, their task is to determine the lawmaker's intended meaning of that text – what the lawmaker intended to communicate through that text which the citizens and officials are and are not bound to do or refrain from doing. We have based our argument on the essential similarity between understanding canonical legal rules and understanding requests from Mom or from our children that we treat as normative for what we should do. Mom and the kids may misspeak or speak in ways that, in the absence of our knowledge

---

[76] To say that there must be some fact of the matter about intentions is not to say that all possible applications must be covered by those intentions. With respect to some applications, it is possible that the authorities lacked any intention, in which case nothing has been authoritatively determined regarding what ought to be done. But in some cases at least, we must be able to say that *in fact* the authorities did determine what ought to be done, even if what they determined they now would believe to be mistaken.

of what they intend to signify, would be ambiguous or incomprehensible. So, too, may lawmakers. But if we take the intended meaning as normative, legal texts containing such infelicities are no more problematic than infelicitous instructions left us by Mom or the kids.

In fleshing out our case for treating reasoning from canonical legal texts as essentially no different from reasoning from other requests or demands that we take to be normative, such as those issued by Mom or the kids, we have pointed out that intended meanings are not undermined by the finitude of all mental states. Nor are they undermined by the possibility that they will be infelicitous vis-à-vis the rule maker's purposes for his rule – either generally, in the case of an ill-conceived rule, or in specific applications. In some cases, the infelicity will be such that we are sure the rule maker did not intend *that* meaning, and in other cases the infelicity will raise doubts in the mind of the rule maker himself whether his intended meaning covers the example. In these cases, the rule does not apply, but the reason is a conflict with or failure of the rule maker's intended meaning, not a conflict with the rule's purposes. Nor are intended meanings undermined by the multiplicity of the rule maker's purposes, or the varying levels of generality at which they might be characterized, or the possibility of conflict among these purposes and between more general and less general characterizations of purposes. Nor are intended meanings undermined by changes in the factual, legal, or moral landscape. Finally, intended meanings are not undermined by Kripkenstein skepticism about rule following.

However, what if the intended meaning of a canonical legal text is quite unjust? Or what if it is quite opaque to the average citizen? Or what if the rule maker is a multimember institution whose members intend different and perhaps inconsistent meanings at the time they enact the rule? We deal with these problems of equating the meaning of canonical legal texts with their authors' intended meanings in the following chapter.

VI

Infelicities of the Intended Meaning of Canonical Texts and Norms Constraining Interpretation

In this chapter we take up three ways that the rule maker's intended meanings of his rules may turn out to be problematic. First, the intended meanings could be problematic as a normative matter because of their content. The rule maker may actually intend a meaning that is absurd, unjust, or quite anachronistic (and thereby absurd, unjust, or pointless). Second, the rule maker's intended meaning may be utterly opaque. The intended meaning of the rule in general may be opaque. More likely, that intended meaning is opaque in particular circumstances of application. Third, and a point much emphasized in criticism of intentionalist approaches such as ours, the rule maker may be a multimember institution such as a legislature, a multimember court, or an administrative board; and it may be the case that there is no single intended meaning endorsed by enough members to enact that meaning as law. We take up in turn these three problems with equating the meaning of a canonical legal text with the rule maker's intended meaning for that text.

I. Absurd, Unjust, and Pointless Intended Meanings

There is no doubt that, on occasions, even the best rule maker will promulgate a canonical legal text, the intended meaning of which will be absurd, unjust, or pointless. This is not an embarrassment for our position on interpretation of canonical legal texts – far from it. Only if one eliminates all vestiges of formalism within law – which we would equate with eliminating law itself – and reduces the meaning of all humanly posited legal rules to the Spike Lee injunction, "Do the right thing," can one escape the possibility of laws that properly interpreted are absurd, unjust, or pointless. And even applying the Spike Lee injunction will, given human fallibility, often lead to doing the wrong thing, thus creating a conflict between the master rule – "Do the right thing" – and the rules that implement it. If the latter are "interpreted" as "Do the right thing," settlement of what to do can never occur. Doing "the right thing" will inevitably lead to doing the wrong thing. On the other hand, settlement inevitably will result in some moral errors – some cases of absurd, unjust, or pointless rules. Our view is no more vulnerable to these problems than any view that sees law as settling moral controversies – that is, any view that characterizes law as positivistic, at least in part.

Indeed, on our view, proper interpretation – recovery of the rule maker's intended meaning of his text – will lead to absurd, unjust, or pointless results less often than would certain other recommended approaches to interpreting legal texts, especially strict textualism. (We take up this point in the following chapter.) For the fact that ascribing a particular meaning to a legal text would make that text absurd, unjust, or pointless is strong evidence that the rule maker did not intend *that* meaning.

There are numerous real life examples of instances where what at first looks like an absurd or unjust result was clearly not the intended meaning of the rule maker. In *Cernauskas v. Fletcher*,[1] the case in which a party cited a recently enacted law that by its terms repealed "all laws previously enacted" to argue that the law relied on by the other party was repealed, it was clear to the interpreting court that the Arkansas

---

[1] 21 Ark. 678, 201 S.W. 2d 999 (1947).

legislature's intended meaning was *not* the repeal of the entire corpus juris, an absurd and surely unjust result. And it is abundantly clear that despite its punctuation, the Seventeenth Amendment was intended to apply indefinitely rather than for only six years.[2] And it is arguable that in the *Holy Trinity* case,[3] the Supreme Court reached the right result in finding that Congress's intended meaning in proscribing bringing foreign laborers into the United States did not encompass religious ministers. (We are assuming for purposes of argument, and in line with the Court's majority, that excluding ministers would have been seen at the time to be a policy error.)

Nonetheless, at times even the best of rule makers will make an error in terms of assessing the present facts, forecasting future facts, or weighing moral considerations. Take another frequently mentioned case, *United States v. Locke.*[4] In that case a litigant filed a claim on December 31 under a statute that required such claims to be filed "before December 31." The litigant argued that Congress undoubtedly meant "*on or* before December 31," as there was no conceivable reason for it to have chosen December 30 rather than December 31 as the last day to file. Nonetheless, the Court rejected the litigant's argument and held the claim not timely filed. The Court may have erred in terms of Congress's intended meaning, as the losing party contended. On the other hand, Congress's intended meaning may have been to require filings by December 30, *although, if confronted with this issue, Congress might have admitted that it was pointless or wrong for it to have so intended.*

Or, to take our hypothetical "no bears" rule from the preceding chapter, it may be the case that the rule maker did not realize that pandas were completely harmless; had he realized that, he would have exempted them from his rule. Nonetheless, he might say that although he intended to include pandas within his rule, he was mistaken to have done so. That is, his "no bears" rule, which was intended to include pandas, is inferior to a "no bears except pandas" rule. The rule maker erred by intending to include pandas. (This type of error – the infelicitous

---

[2] *See* U.S. Const. amend. XVII: "The Senate of the United States shall be composed of two Senators from each state, elected by the people thereof, for six years. . . ."

[3] Church of the Holy Trinity v. United States, 143 U.S. 457 (1892).

[4] 471 U.S. 84, 93–96 (1985).

but intended rule – is different from a felicitous intended rule that has infelicitous applications; for, as we have stressed throughout, almost any rule will have some infelicitous applications or omissions that cannot be eliminated without undermining the value of the rule *qua* rule.)[5]

Infelicities – absurd, unjust, or pointless rules – are ineliminable, given human fallibility. Equating the proper interpretation of canonical legal texts with the intended meaning of the authors of those texts – the rule makers – surely leaves the door open to interpretations that result in absurdity and injustice. Ultimately, however, as we have consistently argued, given the settlement function of canonical legal texts, the possibility of such substantive infelicities is not a point against our approach to interpretation but a point in its favor.

II. Opaque Intended Meanings

Searching for the rule maker's intended meaning may reveal another type of infelicity. As we argued in the preceding chapter, there will be occasions when even the rule maker himself will not be sure what meaning he intended. We gave the example of a newly discovered species of bear that is tiny and docile, and we said that the rule maker might himself be quite uncertain whether he did or did not intend to include such a species in his "no bears" rule. When the interpreter comes to a case where the rule maker's intent is indeterminate to everyone, including even the rule maker, interpretation of the rule by reference to its author's intended meaning yields no answer. In a sense, the rule does not cover the case, either to include it within the rule's application or to exclude it.

When the rule maker's intended meaning is opaque in this way, what should the interpreter do? One thing is clear: whatever the interpreter does to resolve the case, it will not be through interpretation. Beyond that, there are essentially two options, depending on the authority of the interpreter. If the interpreter has lawmaking authority, she can construct a rule to cover the case, presumably one that is normatively attractive

---

[5] Thus, if the "no bears except pandas" rule resulted in too many errors in its application relative to the "no bears" rule – perhaps because too many nonpandas would be taken for pandas – the latter might be the better rule despite pandas' not coming within its rationale.

when conjoined with the remainder of the primary rule maker's rule. If the interpreter has no lawmaking authority, then the case is governed by status quo ante legal rules. If the "no bears" rule were a prohibitory exception to a general permission to keep animals near private residences, the case of the questionable "bear" should be resolved in favor of a permission.

III. Conflicting Multiple Intended Meanings

Perhaps one of the most frequent criticisms of intentionalist theories of legal interpretation such as ours is that they cannot be applied to multimember rule-making bodies such as legislatures, administrative boards, and appellate courts. Individuals have states of mind such as intentions; groups do not. So goes the critical refrain.

We agree that groups do not have states of mind *qua* groups. And we do not posit the existence of group intentions beyond the intended meanings of the individuals who compose the group. Nor do we deny that those individual intended meanings can differ from person to person within the group and can in some cases conflict. Finally, we do not deny that these facts will create difficulties for intentionalist interpretation in some cases. What we do deny is that such difficulties should cause us to reject intentionalism. Instead, what they suggest is that, on some occasions, what appears to be a meaningful law (because its text seems to parse) is actually meaningless.

To begin with, in many cases, the rule makers who possess the authority to create a binding legal rule – say, the legislators necessary to pass a law (usually a majority of the legislature, but occasionally a supermajority) – will all intend the same meaning for the rule they enact. In other words, over the range of real or hypothetical applications of the rule, felicitous and infelicitous, if asked how the rule was intended to apply, each member of the majority sufficient to pass the rule would give the very same answer.

In a large number of other cases, individual members of the majority would agree in terms of intended meaning in most real and hypothetical applications but would disagree about a few such applications. In the cases of disagreement, there is no univocal intended meaning. But so long as enough rule makers for passage would have voted for the rule even if it did not apply in the area of disagreement, the core area of overlapping intended meanings is the enacted rule, and the fringes without the backing of sufficient overlapping intended meanings are not within the rule.

To illustrate this possibility, suppose that groups A and B make up a majority of the legislature, and they enact a rule that A intends to outlaw X and Y and B intends to outlaw X and Z. If neither A nor B is of sufficient size to constitute a majority of those voting aye, but both A and B would approve of a rule outlawing only X (and not Y or Z), then the rule has a core meaning, namely, that of outlawing X.

In both of the preceding examples, the multimember character of the rule maker does not defeat the attribution of *an* intended meaning for the rule, though in the second example the rule is more truncated than many intended. However, a third type of example raises real problems for intentionalism. Imagine that the legislative body that enacts the "no bears" rule is comprised of three legislators, A, B, and C. C voted against the "no bears" rule on the ground that it devalued liberty and property relative to physical security. A and B voted for it. A believed that pandas are bears and intended the rule to cover them. Had pandas been excepted, A would have voted against the rule as unfair to owners of declawed, defanged, friendly black bears. On the other hand, B believed the rule did not cover pandas, pandas not falling within his intended meaning of "bears." Had B believed pandas were included, he would have voted against the rule. ("Who could be so cold or unreasonably fearful as to ban the cute and gentle panda?") A and B did not clarify whether pandas were within the rule before voting.

The results of this disagreement are these. The rule "no bears" admits of two relevant possible meanings: "No bears, including pandas, are allowed" and "No bears, except pandas, are allowed." Although the "no bears" rule itself passed two to one, each of its possible meanings would have been rejected by two-to-one votes. The "no bears" rule has no core of intended meaning that would have been supported by enough legislators for enactment. Neither legislator has been granted authority by the community to settle by herself what the rule should be.

On our view, the "no bears" rule is only apparently meaningful but not actually so. It is no different from the case where a term in a rule is ambiguous and has two nonoverlapping definitions, and some legislators intend one meaning and the others intend the alternative meaning. (Consider: "No canards are allowed in the park," where C votes against the rule on libertarian grounds; A votes for it intending one meaning for "canards" – ducks; and B votes for it intending another meaning – lies. The rule can only mean either "no ducks" or "no lies," and neither meaning has the backing of a majority.)

If we assume that only the intended meaning of a legislative majority regarding what law subjects are obligated to do is authoritative for those subjects, then in these kinds of cases, an apparently meaningful rule is in reality no more meaningful than potential signs produced accidentally – that is, without any intention to signify anything. Monkeys on typewriters, cloud formations, and spilled ink may make what might appear to be words in some natural language. But if the monkeys, the clouds, or the spilled ink produced the shapes *c*, *a*, *t*, it would be odd to ask if that *means* a tabby, any feline, or a jazz musician. Although it could mean any of those – indeed, it could mean almost anything given infinite possible languages with infinite possible ways to signify meanings – without the backing of someone's intended meanings, those unintended shapes have no meaning at all. They are evidence of natural processes, but they are not bearers of meaning.

Our pathological account of the "no bears" rule renders it no different from the natural products of typing monkeys, clouds, and spilled ink. Once we know the intended meanings of A and B, it is a category mistake to ask what the rule means. A's own rule is meaningful, as is B's; but their jointly produced rule is not.

IV. Norms Constraining Intended Meanings as Antidotes to the Foregoing Infelicities

A. SUBSTANTIVE CONSTRAINTS

1. Norms for Avoiding Substantively Infelicitous Results

Substantive constraints on rule makers' determinations, although quite important practically, are relatively unproblematic jurisprudentially. We are used to the idea of substantive constitutional constraints on legislative, executive, and judicial acts. And as we point out in Chapter 8, there is nothing fundamentally different about substantive preconstitutional constraints on the authors of constitutions, that is, constraints assumed by the populace in its acceptance of the authority of those authors. For example, as a preconstitutional matter, we could accept a norm that establishes as fundamental law the determinations of the 1787 constitutional framers, *except to the extent that those determinations are substantively absurd, unjust, and so on.*

Substantive constraints such as one denying the authority of any legal rule that is absurd or grossly unjust (by the interpreter's standards) are different from epistemological principles that help interpreters discover what the legal rule makers intended ought to be done. That some result would be absurd or grossly unjust can be evidence – often strong evidence – that the rule makers did not intend that result. Nonetheless, as we have stressed, rule makers can intend absurd or unjust results, even if not under those descriptions. That is, it is possible that: (1) rule makers wish to require only what is just and not absurd; (2) rule makers intend that X be done; and (3) X is unjust or absurd. Simply put, rule makers can intend unjust or absurd results because they make mistakes. And a norm that directs interpreters to disregard intended absurd or unjust results operates as a constraint on the rule makers' power to determine authoritatively what ought to be done rather than as an aid to understanding what the rule makers did in fact determine.

Substantive constraints on the rule makers' determinations can function as absolute limits, much as do ordinary constitutional norms that limit the authority of governmental actors. Alternatively, they can function as do artificial evidentiary presumptions by directing interpreters to resolve uncertainties about the rule makers' intentions in favor of certain outcomes. Thus, if the rule makers' intentions are not clear, such substantive norms might direct interpreters to resolve the ambiguity in favor of the result that seems most just or wisest, rather than in favor of the result best supported by the evidence regarding the rule makers' intentions, which evidence includes the fact that one result is more just or wiser than the other.[6]

---

[6] Cass Sunstein's canons of statutory interpretation appear to function as substantively motivated, evidentiary presumptions rather than as either norms that define what legislation "means" or norms that act as absolute limits on the authority of that meaning. Cass R. Sunstein, *Interpreting Statutes in the Regulatory State*, 103 *Harv. L. Rev.* 405 (1964). For Sunstein urges the following canons *unless it is clear that the statute "means" something at odds with the*

Both types of substantive constraints, however, must be the product of a decision-making body that possesses higher authority than the rule maker thereby constrained. That is so because both absolute and presumptive constraints on a rule maker result in departures from that rule maker's intended meaning and thus depart from that rule maker's determination regarding what ought to be done.[7] And the norms that are the product of this higher-authority decision-making body – be it a constitutional ratifying body or ultimately, insofar as the substantive norms are preconstitutional norms on which the constitutional norms ultimately rest, the citizens who accept the norms – must mean what *their* authors intended *them* to mean, whether the authors are the constitutional ratifying bodies or the people themselves "authoring" norms by accepting them.

2. Norms for Effectuating Specific Policies

The common law is replete with doctrines that direct judges to disregard the intended meanings of documents that are otherwise thought to be canonical statements regarding parties' legal rights and duties. These include the parole evidence rule for the interpretation of contracts, the doctrine that an ambiguous contract shall be construed against the party who drafted it, presumptions against disinheritance, and many others. In effect, these doctrines direct judges to imagine a hypothetical author who is different from the actual author and to ask what meaning the hypothetical author would have intended in drafting the document. If the hypothetical author's intended meaning differs from the actual author's meaning, the former meaning controls. In this way, the common law makes it more difficult, though not impossible, for actual authors to take advantage of contractual partners, to assert an idiosyncratic intended meaning that would deny the existence of a "meeting of the minds,"

---

canons. *See, e.g.,* id. at 423, 434, 450, 456 (implying that statute could have a meaning distinct from the "meaning" given by the canons). The same point applies to other substantive norms, such as those which direct interpreters to construe statutes in favor of criminal defendants or to avoid constitutional issues: these norms dictate departures from the rule maker's intended meaning and in reality create new rules out of materials that the rule maker provided.

[7] The presumptive constraint results in such departures because it gives the interpreter's view of what would be a wise or just result more weight in affecting the outcome than that view would have as evidence of the rule maker's intended meaning.

to disinherit a spouse, and so forth. Whether or not these doctrines reflect wise policies, there is nothing problematic about them insofar as interpretive methodology is concerned. They merely ask the interpreter what would this instruction in this document likely mean if it had been authored by someone with characteristics that the actual author may or may not have possessed. Or, more precisely, these doctrines are not about interpretation at all; they authorize the judge or other "interpreter" to author the document in question. The interpreter acting as author, however, is not free to apply his or her best judgment about what the content of the document should be but instead must apply the algorithms called for by the governing doctrine. The actual authors of contracts, wills, and the like can anticipate these "interpretive" algorithms and have their documents interpreted in accord with their intended meanings if they are skillful.

Similarly unproblematic are substantive constraints on statutory interpretation that derive from the higher law of the Constitution. The doctrine of lenity, for example, supposedly effects the policies of the due process and ex post facto law clauses that seek to protect actors against being charged with crimes based on nonobvious (to ordinary people) intended meanings of criminal statutes. The doctrine directs the courts to give criminal statutes the most restricted meaning where more than one meaning is possible. In other words, the courts are to imagine that criminal statutes are drafted by hypothetical legislators who seek to limit the scope of criminal liability perhaps more than did the actual legislators who enacted those statutes. This again is just intentionalist interpretation with hypothetical authors inserted in place of actual ones.

As we said, none of these doctrines that constrain the interpretation of canonical legal texts on behalf of substantive policies require departing from the ordinary human endeavor seeking authors' intended meanings. No special craft skill is required by them. Any of us can imagine that a document was drafted by someone other than its actual author and ask what it would have meant in such a case. It takes no special legal training to answer the question what would "I'll make him an offer he can't refuse" mean if, instead of Don Corleone making the statement, it were made by our sweet, good-natured real estate broker.

There *is* an interesting problem here, however. If courts are directed to imagine hypothetical authors who differ from the actual authors along certain dimensions, there have to be additional constraints added to keep from completely undermining the ability of actual authors, whether private or legislative, to have their intended meanings heeded. This is because any symbols can be employed to communicate *any* intended meaning. Thus, as an example, if the doctrine of lenity instructs courts to "interpret" criminal statutes narrowly, what stops them from interpreting those statutes ridiculously narrowly? It would not be the actual intended meaning of the actual author, for we have already dispensed with that in invoking the doctrine of lenity. Nor would it be the actual meaning of the words; for, as we emphasized in the preceding chapter, actual words – certain shapes and sounds – do not carry a meaning if there is no author intending a meaning *by* those words. So the doctrine of lenity and the various other similar doctrines that, in service of substantive policies, constitutional and nonconstitutional, direct judges to disregard the actual intended meanings, need to supplement the characteristics of the target hypothetical authors beyond those we have mentioned. So if the hypothetical legislators of criminal statutes are supposed to be motivated to limit the scope of criminal liability, judges need to know by how much. Or if the hypothetical drafter of a testamentary document is supposed to be disinclined to disinherit the spouse, judges need to know by how much. And so on. Otherwise, criminal liability would disappear, and so would the ability to disinherit spouses.

The most obvious supplement to add here is that the hypothetical legislature or will drafter uses, say, standard English – perhaps definitions listed first in a designated dictionary – and standard grammar. Doing so will in most cases put limits on the hypothetical authors that will prevent courts from undermining all criminal liability in the name of lenity and undermining the ability of drafters of private documents such as wills and contracts to accomplish their ends.

One doctrine that directs courts to disregard actual intended meanings for substantive policy reasons but that raises a worry of a different kind is the doctrine of interpreting statutes to avoid having to resolve constitutional questions – the so-called *Ashwander* doctrine in United States constitutional law.[8] The problem with *Ashwander* is not that it

---

[8] *See* Ashwander v. T.V.A., 297 U.S. 288 (1936).

directs courts to look to what a hypothetical legislature would have meant by a statute rather than to what the actual legislature meant. The doctrine of lenity does that as well. The problem is that, at least arguably, although the doctrine of lenity is a doctrine commanded by the Constitution, the authority of which is superior to that of the legislature, the *Ashwander* doctrine does not implement any higher-order legal norm. Interpreting to avoid constitutional issues is not itself a constitutional command. So when a court following *Ashwander* disregards the actual intended meaning of a statute and "interprets" as if the statute were authored by a hypothetical legislature intending the statute steer clear of any constitutional limits, the court is exercising only the power it has as a court to interpret statutes and not the power it possesses to strike down unconstitutional statutes. And in following *Ashwander*, courts make legislatures go through hoops not found in the Constitution in order to have their intended meanings implemented. It might be concluded that use of the *Ashwander* presumption represents a violation of the constitutional separation of powers.[9]

B. PROCEDURAL CONSTRAINTS

The more interesting constraints on authorities' determinations are procedural constraints. Procedural constraints are norms that dictate the form that rule makers' determinations must take and that handle cases where the rule makers have apparently but not really determined what ought to be done. The norms that dictate form reflect the rule-of-law value of the accessibility of law. The norms that handle cases of failed law reflect both the rule-of-law value of accessibility and the more substantive value of consistent policy.

1. Norms of Form

We are quite familiar with certain formal constraints on rule makers' determinations that must be satisfied before those determinations are deemed to have legal effect. For example, we have norms covering what

---

[9] *See* Larry Alexander and Saikrishna Prakash, *Mother, May I? Imposing Mandatory Prospective Rules of Statutory Interpretation*, 20 *Const. Comment.* 97, 104 (2003).

counts as a "vote" by a legislator to enact a rule, which "vote" not only signifies that the voting rule maker's intention will be counted but also marks the moment in time at which the relevant intention must exist. One who votes aye when the roll is called is counted as in favor of the proposed bill for purposes of determining whether the bill has become law, even if she is subjectively opposed to the bill, and even if, moreover, she believes aye means "opposed."

Notice that in the case of the rule maker who votes aye thinking it means no, if that person provides the necessary vote for passage, the law is deemed to have been passed even though a majority of the rule makers intended that it not pass. In such a case, the law is not what the (majority of) the rule makers determined ought to be done. When the law comes to be applied, what does it "mean"?

We could have a norm that provided that in the case just described, the law means what the rule makers voting in favor intended to mean by it, except that for the person mistakenly voting aye, the law means merely what she thought it would mean if passed. She herself did not intend that meaning because she did not intend for the law to exist as law.

We need some such procedural norm because we have a gap to bridge: the gap between what the (majority of) rule makers determined ought to be done – nothing – and what our norm regarding voting provides is the case, namely, that a law was passed. If we say that because of the mistaken and pivotal aye vote a law was passed but it has no applications, we undermine the norm regarding what counts as aye and no votes. And without that norm, there will be continued uncertainty regarding what laws exist, an uncertainty that undermines the rule-of-law value of the knowability or accessibility of the law.

It is a short step from familiar procedural norms about voting to some similar but perhaps less obvious procedural norms. Consider the following procedural norms that might constrain the rule makers' determinations. (1) All texts shall be interpreted as if they were written in the standard English of the date of enactment, with respect both to the meanings of the words used and to grammar and punctuation.[10] (2) All

---

[10] That the monkeys' marks resemble marks made by writers in English makes no difference. Is the flagpole outside my office the letter *I*? And suppose there were a language Shmenglish that resembled English in every way, except that the nouns and verbs were switched around,

texts more than one hundred years old shall be deemed of no legal effect (or, more limitedly, of no legal effect if the standard English meanings of any of the text's words have changed in the hundred-year period).

Norm (1) reflects the rule-of-law value of legal accessibility. It bars authoring legal texts in the rule makers' private code or in a different language from the populace. It thus prevents recondite law. We discuss norms such as norm (1) more fully in the next chapter when we consider textualism as a theory of legal interpretation.

Norm (2) reflects the same value – that recovering rule makers' intentions becomes more and more difficult as the moment of enactment

so that "dog" meant a domestic animal that meows, and "cat" meant a domestic animal that barks, "whale" meant an ink-squirting mollusk, "harpoon" meant a rapid-firing gun, "walk" meant to move on one's legs as quickly as possible, and so forth. Would we be able to interpret the monkeys' novel in such a case? Because they had no linguistic intentions, how can we decide in which of the infinite possible languages that could employ such marks their "novel" was typed? In this connection, consider the following column by Dave Barry in the *San Diego Union*, Dec. 4, 1993: "Meanwhile, out in Pinedale, Wyo. we have a situation involving ARTISTS PAINTING ON COWS. You may have heard about this. Three artists got a $4,000 grant, some of which came from the federal government, to paint words from a pioneer woman's diaries on the sides of live cows. I am not making this up. The idea was that the cows, with the words on their sides, would wander around and poop on symbolic representations of U.S. taxpayers.

"No, seriously, the idea, as explained by one of the artists, was that the wandering cows would scramble the words so as to 'create a new text.' I think this is a terrific idea, and I believe the government should seriously consider using wandering painted cows to generate the instructions for filling out federal tax forms. I bet the cows would do a MUCH better job than whoever is doing this now (my guess is hamsters)."

For a good sampling of the literature in support of the general proposition that texts *qua* texts mean only what their authors intend them to mean, *see* Steven Knapp and Walter Benn Michaels, *Not a Matter of Interpretation*, 42 San Diego L. Rev. 651 (2005); Steven Knapp and Walter Benn Michaels, *Intention, Identity, and the Constitution: A Response to David Hoy*, in *Legal Hermeneutics: History, Theory, and Practice* 187–99 (Gregory Leyh, ed., Berkeley: University of California Press 1992); Richard S. Kay, *Original Intentions, Standard Meanings, and the Legal Character of the Constitution*, 6 Const. Comment. 39, 40–5 (1989); E. D. Hirsch Jr., *Counterfactuals in Interpretation*, in *Interpreting Law and Literature: A Hermeneutic Reader* 55–68, 57 (Sanford Levinson and Steven Mailloux, eds., Evanston, Ill.: Northwestern University Press 1988); Steven Knapp and Walter Benn Michaels, *Against Theory 2: Hermeneutics and Deconstruction*, 14 *Critical Inquiry* 49, 54, 60 (1987); E. D. Hirsch Jr., *Against Theory*, 8 *Critical Inquiry* 723, 725–30 (1982); Walter Benn Michaels, *The Fate of the Constitution*, 61 *Tex. L. Rev.* 765, 774 (1992). Even Stanley Fish, usually associated with the "reader response theory" of interpretation, which minimizes the role of the author and her intentions – *see, e.g.*, Robin West, *The Aspirational Constitution*, 88 *Nw. U. Law Rev.* 241, 257–58 (1993) – has actually endorsed the centrality of authorial intention to interpretation. *See* Stanley Fish, *There Is No Textualist Position*, 42 San Diego L. Rev. 629 (2005); Stanley Fish, *Play of Surfaces: Theory and the Law*, in *Legal Hermeneutics, supra*, at 297–316, 299–300.

recedes further and further into the past. With norm (1) in existence, norm (2) is perhaps less important but surely not unnecessary, especially if modified as indicated in parenthesis.

Norms (1) and (2) should be contrasted to proposals that might appear to be similar. For example, some have proposed that statutes be given the meaning their words would standardly carry if authored at the time of interpretation or application.[11] One impetus behind such a proposal is to make law's meaning even more accessible than it would be under norm (1), although there are also substantive concerns about policy obsolescence that underlie that proposal. This form of "updating" of statutes, however, has a markedly different effect from norm (1) on the rule makers' ability to carry out their role. Norm (1) forces rule makers to consult the dictionaries and grammars of their time in order to maximize their ability to effectuate their determination of what ought to be done. The "updating" proposal, on the other hand, reduces their control to that of selecting the language (English) and the marks but then leaves the translation of their determination to the fortuity of subsequent changes in the language.[12]

Calabresi has proposed that statutes be declared of no legal effect when they become "obsolete."[13] Unlike norm (2), Calabresi's proposal is not motivated primarily by rule-of-law concerns but rather is based on substantive policy considerations. Calabresi's test of statutory obsolescence is not one of mere age or even obscurity of meaning but is rather one of substantive consistency with more modern statutes and judicial decisions.[14]

Norms (1) and (2) are purely procedural norms that attempt to reconcile the role of rule makers – to determine what ought to be done – with the rule-of-law value of legal accessibility. Norm (2) effects the reconciliation by restricting the temporal scope of the rule makers' authority. Norm (1) effects the reconciliation more or less well depending on the

---

[11] *See* Larry Alexander, *Of Two Minds about Law and Minds,* 88 *Mich. L. Rev.* 2444 (1990); T. Alexander Aleinkoff, *Updating Statutory Interpretation,* 87 *Mich. L. Rev.* 20 (1988).

[12] Query: do we have criteria for distinguishing when a language has undergone a change from when a new language has supplanted it? *See* Anthony Dardis, *How the Radically Interpreted Make Mistakes,* 33 *Dialogue* 415, 420–21 (1994).

[13] Guido Calabresi, *A Common Law for the Age of Statutes* 2 (Cambridge Mass.: Harvard University Press 1995).

[14] Id. at 2, 129–31.

rule makers' skill in drafting so as to communicate their determinations accurately according to the grammar and diction of the time. Where the reconciliation is imperfect – where the rule makers fail to draft so that their determinations are conveyed in standard English – the law will not be what they determined ought to be done. Rather, the law will be a product of their determination regarding marks or sounds and the independent process of codifying standard English meanings and grammar. It will be to some degree "mindless," in that the codification of meanings and grammar will not be a reflection of anyone's determination of what ought to be done in the world beyond dictionaries and grammar books. Unlike the "updating" proposal,[15] however, norm (1) does not deprive rule makers of control over effectuating their determinations. It demands linguistic skills but not linguistic prescience.

2. Norms for Failed Law

The procedural norms in this category are somewhat different from the norms of form in that, instead of addressing the problem of how to make the rule makers' determinations more accessible, they address the problem of what to do when the rule makers appear to have determined an issue but actually have not. Such cases of failed law, as we call them, are phenomena associated with multimember legislative bodies, though they occur as well in other multimember rule-making bodies, such as administrative boards, appellate courts, and constitutional ratifiers. They occur when the rule makers individually intend different applications and thus mean different things, despite having agreed on the language of their legislative text. In other words, norms for failed law deal with the problem of conflicting intentions within a multimember rule-making body.

When the general legislative norm is that rule makers' determinations have the force of law only if a majority (or supermajority) of the rule makers concur, and members of the (apparent) majority have made different and potentially conflicting determinations regarding what ought to be done despite having agreed on the words of a text, then it is possible that there is no majority determination having the force of law. Multimember legislative bodies have no intentions regarding what ought to be done.

---

[15] See Aleinkoff, *supra* note 11, at 13.

Or, put differently, the only intentions such bodies have consistent with the role that rule makers are supposed to play are some aggregation of the individual intentions of the members. Aggregation of individual intentions is not a problem if a majority has identical intentions. Where those intentions come apart, however, the passage of a law may be illusory in this sense: despite the appearance of legislative (majority) agreement that there be such a law, every possible intended meaning of that law would have been opposed by a majority of the legislative body. Put differently, no majority determined any possible meaning for the law.

A norm of form such as one that irrebuttably assumes that all laws are intended to mean what they mean in the standard English of the date of enactment can save some laws from the failure to command a majority of consistent individual intentions. Such norms will not handle all cases, however, for even standard English will leave open the possibility of ambiguity. And in such instances, by application of Arrow's theorem,[16] we face the possibility of majorities in favor of a law and its language but against all possible meanings of that language.

Consider this stylized representative case. Rule makers A, B, and C vote on term T. T is vague and can mean W, X, and Y or W, X, and Z. A votes aye, intending W, X, and Y. B votes aye, intending W, X, and Z. C votes no. A would have voted no had he been presented with B's definition as his only choice. B would have voted no had he been presented with A's definition as his only choice. Moreover, a truncated version of T, one that covered only W and X and neither Y nor Z, would likewise have been rejected. It is clear in this case that we have no majority of the authorities in favor of any possible meaning of T, even though we have a majority in favor of T itself.[17]

---

[16] *See* Kenneth J. Arrow, *Social Choice and Individual Values* (2d ed., New Haven: Yale University Press 1963). Arrow established that democratic procedures for determining policy cannot avoid the possibility of the following dilemma. When the policy choices are A, B, and C, and the voters are V_1, V_2, and V_3, it is possible for V_1 and V_2 to favor A over B; it is possible for V_2 and V_3 to favor B over C; and it is possible for V_1 and V_3 to favor C over A. Id. at 2–3. In such a situation, majority rule produces indeterminate results. Id. at 3, 51–59. Every policy a majority favors can be trumped by another policy favored by a different majority in an endless cycle. Unless restrictions are placed on the voters' agenda, extra weight is given to some voters' votes, or some other objectionable constraints are placed on the voters, this possibility of endless cycling is unavoidable. Id. at 22–31.

[17] *See* Kenneth A. Shepsle, *Congress Is a "They," Not an "It": Legislative Intent as an Oxymoron,* 12 *Int. Rev. Law Econ.* 239 (1992).

Or consider a simple case of ambiguity, such as would occur if there were an ordinance forbidding "canards in the park." A voted for it to prohibit lying. B voted for it to prohibit ducks. C voted against it, as would have A or B had "canard" clearly meant what the others intended by it.

One way to handle such cases of failed law is to bite the bullet and say that, despite appearances to the contrary, those legal texts are not laws. They are only apparent laws.

Alternatively, one might decide that having apparent laws on the books is undesirable for two related reasons. First, the existence of apparent laws confronts those subject to the laws with the specter of uncertainty. In many or most cases, it will be difficult for the average subject of the laws to determine if a particular law is real and meaningful or only apparent. The uncertainty implicates the rule-of-law value of accessibility.

Second, the existence of apparent laws and the consequent uncertainty makes it difficult for legal authorities to carry out their function. For if they are uncertain about the content of the existing laws, they will be severely handicapped in deciding how best to legislate.

It might be desirable, therefore, to have norms that direct official interpreters to breathe meaning into laws that are actually meaningless – in effect, to adopt the language of the existing laws but to "reauthor" those laws so that the laws reflect the interpreters' determinations of what ought to be done (within the constraints of the norms of form). Such norms would make the official interpreters into the primary rule makers, though constrained by the earlier rule makers' choice of language.[18] Although many commentators propose such norms, they frequently make the mistake of conflating actions taken in pursuance of such norms with *interpretation* of the statutes or constitutional provisions that exhibit the failure of law. Those statutes and constitutional provisions are not being interpreted, however, for interpretation would conclude that they are meaningless marks. Rather, the statutes and constitutional provisions are being reauthored by a new set of legal rule makers.

---

[18] Note that the same problem of failed law would arise with respect to the interpreters' determinations if the interpreters were multimember bodies, such as appellate courts.

Again, it should be emphasized that, as with substantive norms, these norms of form and of failed law must be the products of a decision-making body that possesses higher authority than the rule maker to which they apply. That is so again because these norms lead to departures from the norm-constrained rule maker's intended meaning regarding what ought to be done. And, just as with the substantive norms, these norms of form and of failed law themselves mean what the higher-authority decision maker intends their meaning to be.

3. Levels of Generality of Rule Makers' Intentions

It is a common observation that the intentions of legal authorities can be described at various levels of generality. Thus, rule makers may intend a law to accomplish specific results R in order to further a more general purpose P, which purpose furthers a still more general purpose P', which purpose furthers Goodness and Justice. The rule makers think those various intentions are consistent, which is why they passed the law in question. The intentions may turn out to be inconsistent in the view of those interpreting the law, and inconsistent at any level. Thus, R may not in fact further P, P may not in fact further P', and P' may in fact be inconsistent with Goodness and Justice. So some people believe that this raises the question, If the interpreters are to give effect to what the authoring rule makers intended, at what level of generality should that intention be described?[19]

[19] An excellent case for illustrating how the possibility of describing the authorities' intentions at various levels can affect judicial decision making is the U.S. Supreme Court's decision in Home Building & Loan Assoc. v. Blaisdell, 290 U.S. 298 (1934). Blaisdell dealt with a Minnesota mortgage moratorium law that was challenged as violative of the clause in Art. I, §10, forbidding the passage of any law "impairing the obligation of contracts." Justice Sutherland, dissenting from the Court's decision upholding the law's constitutionality, pointed out that not only was the law violative of the contract's clause's literal command, but it was exactly the type of law that the authors of the contract clause had in mind when the clause was drafted, that is, a debtor-relief law enacted in a period of economic depression. Id. at 448–50, 472. Chief Justice Hughes, on the other hand, writing for the majority, characterized the intent behind the contract clause at a higher level of generality. According to Hughes, the authors intended to proscribe debtor-relief laws that were unreasonable (427–43). Although they may have thought all such laws were unreasonable, even in depressions, their intention was only to proscribe unreasonable laws. See also Andrei Marmor, Interpretation and Legal Theory 144–45 (Oxford: Clarendon Press 1992); David O. Brink, Legal Theory, Legal Interpretation, and Judicial Review, 17 Phil. & Public Affs. 105, 126–29 (1988).

Some believe that this question can be answered only by reference to an interpretive norm chosen because of its anticipated good results, and that the question cannot be answered in the absence of such a norm. They believe that when the intentions at the various levels of generality of description are inconsistent with each other, there is no fact of the matter about what the rule makers intended. What they intended is rather the product of whatever norm selects the appropriate level of generality at which to characterize their intention.[20]

We believe that view to be mistaken, as we made clear in the preceding chapter.[21] A norm that directs interpreters to correct rule makers' mistakes regarding how their actual intended meanings square with their more general purposes is one that threatens completely to undermine the rule makers' role of determining what ought to be done. Because rule makers always intend to achieve Goodness and Justice – to "do the right thing" – if they are acting legitimately, the interpreter can substitute his own views about what Goodness and Justice require for any specific intended meaning of the rule makers and still claim to be honoring their (more general) intent. For the interpreter will undoubtedly believe that, had the rule makers been disabused of all their mistakes of fact, mistakes of means-end reasoning, and mistakes in reasoning about values, they would have enacted (intended to mean) what the interpreter would have enacted (intended to mean). In effect, a norm allowing the

For a different constitutional implication of the various levels of generality of the intentions of authorities, *see* Note, *Legislative Purpose, Rationality, and Equal Protection*, 82 *Yale L.J.* 123 (1972).

[20] Perhaps the foremost proponent of the view that what authorities intend is not a matter of fact but rather the product of normative argument is Ronald Dworkin. *See, e.g.,* Ronald Dworkin, *Bork's Jurisprudence*, 57 *U. of Chi. L. Rev.* 657, 663–64 (1990). This is also the official view of Cass Sunstein, though he equivocates at points. *Cf.* Sunstein, *supra*, n. 6, at 10 ("Statutes do not have pre-interpretive meanings, and the process of interpretation requires courts to draw on background principles"), with id. at 423, 434, 450, 456 (implying that statutes do have meanings that are independent of background principles). For a view similar to Sunstein's official view, *see* Note, *Figuring the Law: Holism and Tropological Inference in Legal Interpretation*, 97 *Yale L.J.* 823 (1988).

For a good statement of the opposing view, the one that I now endorse, *see* Paul Campos, *Against Constitutional Theory*, 4 *Yale J. L. & Human.* 279, 281–82 (arguing that interpretation is an empirical matter, not a theoretical one, because it seeks to uncover the "fact" of the author's intention). *See also* Paul Campos, *That Obscure Object of Desire: Hermeneutics and the Autonomous Legal Text*, 77 *Minn. L. Rev.* 1065, 1092–93 (1993).

[21] *See* Chapter 5 at notes 25–44.

interpreter to disregard the more specific intended meanings in favor of more general purposes will convert the interpreter into the rule maker (and, of course, make the interpreter's determination subject to being corrected by a subsequent interpreter, and so on).[22] As we said earlier, in our discussion of Lessig's theory of interpretation,[23] if the rule makers' mistakes are always to be corrected by interpreters, then there will be no rule makers: if the interpreters are tantamount to the rule makers, there can never be rule makers for interpreters to interpret.

One might reply that although a norm directing interpreters to follow the rule maker's most general purposes would undermine that rule maker's role, a norm directing interpreters to follow the purposes characterized at some intermediate level of generality would not undermine that role. The interpreters could correct the rule maker's specific intended meaning by reference to somewhat more general purposes, but not by reference to Goodness and Justice.

There are two problems with such a response, however. First, to speak of levels of generality of purpose as if there were a discrete number of ways the rule maker's purposes could be described is in some ways quite misleading. There is no one way to describe the levels of generality or to count them. Thus, it is impossible for a norm to specify the precise level of generality interpreters should look to in following the rule maker's purposes.

Second, and more important, the choice to correct the rule maker's specific intended meaning in light of the rule maker's more general purposes but not in light of the rule maker's most general ones seems quite arbitrary. In some cases, for example, the rule maker might specifically intend a meaning that is inconsistent with a more general purpose she has, but which is in fact consistent with Goodness and Justice. In such a case she has done the right thing, although she has made two mistakes in reasoning from means to ends that happily cancel each other. The hypothesized norm directing interpreters to follow the rule maker's purposes characterized at an intermediate level of generality would result in

---

[22] *See* Richard A. Epstein, *A Common Lawyer Looks at Constitutional Interpretation,* 72 *Boston L. Rev.* 699, 703 (1992). "The critical point is that theories of . . . interpretation are not theories of substantive transformation. No one should be able to win through interpretation what was lost in the initial drafting."

[23] *See* Chapter 5 at notes 45–64.

the interpreters acting contrary to Goodness and Justice when the rule maker, having made some lucky mistakes, actually intends a policy that is consistent with Goodness and Justice.

Nonetheless, if there were no fact of the matter regarding what the rule maker intended in the sense of at what level of generality to characterize that intent, we would have no choice but to construct a norm that would prescribe the level of generality for interpreters to follow.[24] In our view, however, there *is* a fact of the matter. For example, there is a fact of the matter by virtue of which it is true that the rule maker did not intend to proscribe declawed, defanged pet bears escaping a fire but did intend to proscribe pandas even if that turns out to be a mistaken weighing of liberty and security. If we are correct, then the role of rule-making authorities demands that that fact of the matter be heeded.

This facticity about what the rule makers determined ought to be done in the face of the various levels of generality at which their purposes could be described is what makes formal legal rules – rules that are opaque to their background purposes – possible. If there is a fact of the matter about what the rule makers determined ought to be done, then that fact, possibly as filtered through norms of form and norms for failed laws, should guide interpreters. Otherwise, interpreters are not interpreting, and the role of the rule-making authorities does not exist.

Thus, we believe that despite their having purposes of varying degrees of generality that can come apart, the rule makers' intended meanings are not a function of the interpreter's *choice*. Rather, as we argued in the preceding chapter, there is a *fact* of the matter regarding intended meaning; and the rule makers' intended meaning is, obviously, a function of the *rule makers'* choice, not the interpreter's. Moreover, there needs always to be the possibility for intended meaning and more general purposes to come apart in order for there to be determinate rules that perform the morally demanded settlement function.[25]

It is always possible that the search for the rule maker's intended meaning will result in various infelicities. And it is always possible that

---

[24] Of course, if there were no fact of the matter regarding the level of generality of the authorities' intentions, there might well not be a fact of the matter regarding the words or even the language through which they intended to communicate, which would leave interpretation with nothing to characterize at any level of generality.

[25] *See* Chapter 1 *infra*.

higher-order norms will help minimize or negate such infelicities. Substantive higher-order norms can combat substantive infelicities, such as rules whose intended meanings are absurd, unjust, or obsolete. The higher-order norms could themselves be determinate *rules*: for example, "No statute shall be effective one hundred years after enactment." Or they could be *standards*: for example, "No statute shall be given effect if it is absurd, unjust, or obsolete." In the latter case, the higher-order norm delegates decision-making authority to some other institution – the interpreting one – to determine what is absurd, unjust, and not obsolete. The attempted settlement by the body whose rule is deemed absurd, unjust, or obsolete will be undone. The interpreting institution may itself at least partially settle the meaning of absurd, unjust, or obsolete, or it may just leave the meanings of those standards unsettled except insofar as the particular rule is concerned.[26]

Procedural higher-order norms can deal with rules that have no intended meaning ("failed laws") or that have an inaccessible meaning. Application of these higher-order norms is *not* interpretation of the rules. Interpretation is the recovery of the rule maker's intended meaning. Higher-order procedural norms do not aid in that endeavor and are not meant to do so. They direct "interpreters" to construct rules out of materials that the rule makers have provided. If, in the example of "No canards are allowed in the park," the interpreter treats the rule as outlawing ducks but not lies, or vice versa, or both ducks and lies, that is not because any of those is the rule's intended meaning. And if, in the case of a statute written in a private code, a higher norm directs the "interpreter" to assume the statute's intended meaning is what its intended meaning would be were the legislators to intend the first meaning given in a standard English dictionary of their time, then the meaning that the "interpreter" will assign is not the statute's intended meaning but a meaning that is the product of the marks on the page that the legislature produced coupled with a higher-order norm.

In the next chapter, when we examine textualism, we argue that norms of form such as the hypothetical norm "read as if in standard

---

[26] As we point out in Chapter 8, however, standards that do not constrain their delegations by cabining them with determinate rules threaten to undermine completely the settlement function of law. Therefore, any delegation to a body such as a court to set aside rules on the grounds of their injustice is usually read to be hemmed in by rules that themselves cannot be set aside on such grounds.

English" are less attractive than they might appear. The other higher-order norms we have mentioned may or may not be worth having. We take no position on those. But even if they are, neither they nor the infelicities they are meant to address cast any doubt on our central claim – namely, that interpretation of legal rules is a search for the rule maker's intended meaning and is no different from the interpretation of ordinary demands and requests.[27]

---

[27] Again, we point out that these higher-order norms mean what *their* authors intend them to mean, whether their authors are a higher-order rule-making body, such as constitutional ratifiers, or the people themselves acting through acceptance of preconstitutional norms.

VII

Nonintentionalist Interpretation

We have argued to this point that the interpretation of canonical legal texts, whether those texts are authored by individual lawmakers or by multimember ones, is at bottom no different from interpreting demands or requests in other domains of life. Requests from Mom or the kids, memos from the boss, and indeed all communications that we take to be normative boil down to what the language in its context reveals about what the speaker intended for us to do. In other words, our question is always, What meaning did the speaker or speakers intend? And, we argued, given the role of legal authorities to settle what ought to be done and to do so with expertise and, in the case of legislatures, democratic warrant, the interpretation of legal rules should also be viewed as the search for the speaker's intended meaning.[1]

---

[1] Andrei Marmor, *Interpretation and Legal Theory* 132–39 (2d ed., Oxford: Hart Pub. 2005).

If legal reasoning in the domain of interpreting canonical legal texts is to be "special" – a craft that only legal training and practice can provide – then the intentionalist position we endorse must be rejected. We are all "trained" to practice that, as all of us engage in it all the time. And, indeed, there are challengers to intentionalism in the legal literature. In this chapter we take up the two principal challengers: textualism and dynamic interpretation.

I. Textualism

Textualism is actually a family of theories of legal interpretation. What unites them is their stress on the primacy of the text of the constitution, statute, administrative rule, or judicial precedent in question. For the textualist, the text's meaning always trumps the "private" intended meaning of the text's author(s).

Our reply to the textualists comes in two stages. In stage one, extending the argument of Chapter 5, we show the impossibility of "pure" textualism, meaning the total primacy of text over authorial intent. In stage two, we show that impure textualists, the only possible kind, are either those who would construct – and hence reauthor – legal rules out of raw materials provided by the original author(s) of the legal texts, or those who are intentionalists but who impose limits on the evidence of intent that interpreters may consult.

A. THE IMPOSSIBILITY OF PURE (INTENTION-FREE) TEXTUALISM

Self-described "textualists" hold a variety of positions on how one ought to interpret legal texts. Indeed, there does not appear to be any canonical description of textualism. At most, what unites textualists is their stated refusal to consider the intentions of the laws' authors to determine what the laws mean. We shall argue that such intention-free textualism is a conceptual impossibility – that authorial intentions constitute the meanings of texts. If we are right, a charitable reading of textualists' statements would not attribute intention-free textualism to them. Nevertheless, at times, self-described textualists say things that appear to endorse intention-free textualism.

Consider the most famous modern textualist, Justice Antonin Scalia, and his discussion of textualism in *A Matter of Interpretation*.[2] Justice Scalia's version of textualism seems to have three principal tenets. The first is that a textualist searches for an "objectified" intent – the intent an idealized reader who knows the entire corpus juris would gather from the particular statute.[3] The second is that textualists do not seek to enforce the "subjective intent of the enacting legislature."[4] The third is that legislative history should not be used as "an authoritative indication of a statute's meaning."[5]

The first is the most important principle, as the other two follow from it. The reason for searching for an "objectified" intent is "that it is simply incompatible with democratic government, or indeed, even with fair government, to have the meaning of a law determined by what the lawgiver meant, rather than by what the lawgiver promulgated."[6] After all, "[i]t is the *law* that governs, not the intent of the lawgiver."[7] Legislators may intend whatever they want, "but it is only the laws that they enact which bind us."[8] To govern by "unexpressed intent" is tyrannical in the same sense that Nero's posting of laws high up a pillar was so: people will not be able to make sense of the law if they try to discern the subjective intent of the legislature.[9]

Justice Scalia derives the second principle from an examination of what judges actually do in practice. If the intent of the legislature mattered, then judges would not apply the rule that "when the text of a statute is clear, that is the end of the matter."[10] Likewise, if legislative intent were the touchstone, judges would not assume that the enacting legislature was aware of all existing laws. Instead, they would pay attention to the text and the legislative history of the particular statute in isolation, for that is all the legislators likely had in mind.[11]

---

[2] Antonin Scalia, *A Matter of Interpretation: Federal Courts and the Law* (Princeton: Princeton University Press 1997).

[3] Id. at 17.

[4] Id.

[5] Id. at 29–30.

[6] Id. at 17.

[7] Id.

[8] Id.

[9] Id.

[10] Id. at 16.

[11] Id. at 16–17.

The third principle follows directly from the first. If only objectified intent matters, then legislative history, which yields only indications of *subjective* intent, should not be viewed as relevant.[12] But, argues
Scalia, even if legislative intent were the touchstone of statutory interpretation, we should not look to legislative history to discern legislative
intent. To begin with, on most contested matters brought before a court,
there will be no legislative intent. On relatively detailed matters, it is,
according to Scalia, "a virtual certainty [that] the majority was blissfully
unaware of the *existence* of the issue, much less had any preference as
to how it should be resolved."[13] Moreover, legislative history is likely to
be a highly unreliable indicator of any legislative intent that might exist.
Members of Congress often do not read committee reports, much less
prepare them.[14]

Justice Scalia's explication of textualism raises a series of questions.
Is his version of textualism a quest for the intentions of the legislature with certain evidence barred from consideration (like legislative history), or is legislative intent completely irrelevant even when
known with certainty? It appears on balance that Justice Scalia adopts
the latter approach – actual legislative intent is always irrelevant.[15] We
are unsure whether Justice Scalia is truly an intention-free textualist,
however, because of his use of the concept of "objectified intent." To
speak of objectified intent might be to acknowledge that the intent of
some author matters. Nonetheless, his reference to "objectified" intent,
when placed in the context of the other statements just quoted, can
be taken to mean that the text is meaningful apart from the actual
author's intent.[16]

---

[12] Id. at 30–31.
[13] Id. at 32.
[14] Id. at 32–34.
[15] However, at times Justice Scalia writes as if legislative intent does matter. *See* id. at 20–21
(discussing scrivener's error doctrine and declaring that it is okay to correct statutes where
there is a mistaken expression). We read his discussion of scrivener's error as evincing concern
for actual legislative intent, at least where there is supposedly a clear mistake of expression.
Properly speaking, if legislative intent did not matter at all, statutes could not contain errors.
After all, to speak of scrivener's "error" or of legislative misspeaking is to suggest that what
matters is not the objective meaning of the text but the intent of the person(s) who erred.
[16] That is, if intent plays a role in Scalia's textualism. Scalia might believe that interpreters ought
to search for the intentions of some idealized author.

Our object here, however, is not exegetical. We do not care whether Justice Scalia or other textualists, such as John Manning,[17] really are intention-free textualists. What we want to show is that such a position is a conceptual impossibility. We leave it to others to determine if any self-described textualist actually holds the position we discredit.

1. Argument One: Texts Cannot Declare the Language in Which They Are Written

One cannot attribute meaning to marks on a page or to sounds without reference to an author, actual or idealized, who is intending to communicate a meaning through the marks or sounds. Consider the question of how to identify the relevant language of some communication. Intention-free textualists cannot explain how they identify the language of the text they wish to interpret. Apparently, they assume that identifying the relevant language is unproblematic. Seeing the word "canard," an intention-free textualist who speaks English will assert that the word means "fib." After all, that is the ordinary, public meaning that would come to mind for the well-informed, reasonable English speaker. But a French textualist will attribute a different meaning to the word. To the French intention-free textualist, "canard" clearly means "duck," because that is the ordinary, public meaning for the well-informed, reasonable French speaker. Which of these intention-free textualists is right? We believe that intention-free textualists cannot meaningfully answer this question.[18]

---

[17] Manning has claimed that intent is a necessary concept for textualists. *See* John F. Manning, *Textualism and the Equity of the Statute,* 101 *Colum. L. Rev.* 1, 16–17 n. 65 (2001). He suggests that the interpreter is to imagine a legislature that enacts laws against a backdrop of interpretive conventions establishing the actual legislative intent as irrelevant. *See id.* Thus, the interpreter is supposed to assume hypothetical legislators who intend that their subjective intentions be irrelevant in interpreting the statutes they pass. We doubt the coherence of a legislature's intention that its own intentions be disregarded. The position is paradoxical.

[18] It is possible that if textualists might claim that both textualists in our hypothetical are right. It all depends upon the audience one assumes. If one assumes the relevant audience speaks English, then the reasonable person in that audience would read "canard" as "fib." But this gives up the game because it constitutes an admission that there is no objectified meaning. Indeed, even within a particular language one can narrow the audience in a number of ways and yield different meanings. Of course, it is our contention that the correct audience to assume is *that audience that would attribute the meaning intended by the author(s).*

Along the same lines, consider the following amusingly bewilder-
ing statement: "I am speaking English, not Schmenglish," which in
Schmenglish means "I am speaking Schmenglish, not English." Is this
statement in English or Schmenglish, and how will intention-free textualists decide? Once again, we do not believe that intention-free textualists
have an answer, or at least an answer that does not smuggle in reference
to authorial intent.

Our claim is that we must posit the existence of some author if
we are to attribute meaning to these statements. If we know that the
real author of "canard" generally speaks French, we most likely would
conclude that "canard" in this context means "duck." If the author usually
speaks English, we most likely would conclude that it means "fib." If we
are unaware of (or indifferent to) the author's usual tongue (and likely
intentions), we may imagine what we would have meant had we spoken
the term, imagining ourselves as the authors.

This is not merely a problem across languages. Even within English,
these issues arise. If someone walks into a restaurant and declares "I
would like some chips," what is meant by "chips"? Once again, we
think we should understand "chips" by reference to the intentions of
the speaker. If he is American, we might assume he means something
like potato or tortilla chips. If he is English, we might assume that he
means what Americans generally call french fries. If we do not care about
satisfying the speaker's request, we might decide that the sentence means
what it would had a techie uttered it, in which case "chips" might refer
to microchips.[19]

2. Argument Two: Texts Cannot Declare That They Are Texts

An even more fundamental problem for intention-free textualists is that
texts cannot declare that they are texts or even declare which part of
the putative text constitutes the text. Suppose a monkey typed the U.S.

---

[19] Textualists are likely to respond that modern textualism takes into account the "context" in
which the language was spoken or written, thereby eliminating some of the indeterminacy
and indicating whether microchips, potato chips, or fries is the proper meaning. As we
explain later, we believe that invocations of context amount to unacknowledged invocations
of authorial intent.

Constitution in our casebook. Are the ink marks made by the typewriter keys a text? We think not, unless one posits a hypothetical author with intent to convey a meaning. Without an author, real or hypothetical, intending to convey a meaning through these marks, our seemingly grand Constitution is nothing but a randomly generated mass of inked shapes that merely resembles a text. Or suppose a Martian composed the Constitution in our casebook, and that Martians treat what we take to be spaces between letters and words as the actual letters and words and regard what we take to be letters and words as the actual spaces. If that supposition is correct, then the "text" in our casebook is quite different from the text that we assume. The text that we assume to exist is actually no different in kind from meaningless marks made by waves on the beach or by cloud formations in the sky; it is merely the meaningless residue of the Martian's text.

Our simple point is that one cannot look at the marks on a page and understand those marks to be a text (i.e., a meaningful writing) without assuming that an author made those marks intending to convey a meaning by them. The reason why no one treats the Constitution as a bunch of unintelligible lines and curves is because everyone assumes a particular kind of author for the Constitution. A few originalists latch onto the Constitution's actual drafters (the Framers); others focus on those who purported to make it law (the Ratifiers); perhaps a majority insist on a search for "original meaning," referring thereby to the meaning that an idealized, contemporary reader would have attributed to the document.[20] "Living Constitution" advocates typically assume an author with the desires and fears that animate *them* and hence read the Constitution as if *they* had written it. Still others seem to rely upon multiple authors, sometimes reading portions of the Constitution as it would have been understood by the Founders, and other times reading the Constitution as if it were written yesterday by a modern, well-meaning chap – in other words, by them. Whenever someone reads the Constitution or any other

---

[20] *See also* Abner S. Greene, *The Missing Step of Textualism*, 74 *Fordham L.J.* 1913, 1926–29 (2006). Given our argument about the necessity of envisioning an author, the idealized reader contemplated by some originalists will have to hypothesize an author (actual or idealized) to make sense of a putative text. Hence, the idealized-reader construct does not eliminate the need for some kind of author from which one can derive meaning.

text, he explicitly or implicitly does so with an author in mind. *And he has no choice but to do so.*

3. Argument Three: Meaning Cannot Be Autonomous from Intent – One Must Always Identify an Author

This argument builds upon the previous one. Consider some people who come upon marks on the ground that are shaped like a *c,* an *a,* and a *t.* They begin to debate whether the marks mean "domestic tabby cat," "any feline," or "jazz musician." They are then told that the marks were made by water dripping off a building. Their debate over meaning should now cease: no author, no meaning.[21]

Suppose now that they know that a person made the marks. They encounter him and tell him of their debate. He tells them that he never intended to make letters. Rather, he was marking out the contours of patches of a vegetable garden. The debate over meaning ought to cease: no intended meaning, no meaning.

Now suppose that the person did seek to make a word. The people debate the meaning of "cat." The "author" then informs them that he was writing an ode to his beloved tabby. That should settle the debate: "cat" here means tabby. The alternatives – any feline and jazz musician – are just as much off the table as they were in the previous examples of no author and no intended meaning.

The same point applies to other examples of "mindless" "texts." If "trunk" is produced by an elephant who paints with his trunk, or by legislators each drawing letters randomly from a hat, it is useless to ask whether it means the main axis of a tree, the rear storage compartment of a car, or the nose of an elephant, or even what language it is in. Without an author who intends a meaning, such marks are meaningless. "Texts"

---

[21] If they continue to debate the meaning, they must be debating what the marks would have meant if, contrary to fact, an author intending to convey a meaning had made them. Because they are each free to imagine a different hypothetical author, there is no single correct answer to the question they are debating. Only if they agree on the characteristics of a hypothetical author – for example, what would most jazz columnists have meant by "cat" – does it become answerable. But notice that even if they play this game, they are not debating the meaning of the marks made by the dripping water; rather, they are debating what the marks would have meant had they been made (or appropriated) by particular people intending to convey some meaning thereby.

without authors and intended meanings are not texts; and texts *with*
intended meanings are texts *only with respect to the intended meanings.*[22]

4. Argument Four: Texts Can Have "Deviant" Meanings Because Those Meanings Are Intended

How did "cat" come to mean jazz musician? Because it was used by
some people with the intent that it be understood as referring to a
jazz musician. That is ultimately how all words acquire their meanings.
And the word "cat" meant jazz musician the very first time it was used
with such an intention, even before it was listed as a definition in the
dictionary. Similarly, if a speaker says "Gleeg, gleeg, gleeg," it means
what the speaker intended it to mean, even if to others it sounds like
nonsense.[23] And if your mom is Mrs. Malaprop, and she asks you to make
sure the "autobahn" is pulled next to the sofa when she comes to visit
you – and you know that she intends for you to move the "ottoman" –
then if you are a dutiful child, you will pull up the ottoman and not
attempt to relocate a German highway.[24] "Strategery" has entered into
common use (at least in some circles) as a synonym for "strategy." It
acquired that meaning as soon as Will Farrell of *Saturday Night Live* so
used it; and it continues to have that meaning because President Bush,
his political aides, and the public continue so to use it.

---

[22] Put a different way, texts are individuated by their intended meanings. Consider the word
"cats" that we cut out of a magazine article on "The Big Cats of Africa" and paste it into
our ode to tabbies. In the magazine article, those marks meant one thing – lions, leopards,
and cheetahs – because that is what the article's author meant by them. In our poem,
those identical marks mean something else because that is what we intend by them. The
marks themselves contribute to two different texts, distinguished by two different authorial
intentions. They are capable of bearing an infinite number of meanings, just as an infinite
number of marks, sounds, or other forms of conduct are capable of referring to lions or to
tabbies.
  By contrast, the shape of the marks in the Constitution found in the National Archives
varies from the shape of the marks in the Constitution found in most casebooks or indeed
the Spanish translation of the U.S. Constitution. Yet we take these various marks to mean
the same thing because we assume the same authors with the same intention.
[23] "Gleeg, gleeg, gleeg" is the attempt at a reductio that textualists throw up at intentionalists.
The problem is that it is *not* reductio. "Gleeg, gleeg, gleeg" can be as meaningful as the
third-base coach's pulling on his cap with the successful intent to convey the idea "Bunt!"
[24] Is Mrs. Malaprop misspeaking in English, or is she speaking "Malapropenglish"? Is slang
that has yet to be validated by the *Oxford English Dictionary* "English" or something else?
We cannot see that this is answerable in any way other than by arbitrary stipulation. What
we *can* say is that it does not matter insofar as we are trying to discern what Ms. Malaprop
means by "autobahn."

B. IMPURE TEXTUALISM AND THE CONSTRUCTION
OF RULES BY "INTERPRETERS"

1. The Algorithmic Textualist

When confronted with the conceptual impossibility of pure, intention-free textualism, textualists usually retreat to a less pure position. They admit that we must refer to authorial intentions to determine that the marks we are supposed to interpret do in fact constitute a text – an attempt by some rational being or beings to convey a meaningful proposition to others. And they go further and admit that we must refer to authorial intent to determine in what language the text is written (or spoken).[25] At this point, however, the textualists claim that we should jettison the search for the speaker's intended meaning and rely solely on the textual (utterance) meaning.

So how would a textualist interpret a canonical legal text? After she ascertains that it is in, say, English, she would have recourse solely to dictionaries and books that set forth proper grammar, punctuation, and usage. Those, she argues, tell us what the utterance – the text – means, not what its author(s) intended to mean by the text. And the text is "the law."

---

[25] Walter Sinnott-Armstrong, although not taking sides in the intentionalism-textualism debate, does argue that once we know what language a text's author was intending to use, we can dispense with authorial intent and employ word meanings in that language. *See* Walter Sinnott-Armstrong, *Word Meaning in Legal Interpretation*, 42 *San Diego L. Rev.* 465, 471–77 (2005). We think, however, that leaving aside the normative issues and problems of ambiguity, incorrect grammar, and the like, the position Sinnott-Armstrong gestures toward rests on an oversimplification. Only in unusual cases – say, when a speaker is in a foreign country and must choose between speaking in the local language or in his native tongue – does a speaker or author intend a language. In the usual case, he just intends to say something. And as we pointed out, the line between a language spoken incorrectly and an idiolect spoken correctly will be arbitrary. *See* note 24 *supra*. That we can draw such a line for particular purposes – as, say, when we examine students on their French – does not refute the point.

Consider this stylized case. Frankie, an American, encounters a stranger, Johnny, in Tanzania. Frankie, believing Johnny to be a speaker of Swahili, decides to ask Johnny in Swahili for directions to Arusha. Unfortunately, Frankie's Swahili is terrible. She believes that the proper question in Swahili is, "Wich wā tū Arusha?" Actually, in Swahili that means "I want to flee Arusha." But Johnny, who in fact speaks English, takes her to be asking for directions to Arusha, which was, of course, Frankie's intended meaning. Johnny has in fact understood Frankie perfectly. If, realizing she is attempting to speak Swahili, he tells her what she would have been requesting had she been a competent Swahili speaker, he is being perverse.

The first point to note about this impure textualism is that, if one employs its methodology, "the law" is constructed not solely by the authorities who author it but by those authorities together with a "mindless" algorithm. The mindless algorithm is a function of the dictionary and grammar book that are used to construct a meaning out of the author's intended symbols and intended language. Mom utters the sounds or makes the marks "autobahn"; the faithful interpreter runs a German highway through the den. Mom did not mean *that*, and we know she did not. Nevertheless, the textualist would claim that her *text* meant that. (We leave aside the problem to which we have previously adverted of individuating languages and distinguishing between a language and idiolects thereof: did Mom misspeak in English, or did she speak correctly in Menglish, either her particular idiolect of English or perhaps even a separate language?)

Of course, many words have several meanings, even in standard English. So the algorithm should specify which meaning counts as *the* meaning of the text when the dictionary delivers more than one possible meaning. For example, the algorithm might say that the first listed meaning of the word is the meaning to be attributed to the text.[26]

The textualist's algorithm would, of course, have to be a norm higher in authority than the lawmaker whose texts are being interpreted because the algorithm operates as a constraint on the rule maker's ability to shape the legal universe as he intends to shape it. Textualist canons are to the laws they govern as constitutional rules are to statutory rules, or statutory rules are to administrative or judicial (nonconstitutional) rules.

So let us hypothesize the following textualist algorithm: once marks are determined to be a legal text in English, give them the meaning they would have according to the first meanings given in a particular dictionary and according to particular references for grammar, punctuation, and usage. What would a world governed by textualist algorithms such as this one look like?

For one thing, many legal rules, the intended meaning of which we know perfectly well, would have to be treated as meaningless and thus

---

[26] There is a joke about Justice Scalia asking a genie to grant him the wish that "a million bucks" be deposited in his Supreme Court office and later complaining that he could not enter the building because of all the deer inside.

of no legal effect because they would not parse grammatically or syntactically, or because a word was misspelled and rendered a nonword.[27] Other laws would have to be given meanings that we know were not the intended meanings and that may be absurd. Scrivener's errors could not be ignored, and in *Cernauskas v. Fletcher*,[28] all of Arkansas's laws would have been repealed by some minor law containing a scrivener's error. The Seventeenth Amendment would have expired after only six years.[29] And so on.

Textualists, of course, would argue that legal rule makers, understanding the effects of the textualist algorithms, would be very careful in conveying their intended meanings so that they corresponded to the meanings the textualist algorithms produced. And perhaps, over time, scrivener's errors and errors regarding dictionary meanings, punctuation, and grammar would be minimized. Indeed, putting impure textualism in its best light, interpreters might arrive at the rule maker's intended meaning more often by following the textualist algorithms than by consciously attempting to discover those intended meanings. In other words, algorithmic textualist interpreters, interpreting the words of rule makers who understand that their interpreters will be algorithmic textualists and, accordingly, choose their words (and punctuation marks) with great care, may come closer to the rule makers' intended meanings over the full array of cases than intentionalist interpreters. That all depends on the skills of interpreters at discerning intended meanings and the skills of rule makers at conveying intended meanings in conformance with the textualist algorithms.

Of course, if the textualist algorithms are incomplete – suppose they cannot completely eliminate ambiguity – then they will have to be

---

[27] We are reminded of a Gary Larson cartoon that by itself is a reductio of intention-free textualism. In it, a plane is flying over a desert island on which a haggard, disheveled man has carved in the sand H-E-L-F and is now waving his arms at the plane. The caption, representing the copilot's words to the pilot, reads "Wait! Wait! . . . Cancel that, I guess it says 'helf.'" The copilot is obviously a committed intention-free textualist. *See* Larry Alexander, *All or Nothing at All? The Intentions of Authorities and the Authority of Intentions*, in *Law and Interpretation: Essays in Legal Philosophy* 336 (Andrei Marmor, ed., Oxford: Clarendon Press 1995).

[28] 21 Ark. 678, 201 S.W. 2d 999 (1947) (holding that law containing the fractured boilerplate "all laws . . . are hereby repealed" did not in fact repeal all of Arkansas's laws).

[29] U.S. Const. amend. XVII, § 1: "The Senate of the United States shall be composed of two Senators from each state, elected by the people thereof, for six years; and each Senator shall have one vote."

supplemented. If, for example, the algorithms do not eliminate an ambiguity regarding whether a word in a legal text means A or B, perhaps because the dictionary treats a single spelling as two different words rather than as one word with several definitions, then the interpreter will have to go beyond the algorithms. Indeed, it's hard to imagine that any algorithm can be constructed that will completely eliminate ambiguity. Does "No vehicles are allowed in the park" cover a tank used as a war memorial, skateboards, and shopping carts? Does the "no bears" rule we hypothesized proscribe a stuffed grizzly hunting trophy? If we are told not to decide such issues by reference to authorial intentions but rather to decide them solely by reference to dictionaries and so forth, we will be at sea. Likewise, in cases of ambiguity, the natural question for the interpreter to ask is whether the rule maker meant A or B. But perhaps the rule maker meant neither A nor B. In such a case, authorial intent clashes with textualist algorithms, and the latter fail to settle the matter.

Perhaps textualist algorithms can be constructed so that no cases such as the one hypothesized can arise. No ambiguities will be possible; the algorithms will produce a single answer to every interpretive question. And perhaps following such textualist algorithms will, over the run of cases, come closer to mirroring authorial intentions than attempts to discover those intentions directly. That is a question that cannot be decided as a matter of theory. But even if such algorithms are possible and beneficial, the important point for our purposes is this: to the extent the legally effective meaning is a joint product of authorial intentions (in choosing marks in a language) and textualist algorithms, it is in part a mindless production, and at the interpretive stage a purely mindless matter. And mindless, mechanical construction of meaning for legal texts through such algorithms requires absolutely no judgment and surely no special craft skill possessed only by lawyers. It is not some sort of special "legal" reasoning. Indeed, if it bears the label of "reasoning" at all, it is reasoning of the most elementary, connect-the-dots type. What does require judgment or skill is determining authors' intended meanings. But such abilities are abilities everyone has to varying degrees, and lawyers have no corner on that market.

Moreover, although impure textualism, unlike pure, intention-free textualism, is a conceptual possibility – it is really a form of intentionalism that posits, as the author of the legal text in question, not the actual author(s), but a purely hypothetical author who has perfect command of grammar, punctuation, and usage and who always uses, say, the first dictionary definition given – legal systems with which we are familiar do not employ impure textualism. Surely no jurisdiction within the United States employs it. Clearly unintended absurdities and scrivener's errors are everywhere ignored.[30] So, too, are punctuations that obviously conflict with intended meanings.[31] And context, not the order of listed meanings in dictionaries, is resorted to in order to resolve ambiguities. (The sign located in the window of the drug counselor's office that says "Keep off the grass" is given a different meaning from that given the same sign located on the lawn outside, no matter which definition of "grass" is listed first in the dictionary.)[32]

2. Four Nonalgorithmic Textualisms

Most self-styled textualists turn out in fact not to be algorithmic textualists at all, even of the impure kind. They do not argue for the use of mechanical algorithms to produce textual meanings.

If intention-free textualism is an impossibility because interpreters must always have recourse to some author, real or otherwise, what other positions could textualists be advocating? We know that they are rejecting full-blooded intentionalism of the sort in which interpreters gather all the evidence available of the authorially intended meaning. That position is their foil. Moreover, their position would not be a significant alternative to intentionalism if their claim were merely that one ought to exclude from consideration on grounds of unreliability some evidence of the authorial intent – for example, some forms of legislative history. No full-blooded intentionalist should advocate use of unreliable evidence of authorial intent.

As we see it, this leaves textualists with four possible positions. First, textualists might wish to exclude certain evidence of authorial intent for reasons other than its unreliability but otherwise interpret as would an intentionalist. This position is one that we believe is tenable, although it

---

[30] *See* Larry Alexander and Saikrishna Prakash, *"Is That English You're Speaking?" Why Intention Free Interpretation Is an Impossibility*, 41 San Diego L. Rev. 967 (2004).

[31] Id. at 981.

[32] Id. at 978–79.

perhaps rests problematically on norms that must be deemed superior in authority to those posited by the lawmakers whose laws are being interpreted.

Second, textualists might advocate interpreting laws based on asking some sample of readers – or some median reader – what meaning *they* believe the actual authors intended. This position is unattractive for a host of reasons.

Third, textualists might advocate interpreting laws based on the intentions that a purely hypothetical construct – an idealized reader – would attribute to the law's author. We find this position, to the extent it differs from the first one, to be quite problematic.

The fourth textualist position would have the interpreter read the text as if it were written by, and thus carried the intended meaning of, an idealized author. We find this position to be perhaps the most problematic of all.

Position One: Textualism as Rule-of-Law-Restricted Intentionalism. According to this version of textualism, the interpreter should seek out authorial intent, but in doing so should refuse to consider certain kinds of evidence thereof, even if reliable. For example, we might have reliable evidence that a law, which appears to be written in standard English, and which can be given a sensible meaning therein, was actually written in nonstandard English, or Schmenglish. We could imagine an interpretive norm to the effect that lawmakers will be irrebuttably presumed to use standard English in writing laws. We might tell a rule-of-law story about the justification for such a norm, such as the need for the general public to know the laws, and so forth, or an indirect consequentialist story that pits getting authorial intentions right in the general array of cases against getting them right in any given case. And we might give a similar rationale for excluding even reliable legislative history – that is, that such history is not generally available or that it can lead to nontransparent manipulations of the lawmaking process.

We find this version of textualism coherent and perhaps plausible. To accept it, however, we would need to see clear statements of the specific norms excluding various types of evidence of lawmakers' intentions and to know the provenance and authority of those norms. Notice that because the evidence of authorial intentions excluded by such norms is reliable evidence, the interpreter will end up in a situation in which the *authoritative* meaning of the law is different from what the interpreter knows was *the meaning intended by the lawmakers.* To many, this will not be a devastating criticism; for, in treating statutory and constitutional interpretations by courts as having the force of precedent – that is, as binding even if incorrect – the courts countenance a similar gap between *authoritative meanings* and *actual meanings.* Moreover, if our interpretive norms exclude certain kinds of evidence of lawmakers' intentions, the lawmakers will legislate in light of those norms, thereby narrowing the gap between the meaning they actually intend and the meaning that they will be deemed to have intended. (For instance, if they know their intentions will be interpreted as if they had expressed them in standard English, they will try to use standard English and not Schmenglish in writing the laws.) Still, the gap between what the interpreter knows the lawmakers actually intended and what, according to these norms, the interpreter will deem them to have intended remains a constant possibility under this version of textualism. Indeed, if the indirect consequentialist justification for excluding certain evidence is sound, this gap is no different from the gap between a rule and its underlying justification.

Position Two: Textualism as Man-on-the-Street Interpretation. Textualists could be seen as advocating interpreting legal texts as would some sample of average members of the public. Such a method might be thought by some to have rule-of-law benefits, particularly in giving the average citizen clear notice of what the law means. We believe that any such theoretical benefits are largely chimerical because the position faces a devastating problem of indeterminacy.

One aspect of this problem relates to how much background context we ought to provide to the average interpreter. We might take the law to mean whatever it would mean to a collection of people who are provided no context whatsoever – other than, perhaps, that its authors were English speakers and enacted the law on a given date.[33] Then we

---

[33] The requirement that the language and date be identified – so that those polled know which language's dictionary and grammatical rules to consult – is just a reflection of the general point established earlier, namely, that the meaning of texts is a product of authorial intent and that, therefore, acontextual meaning is an impossibility.

are back to algorithmic textualism and might as well construct a computer program that incorporates datable dictionaries and rules of syntax, grammar, and punctuation and ask the computer to spit out the law's meaning. Alternatively, we might allow those sampled to use their varying understandings of the law's context or to seek further evidence of authorial intent (and if so, how much?). Then, either their readings will converge on the authoritative interpreter's (e.g., the judge's) reading, as their contextual and other evidence of authorial intent approaches the full body of such evidence possessed by the authoritative interpreter – in which case, why poll? – or their readings will vary from one person to the next. If the number of people polled is more than two, and the number of possible statutory meanings is more than two, we may get no dominant meaning from the polling.[34] In that case, the law will have no authoritative meaning, even though the authoritative interpreter (e.g., the judge) will be quite confident about the meaning intended by the lawmakers. Whatever the benefits of such an interpretive method – that is, whatever advance notice, however uncertain, might be provided to the public about the law's meaning – we do not believe that officials should delegate the assignment of meanings to laws to random individuals with varying understandings of what the lawmakers were seeking to accomplish.

Nor does asking one median member of the public instead of several members make the polling method more attractive. It does mitigate the problem of no dominant meaning. But it substitutes an equally daunting problem, namely, that of identifying who is the "median" member of the public. Because there are an indefinite number of dimensions on which one can identify a median member of the public, the concept of a median member of the public is indeterminate. We will derive different authoritative interpretations depending upon the qualities of the median man on the street. Given the indeterminacy of meaning resulting from man-on-the-street interpretation, we view the supposed notice benefits of this mode of interpretation to be largely imaginary. The man-on-the-street method will not make the public more aware of the law's meaning.

---

[34] This is because of Arrow's Theorem. *See* Kenneth J. Arrow, *Social Choice and Individual Values*, 2–8 (2d ed., New Haven: Yale University Press 1963). Furthermore, the number of possible meanings of *statutes*, as opposed to words, typically will be greater than two.

That is because the public will not be able to predict the meaning that will emerge from the method due to the indeterminacy of the notion of the median member of the public on which the method is based. And given that the median member of the public, however designated and however much evidence of authorial intent he is allowed to seek, will be less knowledgeable regarding what the lawmakers meant by a legal text than the judge, it is not at all evident why we would want the latter to defer to the former in the absence of the benefits of determinate advance notice.

Position Three: The Idealized Reader. Textualists frequently have recourse to the construct of an idealized reader who exists contemporaneously with the rule's enactment and ask how *he* would interpret the text. Judge Easterbrook has said that textualists interpret language by asking how "a skilled, objectively reasonable user of words" would have understood the text. Justice Scalia has claimed that judges should read the federal statutes "as any ordinary member of Congress would have read them, and apply the meaning so determined."[35] But textualists do not usually end here but consider the context of the statute and also take into account background legal conventions. Hence, the idealized reader is a lawyer (or at least someone who knows the standard legal conventions) who knows the factual background surrounding the statute's enactment.

We have already observed that supplying the idealized reader the "context" of the statute is but a back-door means of reintroducing the author's intent. Here we wish to make different points about the use of the idealized reader. To begin with, the idealized reader will search for clues illuminating the actual author's intent. Indeed, we think that people, when asked to interpret something, typically seek the actual author's intent as the source of meaning. (Recall the "autobahn next to the sofa" example.)[36] This raises the possibility that textualists, in creating a construct to generate an "objective" meaning, have instead

---

[35] The obvious and profound differences between these two idealized readers highlight the general failure of textualists to specify the characteristics of the idealized reader.

[36] As noted earlier, some people might eschew actual authorial intentions, hypothesize an author, and then seek to divine this imagined author's intentions. But if the actual author's will were authoritative for the interpreter – as it typically is in one's mother's requests, and as it is thought to be when dealing with statutes and constitutions – then the actual author's intentions would be the logical source of meaning.

merely created an abstraction that filters authorial intention. The more (direct or indirect) evidence an idealized reader is given of what an author meant by a text, the more the reader will read the text as meaning what the author intended to mean by it.

Moreover, even if the textualist forbids the idealized reader from seeking the intent of the actual author, the idealized reader will still have to search for some intent. If we are correct that one must envision an author whenever attempting to make sense of text (indeed, even to identify it as a text), the idealized reader will have to imagine a hypothetical author (or authors). Although there may be certain advantages to treating a text generated by a multimember body as if one person created it, one of those advantages is *not* an ability to dispense with the search for intent.

If we assume that the idealized reader selects a hypothetical author (rather than multiple authors), there is a benefit to textualism's abstraction. With the selection of one author, it becomes much more likely that every statute has a meaning. After all, the more authors a text has, the more likely it is that there is no shared intent as to the meaning of the text. And for the intentionalist interested in authorial intent, if there is no intent that is shared by the requisite number of legislators, the text has no authoritative intention to give it meaning and therefore has no meaning. Hence, if one prefers *more* meaningful legislation to less, there is an advantage to hypothesizing one author when there are multiple real authors.[37]

Another potential benefit arises if we require that the idealized reader be an average member of the general public. In this situation, if the law would be incomprehensible to members of the general public, then there is no law, even if a well-versed lawyer would be able to tease out some meaning. Moreover, this approach has the benefit that people generally might know what the law requires without having to consult with high-priced experts or go to court.[38]

---

[37] Of course, this assumes that we *are* better off with more legislation rather than less. A textualist extremely dubious of the concept of collective intent might say that we are indeed better off with more legislation rather than less, and we would have much less if legislation were treated as meaningless in the absence of a collectively shared legislative intent. Other textualists might be happier with less legislation.

[38] This mode of interpretation differs from the mode discussed in the previous section in that, in the previous section, the law means whatever it means to a specific, real, "average" citizen. Here we replace a flesh-and-blood interpreter with a hypothetical one. The judge is supposed to determine what a hypothetical, average citizen would make of a statute. Of course, our

Unfortunately, most modern textualists assume that their idealized reader knows the standard legal conventions and the entire corpus juris. Hence, the meanings generated by this reader are unlikely to have any of the advance notice and rule-of-law benefits mentioned previously, because most average folk are unlikely to know either standard legal conventions or the entire corpus juris. If the average Joe attempts to read statutory text, he is often likely to identify a meaning that is entirely different from the one generated by the textualist's idealized reader. It seems to us that the only benefit secured by modern textualists is the avoidance of the problems with discerning or securing multiple individual intent.

Of course, this "average reader" approach is itself not strictly empirical, nor is it determinate. It requires us to determine how the median reader – not the average reader, because readers and their meanings cannot be "averaged" – would read a legal text. But as we have said, the notion of a median reader is indeterminate. To be determinate, we would have to spell out all sorts of characteristics of the median reader, such as whether he had a median IQ, had a median knowledge of public affairs (which is meaningless, because there is no unitary scale of such knowledge), was of a median age, had a median geographical location (again a meaningless notion), and had a median education (again, meaningless, because there is no single educational continuum). The notion of the idealized reader is, indeed, radically indeterminate. And making it more determinate, without making the idealized reader into someone who actually knows what we know about the authorial intent, is likely to produce arbitrary stipulations, such as that the idealized reader went to public high school in Delaware and reads the *Washington Post* front page cursorily but not the *New York Times*.[39]

Finally, although intentionalists have the aggregate intent problem and must face the fact that, when there are multiple lawmakers, there will be occasions when there is no dominant authorial intent and hence

---

criticisms of the average-citizen approach mentioned in the previous section apply equally here. How the judge constructs the qualities of the hypothetical, average reader will affect the resulting interpretations.

[39] The indeterminacy of the idealized reader is due to the countless ways that her traits can be stipulated. The indeterminacy of the average or median reader considered in the preceding section is due to the countless dimensions along which one can be average or median, some of which (e.g., geographical location) do not admit of averaging or having a median.

no dominant meaning, textualists of the idealized reader type have a mirror-image problem, the problem of a surfeit of meaning. For the idealized reader whom the textualist stipulates, precluded as that reader is from looking to *all* the evidence of *actual* authorial intent, may conclude that a text has two or more meanings that are equally supported by the evidence to which he is restricted. For the textualist, the text then just does have these multiple meanings. There is no deeper metaphysical fact, like intent, of which these multiple meanings are merely evidence. *The multiple meanings just are the metaphysical fact at issue.* The text just *means* two or more things, however silly or pernicious that is as a practical matter.[40]

Position Four: The Idealized Author. The final position that a textualist might hold is that legal texts should be interpreted by reference not to an idealized reader of the text but by reference to an idealized author. In other words, legal texts should be interpreted to mean what they would have meant had they been authored by this single idealized lawmaker rather than by the one or several actual lawmakers.

The problems with this approach should be obvious. In order for it to yield interpretations, we need to specify the attributes of the idealized author. What language does he speak? Does he always use primary definitions of words, or does he sometimes (when?) use secondary definitions, or technical definitions, or terms of art? Are his grammar and punctuation perfect? How rational is he? How just? And so on. How we construct the idealized author will determine what the authoritative interpretation is. And the obvious question then is, Why not construct this idealized author to be ideal? In other words, why not, as Ronald Dworkin advocates, "interpret" every law to be the best law it can be?[41] And if we do not get the best law from assuming the lawmaker is writing in standard English, why not assume the lawmaker is writing in Schmenglish, a

---

[40] Occasionally, intentionalists likewise will face situations where evidence of meaning is in equipoise. Yet intentionalists can take satisfaction in knowing that intentionalism theoretically always yields no more than one meaning, the meaning attributable to the author of the text. (It may yield no meaning when multiple authors mean conflicting things.) So, although textualism sometimes will yield multiple meanings, intentionalism will always yield no more than one meaning, even if that meaning is sometimes difficult to discern.

[41] *See* Ronald Dworkin, *Law's Empire* 348 (Cambridge, Mass.: Harvard University Press 1986).

language in which the law would be ideal from the interpreter's vantage point?[42] We think this natural progression leading to what is in effect the reauthoring of the law by the interpreter is a reductio of the position and surely a horrific prospect for self-styled textualists.

These four positions that textualists could be advocating, given the impossibility of intention-free textualism, appear to us to exhaust the possibilities. Positions two, three, and four are, we believe, difficult to defend, even if they can be made determinate. Position one is at least a tenable position, although it leads to the possibility that the authoritative meaning of the law can differ from the meaning we know was intended, perhaps even by all the authoring lawmakers. That does not mean that the position is normatively unattractive. But it does mean that, relative to a full-blooded intentionalist, a policy-constrained interpreter of the position-one variety is less than a faithful agent of the lawmaker.

Beyond the question of their normative attractiveness, none of these positions require any special form of legal reasoning that is different from ordinary reasoning. The first three positions merely require intentionalist reasoning, albeit intentionalist reasoning that is constrained in terms of evidence (position one) or that is hypothetical (positions two and three). Position four, on the other hand, requires purely moral reasoning, though, as we have said, it can hardly be deemed a method of textualist interpretation as opposed to creation.

---

[42] Textualists have taken Ronald Dworkin to task for arguing that each statute ought to be interpreted as "the best statute it can be" – which will then be equivalent to whatever statute the "interpreting" judge thinks Congress should have written. But textualists who create an idealized author have no principled basis for criticizing Dworkin. In untethering meaning from the actual author's intent and tying it instead to a construct, such textualists have done something quite similar to what Dworkin has done. In both situations, Congress chooses marks; but whatever marks it chooses, judges provide them with meaning without regard to the meaning that Congress meant to convey. The only differences lie in the constraints on the idealized author.

Joseph Raz criticizes the idealized-author approach thusly: "If you regard the Constitution as an uninterpreted jumble of ink scratchings and regard legal . . . [interpretation] as designed to give it meaning in accordance with the best moral theory there is, then there is no gap between ideal law and the interpretation of existing law. Under these conditions, one can interpret the Constitution to mean anything at all." Joseph Raz, *Dworkin: A New Link in the Chain,* 74 *Cal. L. Rev.* 1103, 1103 (1986). Although he denies it, the same criticism applies to Michael Moore's instrumentalist theory of constitutional interpretation. *See* Alexander, *supra* note 27, at 401–2 (criticizing Michael S. Moore, *Interpreting Interpretation,* in *Law and Interpretation: Essays in Legal Philosophy, supra* note 27).

II. Dynamic Interpretation of Canonical Legal Rules

In recent years there has emerged a competitor to intentionalism and textualism as methodologies for interpreting canonical legal rules. That competitor methodology is called "dynamic statutory interpretation" or "practical reason interpretation." The hallmark of this methodology, aside from its rejection of both intentionalism and textualism, is its ecumenical view of the considerations that are material to the correct interpretation of canonical legal rules. Its proponents assert that in interpreting a statute, the interpreter should look at some combination of various of the following items: the meanings of the authors' words, the author's purposes, norms regarding institutional relationships, rule-of-law virtues, social norms, efficiency, and justice. For example, Richard Posner asserts that statutory interpretation is a product of language, purpose, and values.[43] William Eskridge in one place argues that statutory interpretation involves the text, its purposes, and the interpreter's own values.[44] In other places, he and Philip Frickey argue that it is a product of some combination of text, purpose, and current values, and in one place they throw "history" into the list of considerations.[45] And Cass Sunstein maintains that statutory interpretation is a nonmechanical exercise of practical reason that involves the text, history, purpose, and background values.[46]

---

[43] *See* Richard Posner, *The Problems of Jurisprudence* 130–32, 299–300 (Cambridge, Mass.: Harvard University Press 1990).

[44] *See* William Eskridge, *Gadamer/Statutory Interpretation*, 90 *Colum. L. Rev.* 609, 633, 647–51 (1990); William Eskridge, *Dynamic Statutory Interpretation*, 135 *U. Pa. L. Rev.* 1479, 1483–84 (1987).

[45] *See* William Eskridge and Philip Frickey, *Statutory Interpretation as Practical Reasoning*, 42 *Stan. L. Rev.* 321, 351–52 (1990). *See also* Philip Frickey, *Congressional Intent, Practical Reasoning, and the Dynamic Nature of Federal Indian Law*, 78 *Cal. L. Rev.* 1137, 1140, 1208–9 (1990) (arguing that dynamic statutory interpretation looks at language, purpose, current values, and history); Daniel Farber and Philip Frickey, *Legislative Intent and Public Choice*, 74 *Va. L. Rev.* 423, 456 (1988) (arguing that statutory interpretation involves both legislative intent and consequences).

[46] Cass R. Sunstein, *Interpreting Statutes in the Regulatory State*, 103 *Harv. L. Rev.* 405, 497–98 (1989). I am tempted to put Michael Moore into this camp on the issue of statutory interpretation despite his many differences with the authors mentioned here. For when it comes to interpreting legal texts, Moore, too, tells us to look at the meanings of words, legal precedents, purposes, and values. *See* Michael S. Moore, *A Natural Law Theory of Interpretation*, 58 *S. Cal. L. Rev.* 277, 396–97 (1985).

With all due respect, these positions are hopelessly confused. To show why, we need to disaggregate three different things: what the meaning of a statute or other canonical legal text *is* – *the ontological question*; what things should one look to in order best to *discover* the meaning of the statute or other canonical text – *the epistemological question*; and what one should *do* in response to the meaning of the statute or other canonical text once one has discovered that meaning – *the authority question.*

Suppose one agrees with us that, as an ontological matter, a statute means whatever was the intended meaning of the legislature that the statute was enacted to transmit. Obviously then, of all the items on the lists of the proponents of dynamic statutory interpretation, only legislatively intended meaning pertains to the meaning of the statute and, indeed, is synonymous with it. On the other hand, legislative purposes and the text (*qua* utterance meaning) would be material *evidence* of that statutory meaning. The history of the statute's applications might be weak evidence as well, insofar as it reveals what other interpreters thought the statute's intended meaning was. On the other hand, the consequences of the statute and whether those consequences offended currently held (to be true) values would not bear on the meaning of the statute at all, neither ontologically nor epistemologically. They could bear on its legal authority, however, if there are higher-order legal rules or standards that refer to such values and constrain the legislator(s) whose text is at issue. And the history of the statute might bear on its authority as well, either through the doctrine of precedent or through reliance, again if there are higher-order rules or standards that so dictate.

What is surely not a possibility, however, is that a statute could ontologically consist of such combinations of factors. Some of these factors are factual matters, and some are normative. Some are about facts at one historical moment, and some are about facts at different histori-cal moments. If the dynamic-interpretation approach is ontological – if it purports to tell us what statutes *are* – then why is not the meta-physical mixing of facts about one time, facts about another, and moral norms as incomprehensible as asking someone to mix pi, green, the categorical imperative, and the Civil War? Dynamic statutory interpre-tation, were it a real possibility, would most definitely involve a spe-cial form of reasoning not employed outside the law. It is not a real possibility, however.

III. Other Nonstarters

For the sake of completeness we should mention some other views that are thought to be competitors of intentionalism in the interpretation of canonical legal rules. Much of what we say about them here has already been said or has been clearly prefigured in this and the two preceding chapters.

A. ORIGINAL PUBLIC MEANING

Some theorists of legal interpretation suggest that the meaning of a canonical legal text is not the meaning intended by its authors but is rather the meaning that would be attributed to it by (some) members of the public at the time of its enactment – its original public meaning. On one construction, this view is really a version of the form of nonalgorithmic textualism that employs the construct of the idealized reader. We argued that the notion of the idealized reader, if it at all differs from giving canonical legal texts the meanings we determine their authors to have intended, is to that extent indeterminate.

On another construction, this view is really a version of the form of nonalgorithmic textualism we called "textualism as rule-of-law-restricted intentionalism." That view is just intentionalism with certain types of evidence of intent deemed inadmissible. One might argue that "original public meaning" interpretation is just intentionalism, but with evidence of intention that would not be generally accessible to the public at the time of enactment ruled out of bounds (by a legal rule of higher authority than the one being interpreted). That is a cogent notion of legal interpretation; but because it is intentionalist in nature, it is not special to law and legal reasoning.

One statement of original public meaning is that given by Larry Solum, to wit, "the meaning that (i) the drafters of the text would have reasonably expected (ii) the audience to whom the text is addressed (iii) to attribute to the drafters (iv) based on the evidence (public record) that was publicly available at the time the text was promulgated."[47] The

---

[47] Lawrence B. Solum, *Pluralism and Public Legal Reason*, 15 *William & Mary Bill of Rts. J.* 7, 15 (2006).

reference to public availability suggests a concern with secret or inaccessible evidence of authorial intended meaning. But, in our opinion, this is a red herring. The text's authors want their audience to take as the intended meaning the meaning they (the authors) intend. If we say "X" and intend that our audience take us to have intended A thereby, then the meaning of our utterance just is A. It would make no sense for us to claim to have intended a secret meaning B when we anticipated our audience would take us to have intended A.

Moreover, given that authors want their audiences to have the uptake the authors intend, authors will be quite cognizant of the circumstances of and evidence available to the audience.

And the audience will in turn be striving to understand the authors' intended meaning, which is what the authors want, which is why there is no danger of a "secret" intended meaning or even of its possibility. The authors and their audience have complementary goals – the authors to convey their intended meaning, the audience to infer it.

If there is space for a difference between the original intended meaning and the original public meaning, therefore, it must be because of the possibility that the original public might attribute an intended meaning to the authors that was not the actual intended meaning. The proponent of original public meaning over authorially intended meaning must argue that where the original public is in error, that error should nonetheless be controlling.

Schematically, assume the authors' intended meaning is X, but the public misunderstands it to be Y. We would say the meaning is X. The proponent of original public meaning would say it is Y. But why go with Y? The argument cannot be based on "fair notice." We are not dealing with a criminal trial or some other upset-of-expectations case. Those fairness issues can be handled without letting the original public's mistaken interpretation be controlling.

Moreover, not only does fairness not militate in favor of Y, neither does proper deference to the original public. After all, the public itself was trying to get at the authors' intended meaning (X) and would regret that it misunderstood it to be Y.

We have been assuming that the entire public would have interpreted the authors' intended meaning differently from how those seeking authorially intended meaning would interpret it. But that is hardly conceivable.

After all, if those seeking the authorially intended meaning believe the authors' intended meaning is X, presumably some members of the original public would have done so as well – presumably, the most informed, intelligent members of the original public.

So assume some members of the original public interpret the authors to mean X (which is correct), some interpret them to mean Y, some interpret them to mean Z, and so on. What is *the* original public meaning? What the *average* person would have concluded? But how does one "average" people who differ with respect to intelligence, information, motivation, and so on? What the *reasonable* person would have concluded? But why is not the *reasonable* person he who is most informed, intelligent, and so on? The latter, of course, will be the member of the public who would reach the same conclusion as those seeking the authorially intended meaning. And, with fair-notice concerns off the table, why base the meaning on what a less informed, less intelligent member of the public would conclude? We can see no good reason for the proponent of original public meaning to base interpretation on anything other than what the most informed, intelligent member of the public would have concluded was the authors' intended meaning – which will turn out to be the meaning the proponent of authorially intended meaning would give (and which would be the meaning the public was attempting to discern). In short, any plausible version of original public meaning will turn out to be identical to the search for the authorially intended meaning.

B. CONCEPTS, NATURAL KINDS, AND UNDERLYING PURPOSES (SPIKE LEE)

We are going to be brief here because we have covered this ground before in our discussions of Bassham and Lessig in Chapter 5 and of levels of generality of intentions in Chapter 6. Some argue that interpreting canonical legal rules should focus not on authors' intended meanings but on the "concepts" they employed, the "natural kinds" to which those concepts refer, or to the authors' ultimate purposes.

To take the last interpretive stance first, *every* legislator's ultimate purpose in passing *any* law we can charitably characterize as the purpose "do the right thing," aka, the "Spike Lee" purpose. If every statute reflects the Spike Lee purpose and is to be interpreted to prescribe what the interpreter sees as the right thing to do, why not have only one law, the

Spike Lee law? For that is what the effect of "interpreting" all laws by reference to their ultimate purpose will be.

Of course, someone proposing the Spike Lee approach might reply that direct implementation of the Spike Lee injunction by everyone would be disastrous – the "wrong thing." (Too many people would err in determining "the right thing," and their errors would be compounded by lack of coordination.) Therefore, the argument would go, one must implement the Spike Lee injunction indirectly through concrete serious rules that both set up legal institutions and apply directly to citizens. But that reply, although correct, gives away the game. Of course, governance by serious rules – and interpreting those rules by reference to the intended meanings of the authors of those rules (if we assume the authors have rule-granted legal authority to determine what shall be done) – *is* the right thing to do, as we have argued here and elsewhere. If *this* is all the "Spike Lee" ultimate purpose form of interpretation amounts to, we endorse it. But then, it is not a competitor of intentionalist interpretation.[48]

As we said in Chapter 5, when people possessing the requisite legal authority enact canonical rules – whether the rules are constitutional, statutory, or administrative, or are the products of private ordering through contracts, wills, and so forth – they may have in mind some exemplars of the terms they use as well as definitions of those terms.[49] Moreover, the terms might refer to natural kinds. But these items can conflict. The author's exemplars may not match his definition. And his definition may not comport with the best scientific account of the phenomenon picked out by the term. In some such cases, the author may intend his exemplars to control, in others, his definition, and in still others, the best scientific account. Authors do not always intend a particular priority among these items, such as that definitions always trump exemplars, or the "real nature" of things always trumps definitions. And if they do not intend the same particular priority in every case, there is no independent reason for imposing one in the guise of interpreting the canonical rule.

We have looked at the major alternatives to commonplace intentionalist interpretation and found them wanting. They are either incoherent,

---

[48] *See* Alexander, *supra* note 27, at 401–2.
[49] *See* Chapter 5 *supra* at notes 37–40.

normatively disastrous, or just forms of intentionalism dressed up as something else. The interpreter of canonical legal rules may need to learn any legal rules that constrain his access to evidence of authorial intent (as well as the legal rules discussed in Chapter 6 that constrain the legal authority of the rules' authors); however, the interpreter need learn no reasoning skill other than the ordinary human one that we practice every day, namely, deciphering another's intended meaning.

VIII

Is Constitutional Interpretation Different?
Why It Isn't and Is

To this point we have argued that the interpretation of canonical legal rules – whether those rules are promulgated by legislatures, administrators, or judges or by private parties engaged in private ordering through contracts, leases, wills, trusts, and the like – consists, or should consist, of attempting to discover the rule promulgator's intended meaning. Perhaps the search for the rule's intended meaning will be subject to evidentiary constraints in the interest of greater accuracy over the full array of cases, or the intended meaning will be subordinated to substantive or procedural policies embodied in legal norms of higher authority than the rule in question. But however so constrained, the quarry of interpretation of legal rules will be the intended meaning of their authors. And the skill required for legal interpretation – the "legal reasoning" that interpretation of canonical legal rules entails – is the same skill that all of us employ in trying to understand what others are requesting or demanding that we do.

In this brief chapter, we ask whether intentionalism of the sort we have described is the appropriate methodology for interpreting a constitution, the supreme law of the land. As readers no doubt are aware, intentionalism of the straightforward, unsophisticated type that we have been urging is nowhere as much disdained by legal theorists as in the domain of constitutional interpretation. Yet we maintain that intentionalism is as appropriate in constitutional interpretation as it is elsewhere.

We have already in Chapter 7 made our case against textualism, which is often pitted against intentionalism in the battle of interpretive methodologies for constitutional law. And in Chapter 5 we argued that those who author constitutional provisions do not necessarily intend the priority of concepts over specific conceptions, or of the best theory of the thing referred to over its conventional definition, or its definition over its exemplars. The priority relation will vary with the provision because the intent will vary. If the authors intend by a particular provision to enact a standard rather than a rule, then their intent – in effect, their rule – is to delegate authority to the interpreter to decide what should be done. If, however, they intend to enact a rule, then they are attempting themselves to settle what should be done, and their settlement is whatever they intend it to be. This outcome is as true for authors of constitutional provisions as it is for legislatures, administrators, judges, and private orderers.

This, as we said, is ground we have already covered. In this chapter, we discuss four challenges to intentionalist constitutional interpretation beyond those previously dealt with: the methodology of "the living Constitution," the methodology of the "paradigm case," the effect of Supreme Court precedents on interpretation, and the challenge of changes in "the rule of recognition." The first two challenges fail completely. The last two challenges do not affect how the Constitution should be interpreted in the sense of challenging intentionalism, but they do raise questions about the Constitution's *authority* and its *identity*.

I. The Constitution as Super Statute

Our view – and we believe it is the ordinary view – is that interpreting a constitution is not different in any material way from interpreting a

222   REASONING FROM CANONICAL LEGAL TEXTS

statute. The U.S. Constitution is, of course, "higher law" than any statute.[1] Moreover, substantial parts of it are more than two hundred years old (although many statutes are of similar vintage). And, if one deems its "authors" to be not those who drafted it but rather those who ratified it – although the ratifiers were most likely voting on what they believed were the drafters' intended meanings – then the constitutional authors constitute a more numerous and diffuse group than the legislatures that author statutes, though the latter are usually bicameral and include the chief executive in the legislative process. None of these characteristics of the Constitution, however, make it different in kind from a statute. And therefore, there is no reason why the same intentionalism that should guide statutory and all other legal interpretation should not guide constitutional interpretation.

One argument occasionally raised against intentionalism in constitutional interpretation rests on a misunderstanding of intentionalism. Its proponents point out that many clauses in the Constitution appear to invoke moral concepts like "equality," "liberty," "freedom of speech," "free exercise of religion," "reasonable cause," and "cruel and unusual punishment." They go on to argue that these clauses should be interpreted according to the interpreter's best understanding of the moral reality to which those concepts refer, and not according to the Constitution's authors' particular understanding of those concepts and how they might apply.[2] Thus, for example, if the death penalty is really "cruel and unusual," it should be deemed unconstitutional, even if the authors of the Constitution would not have thought that it was. Or, if official gender discrimination is really a denial of "equal protection," it should not matter that the authors of the Fourteenth Amendment did not believe the amendment applied to gender discrimination. And so on.

Now, nothing in this argument is inconsistent with intentionalist constitutional interpretation. As we made clear in Chapter 5, particularly in our discussion of Bassham,[3] and again at the end of Chapter 7,[4]

---

[1] See U.S. Const. Art. VI. cl. 2: "This Constitution . . . shall be the supreme Law of the Land."

[2] See Ronald Dworkin, Comment, in Antonin Scalia, A Matter of Interpretation: Federal Courts and the Law 115–27 (Princeton: Princeton University Press 1997).

[3] See Chapter 5, supra text at notes 32–41.

[4] See Chapter 7, supra text at note 48.

constitutional authors, in using a particular term, may have in mind particular exemplars of that term, which exemplars they believe are consistent with a definition they also have in mind, which definition they believe captures the true nature of the term's referent. Where, from the standpoint of the interpreter, the exemplars, the definition, and the true nature of the thing come apart, it is an open question whether the term's authors intended the exemplars, the definition, or the true nature to control the term's application. We can imagine circumstances that would support the dominance of exemplars of the term, the dominance of the conventional definition of the term, or the dominance of the real nature of the term. The intentionalist seeks the dominant authorial intention.

If, therefore, the constitutional authors did indeed intend for the real nature of the various terms that seem value-laden to control and to dominate the authors' possibly mistaken definitions and exemplars, then the interpreter of those terms must seek their true nature and not what the constitutional authors believed that nature to be. That *is* intentionalist interpretation, not something else. The constitutional authors would essentially be saying to their interpreters, we *intend* by these terms in these clauses for you to seek out the true nature of equality, liberty, and so forth and gauge the validity of ordinary laws by whether they are consistent with what you discover.

We should, however, caution against too hasty an assumption that the Constitution contains terms of this type – that is, terms by which the authors intended to refer to "moral reality." Many legal norms are wholly or in part "standards" rather than "rules." That is, the norms delegate to some other decision maker – the citizen, the administrator, or the judge – the task of determining what should be done. The authors of the hypothetical legal *standard* "drive at a reasonable speed" prescribed such a standard because they would not or did not want to prescribe in rulelike fashion a rigid code of speed limits. The driver, or the judge who must assess the driver's conduct, or the administrator who must post a speed limit for the curve on Elm Street must decide what a "reasonable speed" is at a particular time or place. The authors of the standard did not settle that issue. Rules settle, standards delegate.

It should be kept in mind, however, that ordinarily, standards delegate only within the boundaries set by rules. The "reasonable" speed limit deals only with driving speeds. It does not affect other domains of life. Similarly, a statute instructing a judge to impose a "fair" punishment for a crime deals only with that crime and with the punishment thereof.

In interpreting the "moralized" clauses of the Constitution, we can imagine that their authors intended for them to be rule-bounded standards, delegating to future interpreters the task of deciding what "equality," or "freedom of speech," or "liberty" means within the boundaries established by the Constitution's determinate rules (themselves products of the authors' intended meanings). But the *true* nature of equality, liberty, and so forth may not respect such rule-defined boundaries.

So consider the possibility that the "true nature" of liberty, say, or equality demands that we have a thoroughly centralized government (no state or local governments), a unicameral national legislature (no Senate), a lower burden of proof in criminal trials than "beyond a reasonable doubt," and so on. In other words, it might be the case that much of what our Constitution requires or presupposes is inconsistent with the "true nature" of political morality. If the Constitution's authors really did intend by these moralized clauses for us to implement the true nature of equality, liberty, and the like, then they intended in those clauses to repudiate much or perhaps all of what they intended the rest of the Constitution to establish.[5]

Now their intentions might have been deeply conflictual in this way. But we think one should be cautious before assuming too quickly that they really did intend in a handful of the Constitution's many provisions to open the door to interpreters' repudiating clearly established constitutional rules and structures.

(As an aside, but one illustrative of the problem, consider that the Supreme Court has held that the Fourteenth Amendment's equal protection clause condemns state senates that, like the United States Senate, are not apportioned according to "one person, one vote."[6] And consider that the Court has often held that the principles of equal protection are

---

[5] *See* Larry Alexander and Frederick Schauer, *Law's Limited Domain Confronts Morality's Universal Empire*, 48 *William & Mary l. Rev.* 1579, 1595–99 (2007).

[6] *See* Reynolds v. Sims, 377 U.S. 533 (1964) (holding unconstitutional malapportioned state senates).

part of the "due process" protected by the Fifth Amendment.[7] Finally, consider that the Fifth Amendment was ratified two years after Article I of the Constitution, which article, among other things, establishes the United States Senate.[8] Should we conclude, therefore, that the United States Senate is unconstitutional under the Fifth Amendment?)

In any event, even if the authors of the Constitution intended in certain clauses to delegate to future decision makers the task of divining the "moral reality" to which those clauses were intended to refer, no special legal reasoning is brought into play. Ordinary intentionalist interpretation produces the call to engage in moral reasoning. And the moral reasoning it calls for is just that: moral reasoning. The notion that the Constitution is just a super statute, one to be interpreted like any statute by reference to the intended meaning of its authors, is perfectly compatible with its containing moral referents.

II. Two Opposing Views

A. THE "DEAD HAND OF THE PAST" CRITICISM AND THE NOTION OF THE "LIVING CONSTITUTION"

It is now commonplace to hear the Constitution described as a "living constitution."[9] Intentionalism, according to proponents of the "living constitution" view, accords far too much weight to the "dead hand of the past." After all, the Constitution's authors, leaving aside more recent amendments, lived in a far different time and confronted different problems from those we now face, and they possessed far less knowledge

---

[7] See Bolling v. Sharpe, 347 U.S. 497 (1954) (striking down racially segregated schools in the District of Columbia); but see David E. Bernstein, Bolling, Equal Protection, Due Process, and Lochnerphobia, 93 Geo. L.J. 1253 (2005) (arguing that Bolling did not equate Fifth Amendment due process and Fourteenth Amendment equal protection).

[8] See U.S. Const. Art. I, sect. 3, cl. 1; U.S. Const. amend. V (ratified in 1791).

[9] See, e.g., William J. Brennan Jr., Presentation to the American Bar Association, July 9, 1985, reprinted in Alpheus Thomas Mason and Donald Grier Stephenson Jr., eds., American Constitutional Law 607–15 (8th ed., Englewood Cliffs, N. J.: Prentice Hall 1987) (describing "living Constitution" approach to constitutional interpretation); David A. Strauss, Common Law Constitutional Understanding, 63 U. Chi. L. Rev. 877, 879 (1996) (same); Paul Brest, The Misconceived Quest for the Original Understanding, 60 B.U.L. Rev. 204, 209–17 (1980) (same).

than we now possess. If we interpret the Constitution by reference to their intended meanings, much of the Constitution will turn out to be irrelevant, anachronistic, or perverse. Moreover, the Constitution is remarkably difficult to amend. Why then should interpreters be shackled to a set of understandings that are ill-suited to today's world and its problems? Why not give interpreters the leeway to allow the Constitution to adapt to today's world and knowledge? Why not view the Constitution as "alive" rather than as a fossil preserved in amber?

The complaint of the living constitutionalists is really a complaint against constitutionalism itself and more generally a complaint against entrenching rulelike settlements of controversial matters. Rules settle controversies about what ought to be done by making determinate prescriptions and entrenching them (to at least some extent) against change. Constitutions are merely settlements with a high degree of entrenchment. All entrenched rules are potentially infelicitous when enacted. And even if they are ideal when enacted, they may become infelicitous because of changes in the circumstances to which they apply. One cannot attain the settlement benefits of entrenched rules – benefits of coordination, expertise, and efficient decision making – without the costs and risks associated with entrenched rules. The living constitutionalist is really just someone who thinks that the risks of constitutional entrenchments are too high, but that, despite the absence of constitutional entrenchments, judges should nonetheless have authority to make final decisions on matters they deem "constitutional." The living constitutionalist opposes constitutions under the guise of supporting "living" ones and combines that view with a preference for judicial governance.

The living constitutionalist's arguments, therefore, extend not just to "updating" the constitutional authors' notions of what equality, liberty, and the like demand, but to updating as well the age requirement for the presidency, the composition of the Senate, the terms of elected federal officials, the life tenure of federal judges, and so on. These rules in the Constitution are as much the product of the "dead hand of the past" as are those that living constitutionalists usually target for unshackling from their authorially intended meanings. To repeat, the "living constitution" position is antientrenchment and therefore anticonstitutional. It is not a particular methodology of constitutional *interpretation*.

B. THE "PARADIGM CASE" METHODOLOGY OF INTERPRETATION

In recent years, Jed Rubenfeld has put forward what he deems to be a new theory of proper constitutional interpretation.[10] He calls the methodology supported by this theory the "paradigm case" method of constitutional interpretation.[11] Briefly, constitutional interpreters should ask what particular application was in the minds of the authors of the constitutional provision in question. They then must interpret the provision so that it supports that particular application – the "paradigm case" – but they are free to extend the provision into new areas even if the authors themselves would not have done so. Rubenfeld puts this in the following terminology: constitutional interpreters are bound by application understandings but not by no-application understandings.[12]

Now the binding nature of application understandings is qualified in this sense: if the paradigm case was factually different from what the constitutional authors thought it was, it is not the case as it actually was that is the binding paradigm, but the case as the authors imagined it to be.[13] On the other hand, Rubenfeld rejects the idea that an application understanding should be interpreted by reference to the highest level of generality of the authors' intentions, so that if they made a mistake in terms of values, that mistake should be corrected.[14] Even if the paradigm case turns out to be inconsistent with the Spike Lee constitution – handling it as did the constitutional authors was not "the right thing" to do – it is nonetheless binding on interpreters.

Rubenfeld could, with slight emendations, be read as supporting intentionalism. In most cases, the rules in the Constitution reflect but are more general than the specific applications the authors had in mind. To return to our "no bears" rule, if the authors had in mind a particular sighting of a grizzly on Leo's property next to Claire's house full of children, it surely covers the keeping of grizzlies near residences even if it turns out that Leo's "grizzly" was a stuffed trophy.

---

[10] Jed Rubenfeld, *Revolution by Judiciary* (Cambridge, Mass.: Harvard University Press 2005); Jed Rubenfeld, *Freedom and Time: A Theory of Constitutional Self-Government* (New Haven: Yale University Press 2001).

[11] *See, e.g.*, Rubenfeld, *Revolution, supra* note 10, at 15–18.

[12] Id. at 114–19.

[13] Id. at 127–30.

[14] Id. at 130–34.

Where Rubenfeld departs from intentionalism is in his treatment of no-application understandings. Suppose, for example, that the equal protection clause's paradigm case (for unconstitutionality) was the passage of the Black Codes in the states of the Confederacy in the immediate aftermath of the Civil War. (The Black Codes imposed various legal disabilities on the newly emancipated slaves as well as on other blacks.) And suppose further that none of the authors of the equal protection clause intended for it to go beyond invalidating the Black Codes and outlawing, say, "separate but equal facilities" or, even further afield, official gender discrimination. Indeed, had the authors explicitly announced their intention to have the clause extend to these latter practices, the clause would have been voted down.

Rubenfeld calls the examples of outlawing "separate but equal" and gender discrimination no-application understandings that can be disregarded by interpreters of the equal protection clause.[15] Only application understandings bind. The constitutional authors' values – and value mistakes – if they are embodied in paradigm cases, bind, but not if they are embodied in no-application understandings. Constitutional provisions can be extended beyond the authors' applications but not contracted. Constitutional interpretation is a one-way ratchet for expanding the domain to which the Constitution applies.

It is now obvious how Rubenfeld's paradigm case theory is inconsistent with intentionalism. Rubenfeld starts with the authors' intentions regarding paradigm cases, even when, from the interpreters' perspective, the authors did not resolve the paradigm cases correctly. To this extent, Rubenfeld and intentionalists are on the same page. But Rubenfeld, unlike intentionalists, would ignore intended limits on the application of constitutional provisions. Any and all constitutional provisions become merely the jumping-off points for expansive reasoning. The equal protection clause can be generalized from "no Black Codes" to "racial equality" to "equality" to "a theory of justice," so long as the generalizations respect all extant application understandings. And application understandings that stand in the way of the interpreters' favored expansions can be limited to the precise paradigm cases that underlie them. The constitutional

---

[15] Id. at 125–27.

authors' mistakes of value must be heeded; but they can be read narrowly, perhaps to the point of virtual irrelevance, thus freeing interpreters to impose their own values in the name of the Constitution. This does not describe a method of constitutional interpretation so much as a method of only slightly constrained constitutional *creation* by persons who supposedly lack the authority to create constitutions.[16]

III. Supreme Court Precedents and Constitutional Interpretation

It is well established that courts follow judicial precedents in both constitutional and statutory cases. Although we have made a normative case for the rule model of precedent in common-law decision making, there is really no alternative to the rule model if judicial interpretations of constitutional and statutory provisions are to be accorded authority as precedents. When courts interpret constitutional and statutory rules, they substitute their own canonical formulation of the rule for the formulation they are interpreting. (Where the constitutional or statutory provision in question is a *standard*, it *delegates* settlement authority to courts, which then may "rulify" the standard by formulating rules by which to implement it.) If the courts' decisions are deemed to be binding precedents with respect to future courts, the latter must in effect substitute the precedent courts' rules for the constitutional or statutory provision in question, *even if the future courts believe the precedent courts misinterpreted the provisions in question.*[17]

Following judicial precedents in constitutional and statutory decision making is controversial precisely because the precedent court's authority is elevated by later courts above the authority of the constitutional authors and the legislature, reversing the presumed hierarchy of authority. In the statutory area, following precedent is not terribly problematic given the ability of the legislature to overturn mistaken judicial precedents through ordinary legislation. With respect to constitutional decision making, however, erroneous judicial interpretations are not

---

[16] *See also* Brannon P. Denning, *Brother Can You Paradigm?*, 23 *Const. Comment.* 81 (2006).

[17] *See* Larry Alexander, *Constrained by Precedent*, 63 *S. Cal. L. Rev.* 1 (1989). *See generally* the discussion in Chapter 2, *supra*, at note 47.

easily undone. Constitutional amendment is very difficult to accomplish and, for that reason, is very rare. And as a remedy for every erroneous interpretation of the Constitution that has survived judicial challenge or that was originally promulgated by the U.S. Supreme Court, constitutional amendment is out of the question.

Nevertheless, the practice of following precedents blessed by the Supreme Court in constitutional decision making, even when those precedents are at war with the bound court's best understanding of the Constitution, is well entrenched. Precedents are not accorded absolute weight; they can be overruled, at least by the Supreme Court itself. But overruling constitutional precedents usually requires more than a showing that those precedents misinterpreted the Constitution. The precedents must usually be shown to be harmful as well as wrong, and to cause more harm than overturning them would cause.[18]

In any event, even in a regime in which constitutional precedents compete with correct interpretations of the Constitution, no novel interpretive methodology is required. One interprets the Constitution according to its authors' intended meaning, and one interprets a judicial rule glossing the Constitution according to *its* authors' intended meaning. Whether one follows the Constitution or the precedent will depend on whether there is a doctrine of precedent at all and, if so, whether it is absolute or not. And if there is a doctrine of precedent, but one that is nonabsolute, whether one follows the Constitution or the precedent will depend on ordinary normative reasoning coupled with ordinary empirical reasoning about the factual grounds for the normative determination.

IV. Changes in the Rule of Recognition and the Identity of the Constitution's Authors

The preceding section on how a doctrine of precedent might dictate that courts decide constitutional cases differently from what they believe to be the meaning intended by the original authors of the Constitution opens up a more radical possibility in constitutional decision making. For a doctrine of precedent to affect constitutional decision making, that

---

[18] *See, e.g.,* Planned Parenthood of Southeastern Pennsylvania v. Casey, 505 U.S. 833, 854–55 (1992) (joint opinion of O'Connor, Kennedy, and Souter); Chapter 2, *supra,* at note 47.

doctrine must have authority equal to that of the Constitution. But where would that authority come from if it does not come from the Constitution itself, perhaps through the notion of "judicial power" found in Article III?[19]

Some believe that because the U.S. Constitution is "the supreme law of the land," and because it nowhere mentions the doctrine of precedent, much less bestows on it authority equal to that of the Constitution, precedents should never trump a court's best judgment regarding the Constitution's intended meaning.[20] No matter how harmless or even beneficial the precedent court's misreading of the Constitution, and no matter how harmful its overturning, courts must always disregard mistaken constitutional precedents.

Even if, however, the doctrine of precedent is nowhere to be found *in* the Constitution, there is an alternative source for its possible authority in constitutional cases. Its authority may derive from the same source as the Constitution's itself, including the Constitution's foundational provision, Article VII, describing the process of ratification. That source is, of course, acceptance by the governed. Such acceptance is the "turtle" on which the authority of Article VII rests and, with it, the authority of the remainder of the Constitution and the statutes, treaties, and other governmental decisions that it authorizes. And if acceptance is the source of the Constitution's authority, it can be the source of authority for the doctrine of precedent.

But hence the more radical possibility to which we alluded. Just as acceptance lies at the base of the Constitution's authority, so too can acceptance of mistaken precedents alter the meaning of the Constitution. Nothing, of course, can alter what the 1789 or 1868 authors of constitutional provisions intended them to mean. If, however, a Supreme Court decision misinterprets a provision – but the governed then accept that decision as the meaning of their fundamental law – it is as if the provision's language had been appropriated by a new constitutional author and used to express an intended meaning different from that of the original authors. In such a case, the meaning of the constitutional provision

[19] *See* John Harrison, *The Power of Congress over the Rules of Precedent,* 50 *Duke L.J.* 503; Michael Stokes Paulsen, *Abrogating Stare Decisis by Statute: May Congress Remove the Precedential Effect of Roe and Casey?,* 109 *Yale L.J.* 1535, 1570–82 (2000).
[20] *See* Gary Lawson, *The Constitutional Case against Precedent,* 17 *Harv. J. L. & Pub. Pol'y* 23 (1994).

will have changed because its "authorship" will have changed.[21] Or, put differently, it will no longer be the same provision as before, despite its identical language.

Now we caution against too hasty an embracing of this nonformal method of constitutional change – one that bypasses the formal method of constitutional amendment and which converts mistaken judicial interpretations of the Constitution into the equivalent of constitutional amendments. For acceptance by the governed to be meaningful, there has to be some degree of transparency. The governed must believe the Supreme Court is trying to discern the Constitution's actual intended meaning. And they must accept the mistaken precedent as authoritative on a par with the original Constitution, even if they come to believe it rests on a misreading of the original Constitution.

Still, even with those constraints, the possibility of nonformal constitutional change – constitutional reauthorship, if you will – is always a possibility. And that means that a court, faced with a precedent that it believes misreads the intended meaning of the constitutional provision in question, must decide not only whether that precedent should be followed or overturned under the doctrine of precedent but also whether that precedent has come to be accepted as fundamental law supplanting the original constitutional provision. And *that* decision will require a type of reasoning that is different from discerning intended meanings, deducing results from rules, ordinary moral reasoning (reflective equilibrium), and ordinary empirical reasoning. Deciding whether a new foundational law has been accepted will require *political judgment*. In that respect, constitutional decision making will differ from legal reasoning in all other domains. It will not, however, require a type of reasoning that only lawyers possess. Indeed, political judgment is not something that lawyers *qua* lawyers are even taught.[22]

---

[21] *See* Larry Alexander, *Originalism, or Who Is Fred?*, 19 *Harv. J. L. & Pub. Pol'y* 321, 326 n. 17 (1996); Frederick Schauer, *Amending the Presuppositions of a Constitution* in *Responding to Imperfection* 145–61 (S. Levinson, ed., Princeton: Princeton University Press 1995).

[22] Actually, political judgment may be a form of ordinary inductive empirical reasoning applied to a special sociological question regarding citizens' attitudes. In any event, it is surely not part of the ordinary lawyer's tool kit; nor are ordinary lawyers more competent in answering the sociological question than are social scientists.

Epilogue
All or Nothing

Legal decision making is sometimes described as a craft. To decide cases, judges apply forms of reasoning and techniques of interpretation they have learned over a lifetime of exposure to the decisions of their legal ancestors. They reason by analogy, construct legal principles, and find meanings in canonical texts that differ from the intentions of the authors of those texts. The methods of legal decision making are not accessible to those outside the profession. To some extent, they are inscrutable even to insiders, including judges.[1]

---

[1] *See* Lloyd L. Weinreb, *Legal Reason: The Use of Analogy in Legal Argument* 123–46 (Cambridge: Cambridge University Press 2005); Anthony Kronman, *The Lost Lawyer* 170–85, 209–25 (Cambridge, Mass.: Belknap Press of Harvard University Press 1995); Karl N. Llewellyn, *The Common Law Tradition: Deciding Appeals* 213–35 (Boston: Little, Brown 1960); Brett G. Scharffs, *The Character of Legal Reasoning*, 61 *Wash. & Lee L. Rev.* 733 (2004); Brian Leiter, *Heidegger and the Theory of Adjudication*, 106 *Yale L.J.* 253 (1996); Daniel A. Farber, *The Inevitability of Practical Reasoning: Statues, Formalism, and the Rule of Law*, 45 *Vand. L. Rev.* 533 (1992); Charles Fried, *The Artificial Reasoning of the Law, or What Lawyers Know*, 60 *Tex. L. Rev.* 35 (1981).

The outcome of judicial craftsmanship, however, is widely acclaimed. The methodology of law is believed to constrain judges without displacing their moral judgment or binding them to the terms of legal rules. It prevents judges from imposing their personal beliefs on society but frees them to pursue the spirit of the law rather than the intended prescriptions of lawmakers. Consequently, it has enabled judges to generate a body of common and interpretive law that supports peace and prosperity but also adapts to changes in social and economic conditions and conventional morality.[2]

We do not accept this description of legal decision making. Our own view is much simpler. In our view, there is no such thing as analogical decision making, case to case. Judges who resolve disputes by analogy either are acting on a perception of similarity that is purely intuitive and therefore unreasoned and unconstrained, or they are formulating and applying rules of similarity through ordinary modes of reasoning. To the extent that judges base analogies on "legal principles," the principles on which they rely either are indistinguishable from moral principles or are nonsensical constructs designed to accommodate morally incorrect prior results. "Interpretations" of legal texts that deviate from the lawmaker's intent are not interpretations, but independent exercises of lawmaking authority.

Judges, in other words, have no special decision-making tools. To answer legal questions, they must either follow rules posited by others or rely on ordinary moral and empirical reasoning to reach their own conclusions. Their "craft" consists, at best, of their knowledge of posited rules and legal procedures, their familiarity with the reasoning of past judges on questions of social importance, and a set of conventional practices that enlarge their perspective beyond the exigencies of the case before them and incline them to caution in making rules and altering established law.

We do not mean to suggest that legal training is pointless, although our analysis may imply that law schools should spend more time than they currently do teaching logic and empirical methods. Familiarity with the body of law is important for anyone who reasons about legal

---

[2] See Leiter, *supra* note 1, at 257 (referring to "a presumption that current adjudicative practice is roughly right").

problems, and especially for those who do so professionally. Attention to past legal decisions informs the reader's initial judgments about current cases and enables the reasoner to evaluate the likelihood and extent of reliance on past cases. Legal training is also essential to successful application of precedent rules, because exposure to the body of legal decisions allows judges to grasp the meaning of precedent rules in the manner we associate with interpretation. As we noted in Chapter 3, it is also possible that traditional techniques such as seeking analogies among cases carry indirect benefits for the quality of judicial rules.

We recognize that the position we have taken is contrary to much received opinion. The methodologies we reject as logically unsound have been praised by intelligent jurists and commentators as hallmarks of legal practice. The reason why the notion of "legal reasoning" is so appealing, we think, is that it offers a middle position between unconstrained reasoning and unreasoned submission to authority. The errors of unconstrained reasoning are well known, and submission to authority runs contrary to the ideal of reasoned justice. Explanations of legal decision making that avoid this dilemma are seductive, even if they cannot be explained as applications of reason.

Because we reject the mystification of legal reasoning, we must face the basic dilemma of law. In the common law, there is no compromise between a regime of particularistic natural reasoning and a regime in which precedent rules are binding on future judges. In interpretations of rules, there is no compromise between following the intended prescriptions of past lawmakers and returning to particularism. Efforts to locate law or legal reasoning between these poles are superficially attractive but ultimately unavailing.

Selected Bibliography

Aleinkoff, T. Alexander. *Updating Statutory Interpretation*, 87 *Mich. L. Rev.* 20 (1988).

Alexander, Larry. *All or Nothing at All? The Intentions of Authorities and the Authority of Intentions*, in *Law and Interpretation: Essays in Philosophy* 357–404 (A. Marmor, ed., Oxford: Clarendon Press 1995).

Bad Beginnings, 145 *U. Pa. L. Rev.* 57 (1996).

The Banality of Legal Reasoning, 73 *Notre Dame L. Rev.* 517 (1998).

Constrained by Precedent, 63 *S. Cal. L. Rev.* 1 (1989).

The Gap, 14 *Harv. J. L. & Pub. Pol.* 695 (1991).

Of Two Minds about Law and Minds, 88 *Mich. L. Rev.* 2444 (1990).

Originalism, or Who Is Fred?, 19 *Harv. J.L. & Pub. Pol'y* 321 (1996).

Alexander, Larry, and Saikrishna Prakash. *"Is That English You're Speaking?" Why Intention Free Interpretation Is an Impossibility*, 41 *San Diego L. Rev.* 967 (2004).

Mother, May I? Imposing Mandatory Prospective Rules of Statutory Interpretation, 20 *Const. Comment.* 97 (2003).

Alexander, Larry, and Frederick Schauer. *Law's Limited Domain Confronts Morality's Universal Empire*, 48 *Wm. & Mary L. Rev.* 1579 (2007).

Alexander, Larry, and Emily Sherwin. *The Deceptive Nature of Rules*, 142 U. Pa. L. Rev. 1191 (1994).

Interpreting Rules: The Nature and Limits of Inchoate Intentions, in *Legal Interpretation in Democratic State* 3–28 (Jeffrey Goldsworthy and Tom Campbell, eds., Aldershot: Ashgate 2002).

Judges as Rulemakers, in *Common Law Theory* 27–50 (Douglas Edlin, ed., Cambridge: Cambridge University Press 2007).

The Rule of Rules: Morality, Rules, and the Dilemmas of Law (Durham: Duke University Press 2001).

American Constitutional Law: Introductory Essays and Selected Cases (8th ed., Alpheus Thomas Mason and Donald Grier Stephenson Jr., eds., Englewood Cliffs, N.J.: Prentice-Hall 1987).

Arrow, Kenneth J. *Social Choice and Individual Values* (2d ed., New Haven: Yale University Press 1963).

Bassham, Gregory. *Original Intent and the Constitution* (Savage, Md.: Rowman & Littlefield 1992).

Bell, Bernard W. *"No Motor Vehicles in the Park": Reviving the Hart-Fuller Debate to Introduce Statutory Construction*, 48 J. Legal Educ. 88 (1998).

Bernstein, David E. *Bolling, Equal Protection, Due Process, and Lochnerphobia*, 93 Geo. L.J. 1253 (2005).

Bertea, Stefano. *Remarks on a Legal Positivist Misuse of Wittgenstein's Later Philosophy*, 22 Law & Phil. 513 (2003).

Boghossian, Paul A. *Rules, Meaning and Intention*, 124 Phil. Stud. 185 (2005).

Booher, Troy L. *Putting Meaning in Its Place: Originalism and Philosophy of Language*, 25 Law and Phil. 387 (2006).

Bratman, Michael E. *Intentions, Plans, and Practical Reason* (Cambridge, Mass.: Harvard University Press 1987).

Brest, Paul. *The Misconceived Quest for the Original Understanding*, 60 B.U.L. Rev. 204 (1980).

Brewer, Scott. *Exemplary Reasoning: Semantics, Pragmatics, and the Rational Force of Legal Argument by Analogy*, 109 Harv. L. Rev. 925 (1996).

Brink, David O. *Legal Theory, Legal Interpretation, and Judicial Review*, 17 Phil. and Pub. Affs. 105 (1988).

Burton, Steven J. *An Introduction to Law and Legal Reasoning* (Boston: Little, Brown 1995).

Judging in Good Faith (Cambridge: Cambridge University Press 1992).

Byrne, Alex. *On Misinterpreting Kripke's Wittgenstein*, 56 Phil. and Phenomenological Res. 339 (1996).

Calabresi, Guido. *A Common Law for the Age of Statutes* (Cambridge, Mass.: Harvard University Press 1995).

Campbell, Tom D. *The Legal Theory of Ethical Positivism* (Aldershot: Dartmouth Publishing 1996).

Campos, Paul. *Against Constitutional Theory*, 4 Yale J. L. & Human. 270 (1992).

That Obscure Object of Desire: Hermeneutics and the Autonomous Legal Text, 77 Minn. L. Rev. 1065 (1993).

Cardozo, Benjamin N. *The Nature of the Judicial Process* (New Haven: Yale University Press 1949).

Caroll, Noël. *Interpretation and Intention: The Debate between Hypothetical and Actual Intentionalism*, 31 Metaphilosophy 75 (2000).

Coleman Jules L., and Brian Leiter. *Determinacy, Objectivity, and Authority*, 142 U. Pa. L. Rev. 549 (1992).

Dardis, Anthony. *How the Radically Interpreted Make Mistakes*, 33 Dialogue 415 (1994).

Denning, Brannon P. *Brother Can You Paradigm?*, 23 Const. Comment. 81 (2006).

Dworkin, Ronald. *Bork's Jurisprudence*, 57 U. of Chi. L. Rev. 657 (1990).

Law's Empire (Cambridge, Mass.: Harvard University Press 1986).

Life's Dominion: An Argument about Abortion, Euthanasia, and Individual Freedom (New York: Knopf 1993).

Taking Rights Seriously (Cambridge, Mass.: Harvard University Press 1978).

Ebbs, Gary. *Rule-Following and Realism* (Cambridge: Harvard University Press 1997).

Eisenberg, Melvin Aron. *The Nature of the Common Law* (Cambridge, Mass.: Harvard University Press 1988).

Endicott, Timothy A. O. *Linguistic Indeterminacy*, 16 Oxford J. Legal Stud. 667 (1996).

Epstein, Richard A. *A Common Lawyer Looks at Constitutional Interpretation*, 72 Boston L. Rev. 699 (1992).

Eskridge, William N. *Dynamic Statutory Interpretation*, 135 U. Pa. L. Rev. 1479 (1987).

Gadamer/Statutory Interpretation, 90 Colum. L. Rev. 609 (1990).

Textualism, the Unknown Ideal?, 96 Mich. L. Rev. 1509 (1998).

Eskridge, William N., and Philip Frickey. *Statutory Interpretation as Practical Reasoning*, 42 Stan. L. Rev. 321 (1990).

Farber, Daniel A. *The Inevitability of Practical Reasoning: Statutes, Formalism, and the Rule of Law*, 45 Vand. L. Rev. 533 (1992).

Farber, Daniel A., and Philip Frickey. *Legislative Intent and Public Choice*, 74 Va. L. Rev. 423 (1988).

Fish, Stanley. *Play of Surfaces: Theory and the Law*, in *Legal Hermeneutics: History, Theory, and Practice* 297–316 (Gregory Leyh, ed., Berkeley: University of California Press 1992).

There Is No Textualist Position, 42 *San Diego L. Rev.* 629 (2005).

Wrong Again, in *Doing What Comes Naturally* 103–19 (Durham: Duke University Press 1989).

Frickey, Philip. *Congressional Intent, Practical Reasoning, and the Dynamic Nature of Federal Indian Law*, 78 *Cal. L. Rev.* 1137 (1990).

Fried, Charles. *The Artificial Reasoning of the Law, or What Lawyers Know*, 60 *Tex. L. Rev.* 35 (1981).

Garcia, Jorge J. E. *Can There Be Texts without Historical Authors?*, 31 *Amer. Phil. Q.* 245 (1994).

Goldsworthy, Jeffrey. *Marmor on Meaning, Interpretation, and Legislative Intention*, 1 *Legal Theory* 439 (1995).

Green, Michael Steven. *Dworkin's Fallacy, or What the Philosophy of Language Can't Teach Us about the Law*, 89 *Va. L. Rev.* 1897 (2003).

Greenawalt, Kent. *From the Bottom Up*, 82 *Corn. L. Rev.* 944 (1997).

Law and Objectivity (New York: Oxford University Press 1992).

Legislation: Statutory Interpretation: 20 Questions (New York: Foundation Press 1999).

The Nature of Rules and the Meaning of Meaning, 72 *Notre Dame L. Rev.* 1449 (1997).

Greene, Abner S. *The Missing Step of Textualism*, 74 *Fordham L.J.* 1913 (2006).

The Work of Knowledge, 72 *Notre Dame L. Rev.* 1479 (1997).

Grice, Paul. *Studies in the Way of Words* (Cambridge, Mass.: Harvard University Press 1991).

Harrison, John. *The Power of Congress over the Rules of Precedent*, 50 *Duke L.J.* 503 (2000).

Hart, Henry M., Jr., and Albert M. Sacks. *The Legal Process: Basic Problems in the Making and Application of Law* (William N. Eskridge Jr. and Phillip P. Frickey, eds., New York: Foundation Press 1994).

Hart, H. L. A. *The Concept of Law* (Oxford: Clarendon Press 1961).

Haukioja, Jussi. *Is Solitary Rule-Following Possible?*, 32 *Philosophia* 131 (2005).

Hershovitz, Scott. *Wittgenstein on Rules: The Phantom Menace*, 22 *Oxford J. Legal Stud.* 619 (2002).

Heuristics and Biases: The Psychology of Intuitive Judgment (Thomas Gilovich, Dale Griffin, and Daniel Kahneman, eds., Cambridge: Cambridge University Press 2002).

Hirsch, E. D., Jr. *Counterfactuals in Interpretation,* in *Interpreting Law and Literature: A Hermeneutic Reader* 55–68 (Sanford Levinson and Steven Mailloux, eds., Evanston, Ill.: Northwestern University Press 1988).

Holmes, Oliver Wendell. *The Common Law* (New York: Dover Publications 1991).

Horty, John F. *The Result Model of Precedent,* 10 *Legal Theory* 19 (2004).

Humphrey, John A. *Quine, Kripke's Wittgenstein, and Sceptical Solutions,* 37 *S.J. Phil.* 43 (1999).

Hurd, Heidi M. *Moral Combat* (Cambridge: Cambridge University Press 1999).

Hurley, S. L. *Coherence, Hypothetical Cases, and Precedent,* 10 *Oxford J. Legal Stud.* 221 (1990).

Interpreting Precedents: A Comparative Study (D. Neil MacCormick and Robert S. Summers, eds., Aldershot: Dartmouth Publishing 1997).

Judgment under Uncertainty: Heuristics and Biases (Daniel Kahneman, Paul Slovic, and Amos Tversky, eds., Cambridge: Cambridge University Press 1982).

Kavka, Gregory. *The Toxin Puzzle,* 43 *Analysis* 33 (1983).

Kay, Richard S. *American Constitutionalism,* in *Constitutionalism: Philosophical Foundations* 16–63 (Larry Alexander, ed., Cambridge: Cambridge University Press 1998).

Original Intentions, Standard Meanings, and the Legal Character of the Constitution,
  6 *Const. Comment.* 39 (1989).

Klarman, Michael J. *Antifidelity,* 70 *S. Cal. L. Rev.* 381 (1997).

Knapp, Steven, and Walter Benn Michaels. *Against Theory,* 8 *Critical Inquiry* 723 (1982).

Against Theory 2: Hermeneutics and Deconstruction, 14 *Critical Inquiry* 49 (1987).

Intention, Identity, and the Constitution: A Response to David Hoy, in *Legal Hermeneutics: History, Theory, and Practice* 187–99 (Gregory Leyh, ed., Berkeley: University of California Press 1992).

Not a Matter of Interpretation, 42 *San Diego L. Rev* 651 (2005).

Knorpp, William Max. *How to Talk to Yourself, or Kripke's Wittgenstein's Solitary Language Argument and Why It Fails,* 84 *Pac. Phil. Q.* 215 (2003).

Kress, Kenneth J. *Legal Reasoning and Coherence Theories: Dworkin's Rights Thesis, Retroactivity, and the Linear Order of Decisions,* 72 *Cal. L. Rev.* 369 (1984).

Kripke, Saul A. *Wittgenstein on Rules and Private Language: An Elementary Exposition* (Cambridge, Mass.: Harvard University Press, 1982).

Kronman, Anthony. *The Lost Lawyer* (Cambridge, Mass.: Belknap Press of Harvard University Press 1995).

Kuhn, Thomas S. *Commensurability, Comparability, Communicability,* 2 *Phil. of Science Assoc.* 669 (1982).

Lamond, Grant. *Do Precedents Create Rules?*, 11 *Legal Theory* 1 (2005).

Lawson, Gary. *The Constitutional Case against Precedent*, 17 *Harv. J.L. & Pub. Pol'y* 23 (1994).

On Reading Recipes . . . and Constitutions, 85 *Geo. L. J.* 1823 (1997).

Lee, Win-Chiat. *Statutory Interpretation and the Counterfactual Test for Legislative Intention*, 8 *Law and Phil.* 383 (1989).

Leiter, Brian. *Heidegger and the Theory of Adjudication*, 106 *Yale L.J.* 253 (1996).

Lessig, Lawrence. *Fidelity in Translation*, 71 *Tex. L. Rev.* 1165 (1993).

Levenbook, Barbara Baum. *The Meaning of a Precedent*, 6 *Legal Theory* 185 (2000).

Levi, Edward H. *An Introduction to Legal Reasoning* (Chicago: Chicago University Press 1948).

Llewellyn, Karl. *The Bramble Bush: On Our Law and Its Study* (Dobbs Ferry, N.Y.: Oceana Publishing 1960).

The Common Law Tradition: Deciding Appeals (Boston: Little, Brown 1960).

Manning, John F. *Textualism and the Equity of the Statute*, 101 *Colum. L. Rev.* 1 (2001).

Marmor, Andrei. *Interpretation and Legal Theory* (Oxford: Clarendon Press 1992).

Interpretation and Legal Theory (2d ed., Oxford: Hart Pub. 2005).

The Separation Thesis and the Limits of Interpretation, 12 *Canadian J.L. and Jurisprudence* 135 (1995).

McConnell, Michael W. *The Importance of Humility in Judicial Review: A Comment on Ronald Dworkin's "Moral Reading" of the Constitution*, 65 *Fordham L. Rev.* 1269 (1997).

Michaels, Walter Benn. *The Fate of the Constitution*, 61 *Tex. L. Rev.* 765 (1992).

Moore, Michael S. *A Natural Law Theory of Interpretation*, 58 *So. Cal. L. Rev.* 277 (1985).

Munzer, Steven R. *Realistic Limits on Realist Interpretation*, 58 *S. Cal. L. Rev.* 459 (1985).

Nagel, Thomas. *The Last Word* (New York: Oxford University Press 1997).

Note. *Figuring the Law: Holism and Tropological Inference in Legal Interpretation*, 97 *Yale L.J.* 823 (1988).

Note. *Legislative Purpose, Rationality, and Equal Protection*, 82 *Yale L.J.* 123 (1972).

O'Neill, Onora. *Towards Justice and Virtue: A Constructive Account of Practical Reasoning* (Cambridge: Cambridge University Press 1996).

Paulsen, Michael Stokes. *Abrogating Stare Decisis by Statute: May Congress Remove the Precedential Effect of Roe and Casey?*, 109 *Yale L.J.* 1535 (2000).

Pettit, Philip. *Rules, Reasons, and Norms* (Oxford: Oxford University Press 2002).

Plous, Scott. *The Psychology of Judgment and Decision Making* (Philadelphia: Temple University Press 1993).

Posner, Richard A. *The Problems of Jurisprudence* (Cambridge, Mass.: Harvard University Press 1990).

Postema, Gerald J. *Coordination and Convention at the Foundation of Law*, 11 J. Legal Stud. 165 (1982).

Prakash, Saikrishna B. *Unoriginalism's Law without Meaning*, 15 Const. Comment. 529 (1998).

Rachlinski, Jeffrey J. *Bottom-Up and Top-Down Decisionmaking*, 73 U. Chi. L. Rev. 933 (2006).

Rawls, John. *A Theory of Justice* (Cambridge, Mass.: Belknap Press of Harvard University Press 1971).

Raz, Joseph. *The Authority of Law* (Oxford: Oxford University Press 1979).

Dworkin: A New Link in the Chain, 74 Cal. L. Rev. 1103 (1986).

Ethics in the Public Domain (Oxford: Oxford University Press 1994).

The Morality of Freedom (Oxford: Clarendon Press 1986).

Ripstein, Arthur. *Law, Language, and Interpretation*, 46 U. Toronto L.J. 335 (1996).

Robertson, Michael. *Picking Positivism Apart: Stanley Fish on Epistemology and Law*, 8 S. Cal. Interdisc. L.J. 401 (1999).

Rubenfeld, Jed. *Freedom and Time: A Theory of Constitutional Self-Government* (New Haven: Yale University Press 2001).

Revolution by Judiciary (Cambridge, Mass.: Harvard University Press 2005).

Scalia, Antonin. *A Matter of Interpretation: Federal Courts and the Law* (Princeton: Princeton University Press 1997).

Scharffs, Brett G. *The Character of Legal Reasoning*, 61 Wash. & Lee L. Rev. 733 (2004).

Schauer, Frederick. *Amending the Presuppositions of a Constitution*, in *Responding to Imperfection* (S. Levinson, ed., Princeton: Princeton University Press 1995).

Do Cases Make Bad Law?, 73 U. Chi. L. Rev. 883 (2006).

Formalism, 97 Yale L. J. 509 (1988).

Playing by the Rules: A Philosophical Examination of Rule-Based Decision-Making in Life and Law (Oxford: Clarendon Press 1991).

Searle, John R. *The Construction of Social Reality* (New York: Free Press 1995).

Expression and Meaning: Studies in the Theory of Speech Acts (Oxford: Oxford University Press 1995).

Sebok, Anthony J. *Finding Wittgenstein at the Core of the Rule of Recognition*, 52 S.M.U. L. Rev. 75 (1999).

Shain, Ralph. *Mill, Quine, and Natural Kinds*, 24 Metaphilosophy 275 (1993).

Shepsle, Kenneth A. *Congress Is a "They," Not an "It": Legislative Intent as an Oxymoron*, 12 *Intl. Rev. Law Econ.* 239 (1992).

Sherwin, Emily. *A Defense of Analogical Reasoning in Law*, 66 *U. Chi. L. Rev.* 1179 (1999).

Judges as Rulemakers, 73 *U. Chi. L. Rev.* 919 (2006).

Shogenji, Tomogi. *The Problem of the Criterion in Rule-Following*, 60 *Phil. & Phenom. Res.* 501 (2000).

Simpson, A. W. B. *The Ratio Decidendi of a Case and the Doctrine of Binding Precedent*, in *Oxford Essays in Jurisprudence* 148–75 (A. G. Guest, ed., Oxford: Oxford University Press 1961).

Sinclair, M. B. W. *Legislative Intent: Fact or Fabrication?*, 41 *N.Y.L. Sch. L. Rev.* 1329 (1997).

Sinnott-Armstrong, Walter. *Word Meaning in Legal Interpretation*, 42 *San Diego L. Rev.* 465 (2005).

Sloman, Steven A. *Two Systems of Reasoning*, in *Heuristics and Biases: The Psychology of Intuitive Judgment* 379–96 (Thomas Gilovich, Dale Griffin, and Daniel Kahneman, eds., Cambridge: Cambridge University Press 2002).

Smith, Peter Jeremy. *Commas, Constitutional Grammar, and the Straight-Face Test: What If Conan the Grammarian Were a Strict Textualist?*, 16 *Const. Comment.* 7 (1999).

Solum, Lawrence B. *On the Indeterminacy Crisis: Critiquing Critical Dogma*, 54 *U. Chi. L. Rev.* 462 (1987).

Pluralism and Public Legal Reason, 15 *Wm. & Mary Bill Rts. J.* 7 (2006).

Stavropoulos, Nicos. *Objectivity in Law* (Oxford: Oxford University Press 1996).

Stoljar, Natalie. *Vagueness, Counterfactual Intentions, and Legal Interpretation*, 7 *Legal Theory* 447 (2001).

Strauss, David A. *Common Law Constitutional Understanding*, 63 *U. Chi. L. Rev.* 877 (1996).

Sunstein, Cass R. *Interpreting Statutes in the Regulatory State*, 103 *Harv. L. Rev.* 405 (1989).

Justice Scalia's Formalism, 107 *Yale L. J.* 529 (1997).

Legal Reasoning and Political Conflict (New York: Oxford University Press 1996).

One Case at a Time (Cambridge, Mass.: Harvard University Press 1999).

Verheggen, Claudine. *Wittgenstein's Rule-Following Paradox and the Objectivity of Meaning*, 26 *Phil. Investig.* 285 (2003).

Weinreb, Lloyd L. *Legal Reason: The Use of Analogy in Legal Argument* (Cambridge: Cambridge University Press 2005).

West, Robin. *The Aspirational Constitution*, 88 *Nw. U. L. Rev.* 241 (1993).

Whittington, Keith E. *Constitutional Interpretation: Textual Meaning, Original Intent, and Judicial Review* (Lawrence: University Press of Kansas 1999).

Dworkin's "Originalism": The Role of Intentions in Constitutional Interpretation, 62 Rev. of Pol. 197 (2000).

Willigenburg, Theo van. *Shareability and Actual Sharing: Korsgaard's Position on the Publicity of Reasons*, 25 Phil. Invest. 172 (2002).

Wittgenstein, Ludwig. *Philosophical Investigations* (Oxford: Blackwell 1997).

Yablon, Charles M. *Law and Metaphysics*, 96 Yale L.J. 613 (1987).

Zapf, Christian, and Eben Moglen. *Linguistic Indeterminacy and the Rule of Law: On the Perils of Misunderstanding Wittgenstein*, 84 Geo. L.J. 485 (1996).

Index